THE EROTIC SILENCE
OF THE
AMERICAN WIFE

The EROTIC SILENCE *of the* AMERICAN WIFE

DALMA HEYN

TURTLE BAY BOOKS
A DIVISION OF RANDOM HOUSE/NEW YORK
1992

Grateful acknowledgment is made to the following for permission to reprint
previously published material:

Crown Publishers: Excerpts from *Backlash* by Susan Faludi. Copyright © 1991
by Susan Faludi. Reprinted by permission of Crown Publishers, Inc.
Doubleday, a division of Bantam, Doubleday, Dell Publishing Group, Inc.: Ex-
cerpt from *The Diary of Anne Frank: The Critical Edition,* prepared by The
Netherlands State Institute for War Documents. Reprinted by permission of
Doubleday, a division of Bantam, Doubleday, Dell Publishing Group, Inc.
Harcourt Brace Jovanovich, Inc. and The Hogarth Press: Excerpt from "Profes-
sions for Women" from *The Death of the Moth and Other Essays* by Virginia
Woolf. Copyright 1942 by Harcourt Brace Jovanovich, Inc. and renewed 1970
by Marjorie T. Parson, Executrix. Rights throughout the world excluding the
United States are controlled by The Hogarth Press. Reprinted by permission of
Harcourt Brace Jovanovich, Inc. and The Hogarth Press.
The New York Times: Excerpt from article from March 9, 1989 by Andrée Brooks.
Copyright © 1989 by The New York Times Company. Reprinted by permission.

A small portion of this work was originally published in the August 1987 issue of
Mademoiselle as "The Big, Bad Buy."

The author has changed the names and all identifying characteristics of every
woman and man whose story is told in this book.

Library of Congress Cataloging-in-Publication Data

Heyn, Dalma.
The erotic silence of the American wife / Dalma Heyn.
p.   cm.
Includes bibliographical references.
ISBN 0-679-41339-1
1. Adultery—United States.   2. Wives—United States—Sexual
behavior.   I. Title.
HQ806.H49   1992   306.73'6—dc20   91-51046

Manufactured in the United States of America
24689753
First Edition

For Richard

[Hester] assured them, too, of her firm belief that, at some brighter period, when the world should have grown ripe for it, in Heaven's own time, a new truth would be revealed, in order to establish the whole relationship between man and woman on a surer ground of mutual happiness.

—Nathaniel Hawthorne, *The Scarlet Letter*

Contents

Part
ONE

Chapter One

SEX AND SILENCE

I am writing a story; it is not yet fully developed, but
I show you the beginning so you can get the gist of the
tale.

When Anne tells her mother she is going to marry Alex,
her mother lowers her eyes and takes a long, even, slow
breath, like a gospel singer preparing her body for a
hymn of joy, and says on the exhale, "Thank God." The
privacy of this response surprises Anne, excludes her
even, but she understands her mother's rapture.

She had said the same thing often herself, having
openly despaired of finding such a man—easygoing
and normal, cheerful mostly, with an offbeat sixties
humor but a potential for success that made her think,
yes, I can live with this man; yes, he will make a good
husband.

Four years later—a year after their son is born—Anne,
now thirty-six, goes back to work as a part-time assis-

tant art director at an ad agency. After six months, she hires an au pair to care for her son five days a week so that she can work full time once again. She is tired a lot, but happy.

Her closest colleague, Kurt, is the production manager. He is also the father of a child born on the same day as her son; they compare cuteness and horror stories, and log in, first thing every morning, the number of hours' sleep they get each night. The one with the highest total buys Friday lunch. For six months straight Anne is Kurt's guest.

One day they decide that instead of exchanging boring sleep-deprivation tales yet again, instead of forcing salad and San Pellegrino down exhausted throats, they will do what they really need to do: rent a midtown hotel room and take a nap.

The next Friday they do exactly the same thing, only before the nap they have room service and after it they have sex. It feels as natural as ordering lunch. A surprising passion wells up in Anne for this gentle, playful man, feelings of sweetness and ease and contact she had mysteriously forgotten about.

They monitor their relationship carefully, wary that the sexual addition to it compromise their comfort with each other, or their closeness. It does not. On the contrary, they become even more intimate. Their weekly meetings continue for two years. Anne to this day is amazed at her own sexual feelings for Kurt, and at her overall sense of expansion in his presence. She loves this friendship that leaves her feeling so good. She does well in her new job, is still as grateful for her husband—more than ever, actually, since he is proving to be a superb father. She has developed into a contented woman with many surprising sides to her, a woman whose capacity for adventure will be, she hopes, lifelong.

This is not a trick ending, for my story has no ending at all. I do not know whether Anne will tell her husband about her affair—or, if she does, whether he will forgive her—or whether she will end her relationship with Kurt, or stay in both relationships. What I do know is that she will not hurl herself under a train. She will not be hanged, stoned to death, branded or banished, and she will not swallow arsenic. I do not think Alex will throw her out, or that Kurt will ultimately shun her because of the pleasure he once reveled in; or that her neighbors, scandalized, will ignore her. I hope she will not be fired by a company that cannot tolerate commingling among employees. I do not expect an angry jury, indignant over her treachery, to declare her a sociopath or a nymphomaniac or an unfit mother for her capacity to love her husband and simultaneously sleep with another man. I imagine Anne will continue to have a very nice life, enriched immeasurably by her love affair.

It is a new twist on an old theme, this non-ending. The theme of adultery is hard to avoid if you read at all or go to the theater or to movies or listen to music; it fills Western literature from the time of Homer and obsesses us still. Denis de Rougement, author of the groundbreaking work *Love in the Western World*, observed that "to judge by literature, adultery would seem to be one of the most remarkable of occupations in both Europe and America." But when it is the wife's sexuality that is shared, it usually does her in: Think of Anna Karenina, Madame Bovary, Hester Prynne, Tess of the D'Urbervilles. Their specters hover over every tale of adultery we hear. Their stories, their very names, are synonymous with Sin. With Death. Guilt. Isolation. Shame. Show me a married woman who has an affair—a passionate one, not a desultory indulgence that doesn't particularly engage her—and lives to have any life worth mentioning afterward, and I will show you a tiny oasis in a desert filled with doomed heroines.

Adulterous wives are punished. Adulterous husbands, generally, are not. In our hearts we are not convinced that men who have extramarital sex are doing anything wrong—certainly anything deviant ("You want monogamy, marry a swan," suggests a father to his daughter when she complains of her husband's infidelity in Nora Ephron's 1986 movie, *Heartburn*). On the contrary, we feel men are acting naturally, normally, in accordance with some romantic tale of courtly ardor in which the overcoming of obstacles in pursuit of a forbidden woman is truly noble. British sociologist Annette Lawson, author of *Adultery: An Analysis of Love and Betrayal* (1988), says that such men are actually embarking "on a quest for the good."

But an adulterous woman, confined to a romantic tale in which the only quest for the good is the quest for a husband, cannot be tolerated. The tendency of jealous husbands to kill their wives—along with their children and their wives' lovers—fill the pages of literature just as it fills pages of newspapers: Murder may be a dramatic breach of the marriage vows, but not so unthinkable that even the merest *suspicion* of extramarital sex can't instantaneously provoke and even justify it. Shakespeare becomes obsessed with adultery's monstrous hold on the imagination of even moments-ago trusting husbands, and the resulting devastation such husbands then bring upon even the purest of wives—all in the name of love.

The idea that adulterous women are tainted—an aberration, unnatural, not even human ("O thou thing!" cries Leontes to the innocent Hermione in *The Winter's Tale*)—permeates our consciousness so completely that it is hard to find even an *unmarried* woman having an affair in literature who is not destroyed for her sexuality. Guinevere, Carmen, Mimi, Violetta, Hermione—each of these radiant heroines was killed, banished, or isolated—or she committed suicide.

Sometimes they were punished indirectly: Jane Eyre gets her Rochester, but he is blinded; Sue Bridehead's guilt (in *Jude the Obscure*) leads to her madness; Maggie Tulliver renounces Stephen in *The Mill on the Floss* before even sleeping with him, then—perhaps just for thinking about it—drowns in the arms of her brother. An affair may no longer cost today's female characters their lives (as far as I can tell, Mary McCarthy's *Charmed Lives* was the last tale of adultery in which a woman committed suicide) but it still can cost them their marriages, their stature in the community, and, too often, custody of their children or the finances to support them. Only a handful of novels fail to end with an adulterous heroine's being either annihilated or ravaged by a passionate affair.[1]

The punishment goes on, in literature as in life. The heroine of novelist Jane Smiley's *Ordinary Love* (1989), Rachel Kinsella, admits her affair with her neighbor, and her husband responds first by slapping her to the floor and threatening to kill her if she does not move out of their house by the next morning, then by knocking her down again, and finally by kidnapping their five children and moving to England without leaving so much as a forwarding address. When her lover finds that she has confessed their affair, he refuses to see or speak to her

---

[1] Daniel Defoe's Moll Flanders; Erica Jong's Isadora Wing; Margaret Drabble's Jane Gray; Doris Lessing's Anna Wulf and Martha Quest; Laurie Colwin's Polly Demarest; Gail Godwin's Jane Clifford; Margaret Atwood's "Lady Oracle"; Margaret Laurence's Morag Gunn—these are the ones I'm aware of. There are surely more, but not many.

ever again. In a stunning illustration of the correlation between sex and silence, both husband and lover annul Rachel, cancel her, reduce her to a nonentity. Both abandon her totally—her husband, for having extramarital sex; her lover, for speaking about it.

In all cultures that disapprove of infidelity, women are disapproved of more vehemently; among those that punish, women are punished more harshly. Anthropologist Suzanne Frayser of the University of Denver, author of *Varieties of Sexual Experience* (1985), studied sexuality in sixty-two cultures, past and present, and found that in none of them do men experience the double standard: Of those that permitted adultery, in other words, not one allowed it for women and not for men. In 26 percent of fifty-eight societies, the husband is allowed to have extramarital sex but not the wife. And of forty-eight societies for which she had data, twenty-six—more than half—gave the husband the option to kill his unfaithful wife. Intrigued by the fact that in these societies illicit sex—mainly extramarital sex—ranked only third in importance as grounds for divorce among men, Frayser says, "I realized that in many cases infidelity doesn't get to the point of litigation because the wife has been killed."

Some societies simply define adultery differently for each gender. In Jewish law, still on the books but varying from culture to culture, a married woman is guilty of adultery if she has sexual intercourse with any male other than her husband; a married man is guilty of adultery only if he has intercourse with another man's wife. Since the law allows polygamy for men (but not for women), it was reasoned that his affair with an unmarried woman might lead to his marrying her. It is neither the "extramarital" nor the "sex" of which the adulterous man is guilty, for it is neither his marriage nor his wife's honor he has legally violated. He has committed a property crime against another man.

Depending on the culture, an adulterous woman may be branded or speared in the leg or given over to any other men in the community who want to have sex with her. In the Senoufo and Bambara tribes of West Africa, such a woman is simply killed outright. Under Muslim law, too, a man may freely murder his wife if she is discovered having extramarital sex: In modern Saudi Arabia she could be stoned to death. In parts of Mexico she might have had her nose and ears cut off—*before* being stoned to death.

The story that links female sexuality with punishment is so inflexible that it grips women's fate whether they are inside or outside the sanctified structure of marriage. Anna, the heroine of Sue Miller's *The Good Mother*, is not granted her sexuality after her divorce, although her former husband is ensconced in a new marriage—because she has a child. Even the court-ordered psychologist's report, judging Anna to be a good mother because she has a good relationship with her daughter, is not sufficient to override the stigma of her sexuality and weigh the court in her favor. A sexual woman, in other words, taints her child and does not deserve to keep her. A sexual woman is not a good mother.

THE ROMANCE PLOT

In a lecture Vladimir Nabokov once gave on *Madame Bovary*, he said adultery was "a most conventional way to rise above the conventional." Certainly adultery is as much an institution as marriage, with its own rules and history. Men, who have affairs more often and with more partners than women, have had permissive policies built for themselves into the marriage system; for them it is customary. For women, though, it seems something other than conventional to break the one rule that has been for so long so unconditional, and that guaranteed a punishment of the kind that befell Anna or Emma or Tess or Hester or any other of those irresistible, passionate heroines we loved and lost.

Adultery is, in fact, a revolutionary way for women to rise above the conventional—if they live to do so. The injunction against it—always absolute—is still strong and the stakes are still high, as legions of once-adulterous and now-divorced women whose standard of living has been drastically lowered can attest. While the rules for premarital sexual behavior have loosened dramatically, the rule against extramarital sex is as rigid as it was in Anna Karenina's day—even though we know that many women do not adhere to it. Successful adultery, and by that I mean an affair that enriches a woman's life regardless of its outcome, is an oxymoron—the two words so antithetical, the notion so heretical, it sounds inconceivable.

Because in the one story that has been written about women's lives, sometimes called the marriage plot, sometimes called the romance plot or the erotic plot, the star is Mr. Right. The woman, whether Sleeping Beauty or the Princess of Wales or Jane Doe, is chosen by Mr. Right and whisked off somewhere to live "happily ever after." It is a powerful story, as we all know; it spawned the belief that many women still harbor in their hearts that once they find this right guy and fall in love and marry him they really *will* live happily ever after. In imagining the story of our own lives we cannot help but design it according to the pattern of those tales we already know, the ones we have been told and that live within us. Like children begging to hear the same bedtime stories over and over, we crave the repetition and the reassurance of familiar endings, and we seem inclined to reenact them. "Myth and its little sister, fairy tale, make stories out of what we don't know we know," writes novelist Lore Segal. "They negotiate familiarly with our wishes and nightmares. . . ."

But examine the romance plot closely and you will see that after you cut to the chase—marriage—it is Mr. Right's story that continues, not our heroine's. After her implicit goal of becoming a wife is reached, her story is over. Once inside the little white cottage, the moment after becoming a wife, as Carolyn Heilbrun points out in *Writing a Woman's Life*, "the young woman died as a subject, ceased as an entity," was left there languishing on the page, without a voice, hardly a heroine at all, relegated to a plot that cannot thicken. This story that goes nowhere for her is, nevertheless, the only plot written for a woman's life, just as happily ever after (that is, monogamous marriage) is the only ending that certifies her success as a woman in this society. Modern women, mindful of this, feel torn by both the appeal and the peril of the romantic plot.

If myth and literature are what mold us, popular culture is what defines us in the present—and it is movies, the most popular of all, that provide us with romantic endings which best reflect our current moral positions. In *Fatal Attraction*, a story of a man who commits adultery with a woman who does not (she is unmarried), we get a glimpse of how intolerable any woman's insistent erotic voice is. The movie's ending had to be rewritten three times before one emerged that satisfied viewers' ferocious lust for blood—not of the adulterous man, it turns out, but of the sexually available woman who would not be satisfied with just the one-night stand he offered her.

Ending number one: Crazy and obsessed over her married lover's abandonment of her, Alex, played by Glenn Close, commits suicide. She slits her throat, but manages to frame Dan (the adulterous Michael Douglas character who plays her lover) for her murder, and he is carried off by the police. Trial audiences hated this ending.

In the next version, Alex still commits suicide, still frames Dan for her death, but this time Dan's wife, the virtuous Beth (Anne Archer), comes to his rescue, finding evidence that will save her husband's life. This ending was not so disappointing, audiences felt, but was still not . . . enough punishment for the possessive, predatory, and maybe even pregnant Alex.

In the final version, Alex does not commit suicide at all; she rises from a bathtub—a raging, monstrous creature straight out of *Jaws*—and while Dan valiantly tries to strangle and drown her, it is his wife who delivers the triumphant, fatal shot through her rival's heart. Here, then, $1.3 million later, the audience gets what it wants: The death penalty. For the adulterer? No. For the woman. The sexual woman.

Dan's life is restored. He goes home to his family, the good wife gets her revenge on the bad woman, and we exit basking in the virtue and inviolability of the family framework: The last scene exhibits a photo of Dan, Beth, and child—in a picture frame.

Woody Allen's *Alice* is the closest we have to a film in which a *married* woman has sex outside marriage and ends up intact, physically and psychologically. Alice's affair, however, is first "justified" when she, and we, become witnesses, through an act of magic, to her husband's office dalliance. In *sex, lies and videotape*, too, the sweet heroine, Ann, succumbs to an affair—but only after she discovers that her husband is sleeping with her sister, Cynthia.

Is such manipulation of our sympathies necessary? Could we support Alice without first observing her husband's affair?; Ann without first seeing her sister and husband in her marriage bed?

A BELIEVABLE WOMAN

Which brings me back to Anne and Alex. I must ask you whether you are willing to read about a woman who has extramarital sex if her husband does not "deserve" it; whether you are ready for another plot and another heroine and another point of view. I am really asking whether you want to hear from a sexual woman who is not silent and whose story does not end tragically, an adulterous woman who is not annihilated for her passion.

Because part of what will make my story work is how believable my heroine's fate is—more than believable, how inevitable. Madame Bovary's fate, for instance, feels inescapable: In 1857, women all over the world were living the same story. "Everything one invents is true, you may be sure of that," wrote Flaubert to his mistress, Louise Colet, while in the midst of writing his first and most famous novel. ". . . My poor Bovary, without a doubt, is suffering and weeping at this very instant in twenty villages of France." A character's emotions, behavior, and fate must feel true to readers if she is to become, as Emma Bovary has in Malcolm Cowley's words, "one of those lasting archetypes that people the literary imagination."

It was inevitable, in other words, that Flaubert's poor Bovary suffer and then kill herself, in spite of her creator's passionate identification with her ("*I* am Emma Bovary," he used to say to readers who wanted to know upon whom she was based). It was logical that Anna Karenina do the same, even though Tolstoy admitted to having fallen in love with his character as he wrote her into existence—and even though he had intended to write a simple morality tale. In love or no, the train tracks were Anna's inescapable destination. Thomas Hardy, too, as reluctant as Flaubert and Tolstoy to dispose of his beloved, beautiful, generous Tess, finally succumbed, though as Irving Howe observes, "He hovers and watches over Tess like a stricken father," pointing to the dilemma of the father who loves his vital, sexual daughter and doesn't want her to be hurt. "He is as tender to Tess as Tess is to the world." But not so tender that he can prevent her two lovers from betraying her; not so fatherly that he can rescue her from that horrific threshing machine, or arrange that his adored creation not be hanged. No, the men who created these women and who loved and admired them also killed them. In American literature, too, critic Leslie Fiedler has observed, the only good woman is a dead one.

The reader first coming upon these condemned heroines might well ask, "If they are so wonderful, and if the men loved them so, why are they destroyed?" Unlike the classic tragic hero, whose pride or folly dictate a suffering which then redeems him, the tragic heroine need not have a fatal flaw to warrant her tragic ending: Tess is neither proud nor foolish; neither is Anna. Their suffering comes from without rather than from within; it arises out of the insistence of a social order rather than from any character defect. Our heartbreak results from watching how dearly they pay not only for stepping outside the bounds of goodness but for possessing the very qualities that make men fall in love with them and women identify with them.

And how do we make sense of the real-life tragedy beyond the literary one—that Flaubert, Tolstoy, and Hardy are men creating and loving these vital, alive, sexual women—and then kill them? How does one understand that men want to have and to hold, and that if that possibility is threatened even for a moment, they will kill and that they may well call such murder, as Othello did, the result of loving "too well"?

Most of us know the answers, and do not ask such questions. She is in our bones, this image of the beautiful, strong, vulnerable, tender, kind, silent woman who is both adored for her passion and then destroyed for it (I am reminded that passion comes from the Latin *passio*, which means "suffering"). When she steps out of what Nathaniel Hawthorne, in his masterpiece of crushed passion, *The Scarlet Letter*, calls the "iron framework of [men's] reasoning" she invariably becomes disabled. We no longer question why men kill her, nor why we respond so predictably to her destiny. Perhaps we are attached to her very powerlessness, without which she would lose her heartbreaking status as the beloved victim who brings tears to our eyes even as society demolishes her. Three years before her husband began writing *Anna Karenina* in 1883, Sonia Tolstoy wrote: "He told me that he had imagined a type of woman in high society who had committed adultery. He said that his problem was to present this woman not as guilty but as pitiful. . . ." Perhaps even over a century later, our pity for an adulteress can only be roused if she is sacrificed; maybe only then can she be exonerated for her passion.

If she is not sacrificed, can we feel what she feels, or still feel for her? Is it only sorrow that allows us to forgive a woman who has sex outside marriage, only powerlessness that confers innocence, only punishment that restores goodness, and only goodness that spares her life—as it did for Hester? Can the passionate, strong, sexual heroine who steps outside the framework have as much power to determine her fate as does the society she lives in?

What if we suspend belief, do not rush in with assessments of the woman's morality, doubts about her character, misgivings about her emotional condition? What if our concern and sympathy stay with her and don't shift automatically, reflexively, to her husband and children? What if we reconsider our assumptions about women and love, about marriage and monogamy, reformulate all those old patterns and endings, step outside the iron framework ourselves? What if our adulteress is in no way pitiful: Can we still love her, or at least listen to her?

What if she were your best friend, or your sister, would you still think she was totally bad? Would you still need to see her punished?

The "Riddle of Femininity"

I questioned my own ability to listen when I began research for this book, when I realized how few female voices there were to listen *to*. Girls' and women's erotic needs and feelings, their desire for pleasure—their joy in their own sexuality—is largely an unwritten story. What we know about girls' sexuality at adolescence is this: It is the moment when they become the objects of male passion and worship, a fact that has been charted in coming-of-age novels written by men, from D. H. Lawrence to Philip Roth. As our eye automatically sees the erotic glory of a young girl through the dazzled male gaze, our ear is tuned to men's voices detailing girls' sexuality—to their being desired, not having desire; to their being sexual objects, but not sexual subjects. We know how they look and how they feel and how they taste and how they smell, but only from the perspective of male longing.

How is it that a girl's own sexual feelings have not entered into our culture's imagination? Where in "respectable" mainstream American fiction do we read of a woman's sexual coming of age, described from *her* point of view? Where does this vital young girl speak about her own sexual desire, not her desirability; what feels erotic, not what she hopes appears erotic to others? Where does Sleeping Beauty tell of her own awakening? Where is the female Portnoy? Where does Lolita tell of her own response to Humbert Humbert? Where does Marilyn Monroe tell her own sexual history? How is it we never cared about her silence, connected her "sexy" voice with its little-girlness, tied its very breathy quietness to the fact that it both held back secrets and was so faint it was barely audible?

While the term "male sexuality" conjures up powerful images of men's desire for women, the phrase "female sexuality" conjures up only visions of women's wombs and vaginas, graphic illustrations of women's reproductive systems as depicted in the sea of textbooks in the health section of the library or bookstore. But few female voices speak out to describe their *pleasure*, to define precisely what feels good and what does not, to delineate girls' sexual maturation in terms other girls can relate to.

No wonder Freud lamented in 1933 that "the riddle of femininity" remained unsolved. The erotic life of men had become accessible to research, he noted, yet the erotic life of women ". . . is still veiled in an impenetrable obscurity," and was therefore, he concluded, a "dark continent." It is still. It is a whole world marked by women's silence.

Explanations for the silence suggest that women don't really know what they want, or don't say what they need, or don't say what they mean, or don't mean what they say. Those who have noticed the difficulty women have in speaking about what is most precious to them—love and sex—may also suggest that the silence is not cultural but inherent; that women, even when they know what they want, will not speak of it because they are "secretive" or "manipulative" or "tricky." They not only lack a voice, these explanations imply, they lack much more: a morality; a self; a soul. Or they suggest that what women want is indecipherable—Freud's conclusion—even when they do speak. "What do women want?" he asked, but implied that the question was fundamentally unanswerable, that probing such a mystery would uncover only chaos, that women's desires inhabited the realm of the unfathomable.

Women are not by nature silent; they have been silenced. They do not lack a voice; their words are unwelcome. Women have long seen the correlation between female passion and punishment, and noted well that the two remain inextricable. They have witnessed the result of men's intertwined adoration and jealousy in the stories of Anna and Hester and Emma; noticed what happens to "aggressively" sexual women in movies and in life; observed the decision of kings to kill their "beloved" queens, noticed the decision of authors to follow society's lead and kill off their heroines. They have seen dead bodies of desirable, passionate, vital women strewn all over books and the stage, splattered across newspapers and on TV and movie screens, and they got the message long ago: *Pas-*

sion doesn't pay. Sex kills women. And they made a smart decision: They shut up.

Those few who do speak sound to our unaccustomed ears—to use a word that most often describes women's unquiet voices—shrill. Women talking about their own sexual desires sound different from other women; a crashing wave in a calm sea. When they attempt to articulate their erotic pleasure, many sound as though they are translating from a foreign language. They are. When they speak, they do not sound like *women* to our ears. Because to sound like a woman is to say nothing erotic at all.

If sex alone silences women, illicit sex (the Victorians aptly called it "criminal conversation") intensifies the stillness. Intrepid women writers must confront the fact that their heroines have no codified erotic language; that the words in sexual conversation are male, and while we admire male writers who use them, women writers who do the same thing are called obscene, vulgar, cold, threatening, predatory, unfeminine, or, at best, inauthentic.

And there is this relentless death-sentence to contend with. Although Erica Jong's famous heroine Isadora Wing neither drowned nor poisoned herself, it was not because Jong wasn't tempted. "I spent six months writing and rewriting the ending of *Fear of Flying*," she says. "It was 1973 and the novel was due, and I couldn't let go of it. I kept thinking, 'She's got to die, she's got to die,' and I came to understand that I had internalized the patriarchal paradigm, and that while I finally broke with it, something in me wanted to fulfill it."

It is difficult for wives to speak about their adultery: How can they sound like "women" if they do—not only breaking the silence about their own sexuality and desire, but the one sacred rule of marriage? Adultery is forbidden—unmentionable, as historian Tony Tanner points out in his book *Adultery in the Novel* (1979), "a crime unlike, for example, murder, which is arguably a greater threat to person, property and law, but was never *unspeakable* in society . . ." (italics mine). Knowing they are defying a hallowed social norm and that their experience should not be spoken of, women express their feelings defensively, hesitantly, defiantly, or timidly. Their words are then processed through the disbelieving ears of the listener, finally reaching the shocked eyes of the reader. The truth so easily reads false; the speakers, uttering such unexpected information, become untrustworthy. Are these *whores* speaking, or what? we wonder.

"I Didn't Know Who To Tell—or Who Would Listen"

And so the erotic voices of women are silenced. We do not hear them. For too long, this silencing has left a grievous void, an abyss filled only with distorted notions about women's character and lives and sexuality. How often have we heard:

Women are by nature monogamous.

Happily married women don't have affairs.

Women do not desire a variety of sex partners.

Women must love a man to have sex with him; women fall in love with any man they have sex with.

Women can't love more than one man at the same time; women dislike casual sex.

Women like married sex better than unmarried sex; women can't separate sex from love.

Women who have sex with men other than their husbands feel overwhelmingly guilty.

Women are not aroused by men's physical appearance.

From these aphorisms arise a host of comparisons between male and female motives for seeking extramarital sex: Men do so for urgent, biological reasons that have little to do with another woman—either his wife or his mistress; women do so for exclusively emotional reasons. Women's affairs, linked as they are thought to be to unhappiness in marriage rather than to anything intrinsically sexual, are thus explained as merely retaliatory, a weapon used either to diminish or imitate or punish men. If wives' affairs are premeditated, then they are also preventable, whereas husbands have their uncalculated, uncontrollable, and urgent passions as well as their biological need for variety to contend with. And if women's affairs are attacks on men, or imitations of their behavior, or means to avenge an adulterous husband, then they are hostile—whereas men's are innocently and exclusively sexual.

It is impossible to study the early literature on sexuality, which for the most part is written by men, based on a model of men's sexuality and men's relationships, and viewed through cultural stereotypes largely established by men, without being overwhelmed by this ineradicable portrayal of who women are and of what their motives consist. Sex statistician Alfred Kinsey, for example, attributed his finding that women had fewer extramarital partners than men to their lesser sexual needs. Another researcher, Robert R. Bell, saw aging and the desire for reassurance about physical attractiveness as a motivation for women's affairs but not for men's. Sociologists Gagnon and Simon, in discussing the socialization of women that leads them to envision sexuality "as a form of service to others" wrote, in 1975, "For the female sexual activity does not occur for its own sake, but for the sake of children, family and love" and added that "the body (either of the self or of others) is not seen by women as an instrument of self-pleasure."

The Lie of Female Adultery

Add up all these "facts" about a woman's sexuality and motivations and you get the following calculation about a woman having extramarital sex:

She has a bad marriage.

She is in love with the man she is having sex with.

She is eager to marry him; and she is torn apart by guilt.

She is either hopelessly in love or, worse, she is not a one-man woman at all, in which case she must have problems with intimacy, or a narcissistic need for sexual attention, or a repetition compulsion demanding that she unconsciously recreate the Oedipal triangle or some pre-Oedipal, split-object relationship.

She wants to have her cake and eat it too.

She is hysterical, commitmentphobic, a nymphomaniac, a bad mother.

She hates men.

She is not a good woman.

Equally disturbing is the tendency on the part of some women to believe what they have been told: that while men really want sex, women really want relationships. I question this: it is often a semantic distinction men and women are socially taught to make when in fact they both may want both, and because it implies that sex is not an integral component of women's pleasure in relationships; that an adult woman is content with a closeness which is not deeply sexual; and that the sexuality found in a relationship eventually and necessarily loses its intensely sexual edge.

WHAT WE DON'T KNOW ABOUT WOMEN'S SEXUALITY

Although recent studies suggest that sexual practices among American women are different from what earlier studies revealed, the truth is not easy to uncover. Statistical knowledge about the rate of extramarital sex is notoriously difficult to obtain. No numbers have officially replaced those of Kinsey, who surveyed 12,000 men and 6,000 women in 1948 and 1953 and found that 50 percent of married men and 26 percent of married women in this country had had affairs.

As hard as public health officials and scientists and therapists and sexologists have argued for a major nationwide study of American sexual behavior, and much as we need new information for such vital tasks as combating the spread of AIDS and other sexually transmitted diseases, lowering the rates of teenage pregnancies, and sexual abuse of children and rape, there is enormous resistance to such a survey. Indeed, in July 1989, in the middle of my research for this book, federal plans for an $11 million survey on nationwide sexual practices were squelched; *The New York Times* reported that conservative religious groups were in an uproar over the idea of government researchers asking questions about individuals' sexual practices, and that the House Appropriations Committee had withheld the money and directed the Public Health Service not to conduct the research. Again in September 1991, the National Institutes of Health canceled a survey of adult sexual behavior because of pressure from conservative politicians.

Certainly the theme of sexually joyous women—those who might commit adultery for their own pleasure—is a subject so taboo, our resistance to it is so profound, statistics about it are so inconsistent, that what *is* written about such women outside the novel, the movies, and popular music, emerges as alien and alienated and as easily dismissed as the women themselves. Our national silence about sex, particularly when it is women who are having it, reflects our ambivalence about both it and them, and has bred remarkable sexual ignorance. In fact, the first chapter of the sexual literacy study included in the 1990 *The Kinsey Institute New Report on Sex* is entitled, "America Fails Sex Information Test."

In this test, the "first nationally representative survey of what people know about sex," the majority of the 1,974 statistically representative American adults polled—55 percent—failed to answer correctly such basic questions about sexual knowledge as whether women can get pregnant during menstruation (yes), at what age the typical American first has sexual intercourse (sixteen to seventeen), and what percentage of women have had anal intercourse (40 percent). In fact, the majority failed the test entirely, unable to answer ten out of eighteen questions, which shows, notes Dr. June M. Reinisch, director of the Kinsey Institute and one of the authors of the book, that "Americans either don't have the facts or are misinformed about a range of sexual topics, including AIDS, contraception, homosexuality, erection problems, infidelity and menopause." Our population, she says, "does not know the facts that we need to be sexually healthy."

In a nation obsessed with sex, how is it possible that we so diminish its importance that we can justify our ignorance and denial over and over again? We still resist unearthing the numbers that might prove and help us cope with what we already know: that most teenagers have intercourse by the time they leave high school; that many girls don't protect themselves from pregnancy or disease. Yet in September 1991, Dr. Louis W. Sullivan, the secretary of Health and Human Services, defended the cancellation of a survey aimed at teenagers that was already financed by the National Institutes of Health. He worried that the questions aimed at uncovering reasons for teenagers' sexual attitudes and practices might appear to be condoning "casual" sex, a position seconded by William Dannemeyer, Republican of California, who called the survey an example of "wasteful government spending."

"Sex education does *not* promote increased sexual activity among young people," say the authors of the new Kinsey Report, "and a young person's attitudes about sexual behavior do not change to become either more or less liberal after sex education."

As for adult women's sexuality, perhaps we are afraid that asking questions aimed at eliciting information about wives' extramarital activity is tantamount to condoning it. Certainly books and magazines continue to report endlessly on the one sliver of truth we have not felt compelled to be quiet about: *men's* extramarital affairs. They continue as they always have to focus on helping unhappy wives deal with the heartbreak of infidelity—their husbands'—and promise to help them save their marriages, confront straying spouses, restore monogamy, even cope with a husband's bisexuality. By reiterating still the status quo, by recycling one half of the story, we are lulled into thinking that women's extramarital sex is not an issue.

But it is an issue. Women are having extramarital sex in numbers that might surprise Kinsey—although he was the first to admit thirty-five years ago that his own figures on adultery were affected by women's reluctance to speak up, and by men's eagerness to be counted as adulterers even when they were not. In the absence of a nationwide report, the numbers vary from study to study. In 1978, Paul Gebhard, one of the authors of the early Kinsey reports, summarized the existing data, saying he believed that the change since Kinsey was an increase in the number of women having affairs to around a third, with the figure for men remaining at a half. In 1980, *Cosmopolitan* conducted a landmark survey of 106,000 women and found 41 percent had extramarital affairs. In 1982, *Playboy* surveyed 100,000 married women and men and found 38 percent of the women and 48 percent of the men had had affairs—with married women under thirty more likely to have had affairs than married men of the same age.

Of the 12,000 people surveyed by Pepper Schwartz in preparation for her 1983 book (coauthored with Philip Blumstein), *American Couples*, she found "equal amounts of extramarital sex: 25 percent for both men and women. They're starting earlier," she said, "and equally."

A 1986 national survey by Thor Data of New York City included 2000 college-educated working women aged from twenty-five to fifty and found that of the 36 percent who were married, 41 percent were having or had had affairs. According to The Kinsey Institute, 29 percent of wives—and 37 percent of husbands—interviewed for its 1990 report had had extramarital sex.

Although we as a nation still uphold the ideal of sexual fidelity, it appears that approximately the same number of women as men fail to practice it, according to Frederick Humphrey, a sociologist and family therapist at the University of Connecticut who has been studying the subject of affairs for thirty years. "It's statistically 'normal' for people of both sexes to have an affair if we accept the fact that half or more of the people are doing so," he says. "And I'm willing to guess that half of American wives will have an affair—and that's a conservative guess."

That it is not men's sexuality women are interested in but their own will continue to be a cultural secret as long as women's sex lives as they really are, not as we think they should be or wish they were or hope they become, is a topic that makes us so deeply uncomfortable. As long as we feel it necessary to reduce a woman who has extramarital sex to a nonentity, and to declare her voice, when she speaks about desire and about sex, unnatural, unreal, and unbelievable, any discourse of desire will remain stuck in women's throats. Because to acknowledge the existence of the increasing number of women who have extramarital sex means to acknowledge women's sexuality in the first place; and to do that is to throw open the question of who women really are, what their nature really is, what their values really are, and what women really want, right here, now, today.

WOMEN'S DESIRE: A NEW LANGUAGE

I was about a year into the research for this book when I arrived at an unsettling impasse that put me in the center of this very question. During the more than twenty years I have been writing about relationships, dating, marriage, divorce, and remarriage—including my years as an editor at *Redbook*, *Family Health*, and *McCall's*, and a columnist for *Mademoiselle*—I have interviewed hundreds of women about sex. Yet it was only in the past ten years that I began hearing something new: about pleasure, and the insistence on it and the effects of it even if it is not found in marriage.

I already had information showing that women were having extramarital sex younger and earlier in their marriages than they once did: Kinsey estimated that his 26 percent of women who had affairs would have them by age forty. Close to twenty years later, in a study of 2,372 married women, researchers Robert R. Bell and Dorthyann Peltz found the same number of women having affairs by age thirty-five—with the figure rising to 40 percent by the time they reached forty. And in another large-scale study of sexual behavior conducted in 1972 by the Playboy Foundation and published as a book in 1974 with a text by Morton Hunt, 24 percent of the wives under age twenty-four reported having had extramarital sex—three times Kinsey's figure of the same age group.

In 1989, I widened my net, going back to the women I had interviewed over the years and speaking with them again—talking to their friends, and to my friends, and friends of friends—about extramarital sex. I did not expect such an enthusiastic response. Everyone seemed to know a woman who would participate: I would mention the subject at lunch or dinner, and someone would say, "Call me." Once, when I advertised in literary and city journals and newspapers in order to hear from women across the country, I got responses from women of all ages, from the early twenties to the late sixties. They all had a story to tell about adultery.

Many women had never uttered a word about their affairs to anyone else and were happy to have a chance to talk; some told me later that I, a stranger, known to need their help for a book, was a more appealing and possibly less judgmental confidante than even a close friend or therapist would have been. Many wanted to explore their feelings with another woman, and to find out what other women felt and how their lives turned out. Many hoped that in sharing their experiences, others might feel less stigmatized and less alone.

What is said about women was not what women were saying. In fact, much of what I was led to believe about women and extramarital sex from the literature neither illuminated nor corroborated what these women were telling me. I was listening to articulate, passionate women speaking about their sexual selves outside of marriage, breaking the silence and struggling to make sense of it all, and found other voices like theirs conspicuously absent in the scholarly work. Even in the psychoanalytic literature, which abounds with theories of women's sexuality and interpretations of women's deepest motives for extramarital sex, few women are doing either the talking or the interpreting. I discovered that the women's own stories did not resonate with the stories I "knew"; and that what they were saying might be something other than what I had been taught to believe.

I had to make a decision: Either fit the women into the literature, in which case I would have to disregard a good deal of what they all said as irrelevant or untrue; or believe what they were telling me, in which case I would have to attempt to rethink some deeply entrenched notions about women and their desires. I decided to stay with the women, because what I was hearing from them was consistent and urgent; it felt viscerally right to me, inescapably meaningful. Their voices would be the primary voices in this book.

Once I made that choice, my interviews with the many psychologists, psychiatrists, sociologists, and marriage therapists became secondary to those with the women themselves. A new story was being told; if I was to make sense of it, I could not superimpose on it my own or anyone else's more familiar story.

I must emphasize that this book is not a scientific study. My questions and results are not analyzed by computer, but by me; and my conclusions, coming as they do from the women themselves and interpreted by me, are therefore completely subjective. These women do not represent all American women, nor even all American middle-class white, heterosexual women, and I do not claim their stories are necessarily typical. I believe that interviewing women in depth the way I have has permitted me to find out a great deal about their marriages and their lives, and far more about their thoughts, hopes, and dreams than even I had hoped.

The women who talked to me did not do so, it soon became clear, with the intention of telling a story with some horrible ending. (Perhaps those who had sad stories to tell would not have been so willing to talk to me, or to anyone.) They came—and I don't think they knew this at the time any more than I did—because they had made an amazing discovery about themselves, and the catalyst for that discovery had been an extramarital relationship. I stress extramarital *relationship* rather than extramarital *sex* because it was ongoing friendships rather than casual encounters that deeply touched women's lives. It is interesting to note that while AIDS has diminished the frequency of one-night stands, and increased the interest in sexual exclusivity, research shows that it has not affected longer-term relationships.

"LAWLESS PASSION"

A few notes:

Technically, the term "monogamy" means marriage to one partner—its opposite is not "infidelity" but "polygamy"—but I use it here loosely, in the vernacular, to mean sexual exclusivity within a marriage, because the women do. I've taken into account the connotations of the various words that describe sex outside of marriage—"adultery," for example, suggests to me the completion of an extramarital sexual act that is legally as well as emotionally a crime, whereas "infidelity" seems to weigh in emotional dishonesty, while "straying" suggests a pattern of unemotional encounters. EMS (for extramarital sex) is what much of the scholarly literature now uses, and this term alone seems essentially without the judgment implicit in the others, but I have used most of these terms synonymously in this book, keeping the words used by the women themselves and allowing them to explain the meanings of their liaisons.

I have limited my attention to sexual relationships outside marriage, although sociologists and psychiatrists assure me that nonsexual extramarital affairs do exist and are as complicated and affecting as sexual ones. I have also limited my consideration of affairs to those that are heterosexual, although of course many women have extramarital sex with other women. I have not included women who were in "open" marriages, because the rules for conduct in such marriages are specifically opposed to the rules for couples in "closed" marriages, and this book is about the latter.

To report extensively on the men or the children involved in this drama would have been to write a different and more conventional book. My concern here was the women, their emotional state as a result of their affair or affairs, not their marriages or their families. This effort has uncovered something surprising: For if it is true, as psychiatrist Jean Baker Miller suggests, that most women spend their lives constantly "doing good and feeling bad," I was seeing the opposite: women who were doing "bad" and feeling good.

I am now more than ever interested in the extraordinary power of transgression for women. And extramarital sex, or "lawless passion," as Nathaniel Hawthorne called it, is the single most emphatic form of transgression available against a historical framework that has defined and confined women, and still does, despite the obvious changes in their lives, their environment, and their expectations—changes that their mothers, just a few decades ago, would not have been able to imagine.

I am asking you, as you read on, to suspend belief, and to listen. The following women are real.

Chapter Two

"I WANTED THEM BOTH"

*S*he had lost consciousness for an instant this time, which signified to June that her capacity for orgasm had finally, blessedly, returned. For the entire year she had been sleeping with Jonathan, it was only now that she felt able to fully surrender to her own physical sensations, to recognize a responsiveness that seemed to have left her some time ago. He had accused her of being anhedonic, a word she'd never heard of and that no one in the universe but Jonathan would use. "It's the opposite of hedonism," he told her, an explanation she sensed hid some irritation. She took it as criticism, a refined version of the old attack—calling a woman he was unable to please frigid.

Now she'd been vindicated. He was as thrilled as she at their victory, but they didn't celebrate loudly, they just looked at each other gratefully. They went through their postlovemaking bathroom ritual giddily, exaggerating their usual noisy protest at having to negotiate the cramped, tiny space together. They showered. She got

33

out before he did, as usual, leaving him alone with the dismal water pressure.

Inside June's travel kit, with its dwindling supply of her various ablutions, was a big green can of shaving gel she had mistaken for her green can of styling mousse. This sudden reminder of her husband was like a cut with the razor blade itself, the perfect sabotage of her orgasm celebration with Jonathan. Ah, she thought. The tritest of all tricks. The Freudian slip.

Her guilt—or whatever it was, since she would not have said until then that she even felt a twinge of it— lasted the duration of Jonathan's shower. The moment he stepped out, the stocky body she had moments before been lost in, the dripping black hair into which she had buried her face, reminded her: This man, this intense, demanding, fierce man, this respectable psychologist who seemed quite crazy most of the time, was irresistible.

The reason June got married nine years ago in the first place, she told me when I began interviewing her on June 1, 1988, was because she wanted to have a baby. She regarded this truth with more anxiety than she did her upcoming fortieth birthday, as if it invalidated her choice of partner, as if the decision had been cold-blooded, unromantic, reminiscent of couples she knew who decide to get married when one of their leases expires, who conceive of their nuptials as a tax-defying, money-saving life-style strategy. She reminded herself that Russell had long defended the pragmatism of their decision, that he had wanted a child too, and that he had since reiterated the soundness of their reasoning. It had not been unromantic, he assured her—they had both been, after all, twenty-seven years old—there was nothing faulty or mergerlike about their motivation, and of *course* they would have gotten married anyway.

But his assurances of the inevitability of their union failed to soothe her, and she didn't quite know why. She knew that her recent obsession with the reasoning behind their long-ago decision to marry clearly was dangerously displaced. She told herself her thinking was weird; it was as if she were preoccupied now, eighteen years after the fact, about her decision to go to UCLA or to become a reporter, both of which also were practical decisions. She still loved Russell; she loved their eight-year-old Chloe. So it was deranged to be investigating so intensely the emotions of an event that happened nine years ago, as if to successfully dissassemble the motive from the choice would provide a clue to some fundamental flaw in her thinking that could explain the one astonishing fact of her life for which she had no explanation: her affair.

What particularly disturbed her was that it was so easy, this business of being unfaithful. She'd always hated that mindless explanation of straying spouses—"I don't know, it just sort of happened"—because she knew nothing just happened. There were reasons. It took a complicated combination of vulnerability and intention and dissatisfaction and planning and lust and need, all that and more, to turn an acquaintance into a lover, and if that added up to an explanation of something that just *happened*, then someone was seriously out of touch. But while she didn't feel out of touch in that particular way, she did in another: She couldn't locate exactly what her dissatisfaction was about, quite what the enormity of her need was about, how, exactly, she had arrived where she was.

She and Russell both felt strongly about monogamy, at least within their own marriage. She had often delivered long speeches about the irrevocable damage of affairs, about the moral imperative of sexual commitment, how just because they lived in a society that was shaky about its values didn't mean that they themselves had to be. And yet for months, for maybe even a year, she'd been thinking a lot about extramarital sex, even though she wasn't unhappy with her own sex life. But there they were, these general and disturbing thoughts. How do women do it? How do they have time? Where do they go? More specifically, how would it affect her, if she ever did anything so rash and forbidden—how would it affect Russell? How would it affect Chloe, if she knew; how would it affect Chloe even if she didn't know? How would it affect her marriage if she were to have an affair and be found out? Would she deny it? Beg forgiveness? Regret it? What did other women do? But at this moment she was thinking, Oh, yes, I'm a true model of conjugal decency: I'm screwing my husband on some days, my lover on others, and on some, unavoidable, awful days, both—one right after the other.

As a reporter for medical magazines, specializing in psychological news and breakthroughs, June was at least aware of her own tricks, even if she didn't know exactly what she was tricking herself out of facing. She knew that question she posed to herself endlessly, like a mantra—Would I have married Russell if I hadn't had baby lust?—was not going to change anything, regardless of whether the answer turned out to be yes or no. But it amused her, in a dark sort of way, to discover she was as capable as any of her friends of obscuring the more pressing question, the one she knew she should be resolving rather than trying to figure out her exact emotional circumstances at the time of her marriage. And that question was: Why, if she was so damned happy with Russell, so contented in her marriage, was she sleeping with Jonathan?

She'd met Jonathan at a psychologists' meeting in San Diego eighteen months before. Jonathan was a psychologist; both lived in L.A. The paper he delivered was brilliant and she ran up to him after the morning session ended to tell him so. They became friends during that meeting, chatting both about their own specific interests in psychology as well as the future of psychoanalysis; gossiping about the speakers at the meeting, their reputations, and, of course, who was supposedly sleeping with whom. Jonathan's take on things astonished and thrilled her; June's easy, instinctive comprehension of all the essential psychological theories impressed him. They both thought the other absolutely adorable.

He was forty-four, divorced five years. He'd been married eleven years, had two boys, nine and seven, and was on good enough terms with his ex-wife to have flexible and frequent visitation rights. He had no plans to remarry: His practice, his children, and his passion for travel kept him busy and emotionally satisfied enough so that he did not miss marriage, although he said he had nothing against it, it was a good thing. It wasn't that he wouldn't marry again, it's just that he didn't have a yearning to right now. Sometime, maybe.

"I can't explain how I was able to drop my long-held beliefs about monogamy and instantly adopt a Go For It! attitude toward sex," June tells me, "but I did. Everything I thought I believed in simply dissolved and I did the quickest turnaround you can imagine. I went to my room the night I met him and thought, 'I want that guy; I'm going to have an affair with him' as if I were a practiced . . . adulteress. I was clear as I'd ever been. I shocked myself, and double-checked my thinking, kind of like, 'Come on now, June, that's not your style, that's the *opposite* of your style.' 'Are you sure?' I kept asking myself. And 'You bet!' was my answer. So much for my superego.

"I felt more than tempted to sleep with him, I felt determined to—I was on a mission—as if I'd found something I had to have and I'd be damned if I wouldn't have it. I felt greedy. Needy. All those words I'd scoffed at, words like 'growth' and 'experience' came to me in a rush: I suddenly felt my own life was a human-potential movement and this was the only way to develop my human potential and I'd be throwing away what I knew was right for me if I didn't pursue it. I'd be a woman with no life in her, a silly, scared wimp. All my 'Grab the Moment' impulses; all my 'Don't Let Opportunity Pass You By' feelings came up and squashed my puny little 'Don't Because You're a Married Woman' prohibitions, which suddenly felt about as compelling as my 'Don't Eat Sugar' vows. I was surprised by my own vehemence, and about the stupidity I was able to ascribe to my own prohibitions. It wasn't as if morality didn't exist; it was as if a greater morality, one I hadn't yet been aware of, had finally made itself visible to me. This must be how people rationalize murder, I thought. They tell themselves: It Is Good. God wants it that way. Do it.

"And so I decided, since I wasn't even on the fence about this, that I wouldn't dredge up some fatuous rationale to try to justify it or dissuade myself. I'd go with it, and deal with the rest later." This was peculiar, since for nine years June had had no desire whatsoever for another man, although she had had a vibrant sexual history, recalls her delight when, at seventeen, she slept with her beloved boyfriend Frank; remembers "these explosive feelings" and how much pleasure they brought her—how she and Frank "had sex everywhere."

She'd had several sexual relationships before she married Russell, at which point she said she entered a state of "unawareness" about the possibility of sex with other men—a feeling she didn't think came so much from sexual satisfaction as it did from "being off the market." For the nine years she was married, she felt her sexuality was reserved for marriage, that she "had handed it over" to her husband like a gift, and that it now belonged to him—and in fact she didn't experience sexual feelings much outside of intercourse with Russell. She did reach orgasm with Russell. What seemed to have left her was an ongoing sense of being connected to her sexual feelings, a sense of herself as a sexual being, the owner of all those sensations.

"You know, I used to feel like a really sexual person, I was always thinking about sex and feeling just sort of sexy in general. I don't mean sexy like men always looked at me or anything, but sexy inside myself. I'm a dancer, not professional, but I've taken some kind of dance classes, either modern or jazz or ballet, since I was little; and I'm in tune, sort of, with my body."

"You lost that feeling?"

"Yes. I lost it even before Chloe was born, like around when we got married. It was very subtle, though. I stopped taking classes. I stopped connecting with other men. And I didn't feel bad about it; I figured, well, that's what you do when you get married, what's the matter with that? It's a nice gift of love."

Her first night with Jonathan was not so much gratifying as intense. She got scared after all, suddenly realizing how impulsive this was, how outrageous, how she hadn't weighed, with her normal caution, what she was doing. So her determination—that go-for-it feeling, and her sense of the rightness of it—fizzled the moment they started undressing, at which point she thought, What the hell am I doing? I'm a married woman! And the fiercely negative feeling she'd had at that moment was exactly the opposite of the positive rush of guiltless delight she'd experienced earlier when she first invited Jonathan to her room.

"So what did you do?" I ask.

"I asked him to leave," she says.

"What did he say?"

"He paused a long time, there in his Hanes briefs, and said, 'Hmmm. I see.'"

"A shrink."

"Yeah. And he got dressed and left. I was paralyzed. 'Whaddaya mean, you *see*?' I wanted to say to him. 'How can you *see*? You don't know how much I want this. You're not married, you're not a woman, so how do you know how this feels? You don't know anything about me. You think I'm a lonely woman on the town, a bored person looking for kicks. You think I'm a . . . cock-teaser!' And so, in a frenzy, I called his room."

"You said this?"

"Yes. He was four doors down from me and I shouted at him like a madwoman over the hotel phone, like Sophia Loren and Marcello Mastroianni in one of those terrible farces. He said, 'Do you want me to come back?' and I said, 'Well, of course I do! See? If you *saw* you'd know that. Yes! Yes, I do!' And he did."

And she liked him, liked his body, his way with her, liked how willing he was to take her on, how much he really did seem to see what she accused him of not seeing. She liked his lovemaking. "The business about my being anhedonic didn't come up for months," she adds. "I think he was worried that I'd never give in to this, that I'd never feel relaxed with him, never have an orgasm. I was pretty sure he was right, not that I wasn't comfortable with him, but something in me definitely wouldn't play. But I figured, I'm enjoying this consciously, what my unconscious is doing, given the circumstances, I can't control. What can I do about it—go into therapy to see why I don't come with my extramarital partner?"

It was clear to both of them that this was an affair that had no future. So they grabbed their temporary love, orgasm or not. Their relationship was extremely intimate; June felt his interest in her, his desire for her, and they played together, played the way she and Frank had, years before. His interest in her moved her; she couldn't quite believe all the attention and concern he gave her, the way he remembered what her days were about, what she had to do, what she thought, whom she was interviewing and for which publication, what her problems with each article were, and how he tried to help her. She adored it.

"There's something to this business of sharing interest in a profession," she told me. "It makes me more sympathetic to all those businessmen-and-their-secretaries stories I've heard all my life that sounded so predictable and so dumb. It's not just proximity that takes hold, or idle lust. Having a common interest is uniting—the interest in each other grows naturally, it doesn't have to be cultivated or feigned. We're interested in this thing together; so you get to concentrate on something other than yourselves . . . and all the while you are concentrating, on some other level, on yourselves."

"Well, so anyone thrown together with a common cause would make good lovers? That's the old Opportunity theory of affairs."

"Yes, right. I mean wrong, that's not right. That's not what I mean. We just were having such a good time. We . . . *played*. Sex, I think, is just one of the ways adults play."

Jonathan became the mentor June never had, the close male friend she felt she hadn't had since before she got married. Not that Russell wasn't a friend. But it was just different. Russell, she said, saw the psychological community as stuffy and boring, her reporting as taking too much of her time, and the subject matter unappealing, and Jonathan's support thrilled her. It was a relief to be able to confide in someone else, because she felt her career concerns had to be hidden from Russell, whom she felt to be always on the verge of saying, 'For God's sake, why don't you drop that crazy profession?' Russell probably was pleased she'd stopped talking about it so much, she figured. He certainly hadn't asked any questions about it lately.

Not that Russell was unsupportive, June assured me. It was just that medical reporting as a profession—as an interest, even—baffled him, and while at first he was intrigued, it was just not a field he could fathom. It bored him, really. The brain, the emotions, were not his specialty. He was the owner of a small construction company, an elegant little firm that had built some of the most innovative small buildings in Southern California. He was a businessman; June felt sometimes that what made her profession palatable to him was its potential for a high income.

"What does Russell like about you?" I asked.

"Oh, dear. I don't know. Something, I guess, that I don't think I notice in myself, or value too much. I think he really likes the fact that I'm sort of a regular gal. Not too neurotic. Not too hard to deal with. He said once, 'You're not like most women,' and meant it as a compliment. I didn't ask why I wasn't like most women because I was afraid if he told me it would annoy me, either because of his assessment of 'most women' or of the way he supposed I differed from them. What he means is that I'm relatively easy to get along with. Not crazy. Not clingy. Independent. Something like that.

"And he thinks I'm a good mother. I *am* a good mother. Our relationship is solid. A little boring; kind of etched in stone, somehow. We're a perfect couple, according to our friends. We don't fight a lot, we don't torture each other. A little on the tepid side, but we're sort of proud of that; we've always thought that was a good thing for a marriage. Not too much intensity. We were very smug at the beginning—like it was all so wonderful, so perfect, so rational; and we never fought. And I really felt odd, like 'Oh, so *this* is what it's all about?' Like I wouldn't ask him something that I knew would provoke a fight—or, like I don't ask why he likes me because I know his answer would bug me. My sense of Russell is that he likes me fine—no, that he loves me—but that if anyone stopped to ask him what it was about me he really loves, he might be baffled. It's like the guy who says, 'Hey, I *married* you, didn't I?' when his wife asks whether he loves her. But I accept that about him, and don't feel he loves me less because it's unarticulated. I never really expected him to be perfect, or anything. You know, knight on the white horse."

"But he doesn't love you according to your criteria?"

"You mean the real me? Oh, God, who knows? He doesn't mind the real me, I suppose. I mean I don't hide it particularly. But listen, the strangest thing happened about a month ago. I went to a three-day meeting in Chicago—Jonathan was giving a paper and I was scheduled to go anyway—and I called home the day after I arrived. Russell isn't great on the phone—our conversations have always been clipped, since he thinks phone calls aren't the place to chat, and I've sort of picked up the cue. So here I was prepared for a brief rundown on my plans—what time I'd be going home; how the hotel was. But Russell sounded strange. He said he missed me, could I come home the next day? I was floored. I couldn't—it was the day Jonathan was reading his paper, and we'd agreed to drive to Evanston that afternoon to go to the Northwestern–Michigan game. So I said no, I couldn't come home Saturday, expecting him to say 'Fine.' He asked would I come home Sunday, then, instead of Monday night? Well, I couldn't really say no to that, although I'd looked forward to the whole weekend with Jonathan.

" 'Sure,' I told him, 'I'll check Sunday flights.' He said good, he'd like that. Was there anything wrong? I asked him. No, he said. He just wanted to see me. All delivered in Russell's rather affectless way. I wasn't sure whether he was upset or not; it's all so . . . flat—you have to understand—I've known this man for a decade and great bursts of emotion are not his thing—and to be honest, I didn't want him to be, so I didn't probe. He'd never rushed me before, so something was up, even if I didn't know what it was. Even if *he* didn't know what it was.

"When I got home he came toward me and held me close for about a minute. Chloe was standing there looking surprised and sort of weirdly happy—her father isn't the gushy type, as you may have gathered. That night he told me—still in that flat, affectless tone—that he'd been scared; that he thought something might happen to me while I was in Chicago, that he'd been feeling nervous since I left that he might lose me.

"I was as much surprised as moved by his vulnerability, and by that eeriness of someone's picking up truths as if from the air, and I reassured him that he wasn't about to lose me. I mean, he wasn't. His anxiety lessened soon after that, and he was back to being the same self-possessed, vaguely preoccupied husband I knew. He didn't want to talk about it, then or later, when I asked what brought on his terror, fascinated as I was by this. I would have nagged him to tell me, under normal circumstances—you can imagine that I'm not the person to leave a scary dream alone without trying to analyze it—but I was too guilty to push it. But I tell you, I was moved, the way you are when a child has a terrible nightmare that clearly arose from the day's events, and you know what your own part was in it, who the Wicked Witch is in that dream and why. I thought to myself, what the fuck are you *doing*, June?

"And still, I can't let Jonathan go. I know that to really explain my affair, to justify it, it would be more understandable if I could portray Russell as bad, somehow—you know, the way men always say they sleep with other women because their wives don't understand them. But Russell is okay. He really *doesn't* understand me, but I don't think that's the point. But I don't know. I'm used to him. He's a little bit more conservative than I am—more domestic, even—I mean he likes being with Chloe and me a lot. He's a very good man. He . . . touches me, with that straightforward midwestern style of his. He's like Gary Cooper. Very straight, very good. A deal on a handshake type. No theatrics. I can't even imagine Russell having an affair—isn't that strange? I really can't."

"No woman I've ever talked to can imagine her husband having an affair—not if she's having an affair, too," I say. "There seems to be some psychological insistence on the *other* partner's fidelity."

"Oh, I used to hate men who said about their wives, 'She'd never sleep with anyone else. She'd never want to, or she doesn't like sex, or she only thinks of the family. . . .' "

"Well, so why do you think Russell would never have an affair?" I ask.

"It's not that he wouldn't ever have one, just that I don't get the sense that he connects with that many people. And if you think I'm going to say something like 'Because he only loves one woman and that's me,' you're crazy . . ."

"Right. But if you thought he would have an affair, would you be uncomfortable?"

"Yes. I think so. I'm uncomfortable as it is. But then it would mean that our family would be in trouble."

"This way, you figure, someone is minding the store."

"Yes. Exactly. That we won't fall apart. And I want to be married to him. I can't imagine not being with him, really. I know that I care deeply about Jonathan, but that doesn't mean I want to end my marriage. Again, I know I sound like a man, but my marriage is a separate thing. Jonathan doesn't alter that."

It is this that is ultimately the most baffling to June. "I guess I love two men," she says. "I've always heard that that's impossible—that a woman only has the capacity to love one man, and if she thinks she loves two, she probably doesn't love either. Or she's running away from love, or she's not in touch with her anger. In fact, I *am* in touch with my anger at Russell. I *do* wish he were warmer, funnier, more accessible. I *do* wish I wanted to share my feelings with him. I wish our sex life was fabulous, and that we played together, if you know what I mean. I do wish our marriage weren't so . . . bland. So, yeah, I guess I'm angry, but only because I'm married to someone who doesn't fill all my needs, which of course we all know no one can do anyway. I'm not so angry I want out. I'm not thinking every day, oh, my husband's this withholding jerk. I just know his limitations, don't have much hope of changing our dynamic, and don't really love him a whole lot less than I ever did. Isn't this just the reality of loving someone for a long time?"

Meanwhile, Jonathan's intensity has won her over. "He's like this wild creature who wants to know everything—what I think, what I feel. He notices everything—when I have an inch trimmed from my hair, when I get too little sleep. 'You look pale,' he tells me. 'Why do you have those rings under your eyes? Why haven't you been sleeping?' I always tell him to back off, to take it easy, that I'm fine. But I love it.

"I mean, Jonathan isn't every woman's cup of tea. He's got a ferocious quality that would drive a woman mad who didn't like his kind of intimacy. He's sort of always on me, excuse the pun. His sexual involvement is ridiculous, it's so intense—as if nothing short of merging is good enough. 'I don't just want part of you,' he says, to which I inevitably respond, 'Yeah, I know, you want to smother me to death.'

"But you know, after about a year, during which time I responded to his intensity by tuning out a lot, by refusing to merge, by shooing him away a lot, something weird happened. I began to crave his kind of closeness, overbearing as it may be. It scared me less. It felt alive—I felt alive. I loved playing with him—he was so funny, so involved with me. He knew me so well and was so attentive. Instead of feeling overwhelmed, I started to feel free, like some weird, deep need I didn't even know I had had been met. I'd sit at the institute and just crave him. I began to feel his kind of involvement not as a terrific, temporary insanity, but as a normal way to live, the right way to love. I feel like being with him all the time now, having sex with him, particularly now that I'm having orgasms. There's nothing to hold back

47

anymore. It scares me—but not because I feel scared, because I feel so *unscared*—I feel awake, being this involved with someone. I feel alive.

"Maybe I can afford to be . . . a Jonathan junkie . . . because of Russell's aloofness. Maybe all I'm doing is filling in the blank spots in my life. You know, they say that many affairs merely exist to stabilize the primary relationship—maybe that's what I'm doing. Or maybe I'm hoping it will burn out. Explode. That the situation will become untenable. That's the script, right? You can't have both. But what really worries me is the fact that I can't imagine being without either man. I feel strangely complete: Something is mine again, something I used to like about myself that I just lost. I'm happy in my marriage. And happy in my affair. It's supposed to not work, or I'm supposed to be deeply troubled, and here I am, feeling better than I ever have and I'm not supposed to. I know intellectually something's got to give, but then I think, why? Who said?"

That "sudden" decision June made in her hotel room to sleep with Jonathan wasn't so sudden. It had been fomenting over the past few months in the form of those theoretical questions about her marriage and about sex in general—did she marry Russell *only* to have a child? Would she have married him otherwise? How does a woman who has an affair handle the deceit? How would her own affair, were she to have one, affect Chloe, Russell, their marriage? She remembered that they began, these idle fantasies that seemed to have no source, no point, right after she met Jonathan. But she certainly did not intend to have an affair; that was something other women did, friends even, but not she.

Like June, all the other women I would meet had had

premarital sex, either with their future husbands or with several men, so it was monogamy that was new to them, not multiple relationships. This sociological shift characterizes research that shows a woman is more likely to have extramarital sex if she has had premarital sex. Yet these women—like women all over the country, polls reveal—tend to disapprove of extramarital sex. They believe in the sanctity of the sexual exclusivity clause in marriage. They believe that adultery is wrong. So in order for the "go" signal to be as compelling as it was for June, to make her feel it would be denying the deepest of her needs to ignore its insistence, she had to make an emotional and intellectual about-face, undergo an intricate but powerful self-administered conditioning process that allowed this disapproved-of behavior to supplant the desired and acceptable one. For her, as well as for the other women, there was this repositioning, the emotional negotiation of which was inevitably prompted by a man.

That men actually still pursued her after marriage surprised June, as it did the other women. "I mean, look, I knew men still *existed*," Sarah, twenty-eight and married one year, told me, "and I was even sort of attracted to some, but something had changed for me, deep inside. Something had clicked off." But that something had not necessarily changed for the men. "My old boyfriend kept calling me, wanting to see me, even after I got married," she told me. "I kept saying, 'Todd, I'm *married*.' He kept saying, 'Yes, Sarah, I *know* you are,' as if I were making some totally irrelevant observation." Here she was, with an automatic monogamousness setting in and a feeling of spontaneous sexual stirrings "deep inside" clicking off—what Sarah called the odd sensation of walking around with a Day-Glo "Sold" sign on her chest—and yet it didn't have the effect of discouraging men from putting in a bid. One explanation, according to sociologist Lynn Atwater, who studied women's extramarital affairs in her 1982 book, *The Extramarital Connection*, is that

> Men, by continuing behaviors they have been taught so well, become unwitting socializing agents in the transitional process to the first extramarital involvement. Women are not completely passive in this process, of course. But male sexual initiative, especially to the degree that it is forthright rather than ambiguous, raises the opportunity for extramarital sex to a woman in a way that she must *consciously* be aware of and respond to [italics mine].

But what could make a woman who has been responding to sexual advances all her adult life, lived comfortably in her body and had other sexual relationships, negotiated familiarly in the territory of her own desire and regulated it for years, *unconscious* of the opportunity? During the ten-year period between her twentieth and thirtieth birthdays, June had felt desire for other men even while having sex with one; she'd had sex with two men simultaneously, even while feeling love for neither; she'd negotiated the intricacies of sexual etiquette and sexual feeling in all her complicated premarital relationships. She knew, in other words, the workings of her own sexual desire—how it operated independently from what she willed it to be, how it flooded her, was part of her—none of these feelings was scary. She knew the vagaries of her own sexual nature; *knew* it was absurd to think desire and desirability vanish once a ring went on her finger—yet that is precisely what happened.

It is one thing, I tell June, to voluntarily choose sexual exclusivity, to declare herself out of circulation—that is a decision both men and women often make when they marry. It is another to have become involuntarily out of commission—to suppress sexual feelings, to block them from awareness, as if sexual exclusivity were not a decision but a nonnegotiable fact—an edict issued by the body: *Now you are no longer noticeable. Now you no longer feel.*

Yes, June says, she wondered about that, wondered why she couldn't be married but still keep that nice, sexy feeling she'd always had around men. Why had becoming a wife clamped down on that feeling instead of freeing it? Why, now that she was having "permissible" sex—did she feel vaguely invisible, the way Sarah felt when her former boyfriend kept calling her "even after I got married."

Why, suddenly, would this profound knowledge of herself and of her body, her unique understanding of sex and of relationships, all gained from years of having been in connection with her body and with men, of having many erotic experiences, go underground? How could it get pushed out of awareness—in the language of psychology, dissociated or repressed, but in any language, no longer known, no longer her own? What could be so powerful as to make a modern, experienced young woman disavow her own pleasurable feelings this way? And why would marriage, the one place where she thought her sexuality would be at home, be the very place where it felt "no longer my own"?

Chapter Three

THE PERFECT WIFE

The eyes of others [are] our prisons; their
thoughts our cages.

—Virginia Woolf, "An Unwritten Novel," from *A Haunted House and Other Short
Stories* (1944)

When you think about it, giving up your
"real" personality is a small price to pay for
the richness of "living happily ever after"
with an actual man!

—Lynda Barry, cartoonist

*W*hat is marriage? I ask each woman. They laugh.
Their responses are remarkably similar: A man and a
woman in love. Closeness. Happily ever after. The blissful picture is the same today as it was yesterday, despite
the sexual revolution, despite divorce statistics and increased life spans, despite their own self-deprecating
jokes about how naive the vision is—even despite chilling reports, like the one that analyzes fifteen years of
data compiled by the University of Chicago's National
Opinion Research Center and concludes glumly that
marriage in the U.S. is a "weakened and declining insti-

tution" because "women are getting less and less out of it." The women's emotional reaction to the word was fixed ages ago, when they first learned to idealize—to "attribute ideal characteristics and excellences to"—marriage; it has been promising happily ever after too long for reality to interfere with it much.

Next I ask how long they expect to stay married once they get married, and each woman answers "forever." Sociologist Annette Lawson asked her students at Berkeley, "How many of you expect to be married?" All put up their hands. "How many of you expect to be divorced?" Very few hands. "They know the figures," says Lawson, "but it is not going to happen to them." My women, like her students, know that the original immutable marriage contract, a commitment to permanence, has shifted to a commitment to the quality of the relationship—a mutable phenomenon if there ever was one—so if one partner or other decides the quality has diminished sufficiently, all the court has to do is simply agree and the marriage is over. That alone has done for the life span of marriage what the hole in the ozone layer has done to the life span of our rain forests: changed the meaning of "forever" from Webster's "for a limitless time; eternally" to "for a while"; made its duration subject to our whim. Nevertheless, the dream of happily ever after women have always cherished is so persistent that Lawson, calling it "The Myth of Romantic Marriage," observes, "Romantic love has become the most desired experience of life—the fantasy of the West," and that "especially for women, to love and to be in love is to become the good and whole person, a hero."

Every woman I spoke to had aspired to being this good and whole person, this hero, the minute the word "marriage" was in the air. They began to emulate her, or at least what they imagined her to be. Their picture of this Perfect Wife, drawn long before, was an image both deeply familiar, repeated endlessly in stories of love they had heard and read, yet foreign—for none of them actually knew such a woman. Again, they know she is a dated prototype, just as they know marriage rarely lasts forever, although they do not really believe this. They choose to heed the myth rather than the reality, notes sociologist Dr. Norval Glenn, of the University of Austin, "in spite of what they know, think, feel and anticipate." They are "totally unrealistic," he says, but prefer nevertheless to convince themselves that they will avoid the pitfalls. The Perfect Wife is an image as resistant to change as that of Happily Ever After; she is part of the same vision.

Who is the Perfect Wife? What effect does she have on the women who aspire to become her? And why does she exist now—still—for these sexually sophisticated women who would appear to have no more use for her? The answers may begin to explain the origins of June's disconnection, her sense that she had "handed over her sexuality" to her husband right at the onset of marriage.

BECOMING DONNA REED

The Perfect Wife is, of course, Donna Reed.[1] She is beautiful, smiling, supportive, contented, giving, feminine—she is, in a word, good. "Good" as it applies to the Perfect Wife inevitably modifies and diminishes the word "self"—as in self-sacrifice, self-abnegate, self-restraint, self-denial—the suffix always restraining or

[1] Donna Reed of *The Donna Reed Show*—even more than June Cleaver of *Leave it to Beaver* and Harriet Nelson of *Ozzie and Harriet*—embodies the virtuous qualities of the Perfect Wife as well as the Perfect Mother.

containing or constraining in an effort to make that woman's self a little less *something*. Her virtue exists in direct proportion to how much of her self is whittled away, and how much of what is left she is willing to not keep to herself. If she is amenable to expunging the self altogether—to be self*less*—then she has succeeded in accomplishing the highest goal, attaining what many believe to be woman's best self, often calling it her "true" self, obviously empty of her true self though it is.

If she can annihilate her self altogether and still manage to seem contented, then she has achieved the additionally heroic feat of holding on to her femininity—that elusive quality women are always in danger of losing whenever their selves threaten to burst through all the constraints. In her book *Femininity* (1984), Susan Brownmiller suggests that the specter of lost femininity hovers over every woman at all times, a constant reminder of this "inherent nature" she "seems to misplace so forgetfully whenever she steps out of bounds." Certainly femininity is something women are thought to have had more of in the past—Brownmiller even defines the term as "a nostalgic tradition of imposed limitations"—and indeed with every new sign of budding self-possession a woman displays—assertiveness, say, or ambition—her "femininity" dwindles accordingly.

It diminishes most dramatically when she displays her sexuality openly, for overt sexuality is antipathetic to femininity. She is thought to have had more femininity in the past than she does today because the constraints on her sexuality were so much greater then, and because there is, theoretically, anyway, so little these days to stop her from coming right out and getting her sexual desires filled, or for showing how great her erotic appetite is. Wrote psychiatrist Dorothy Dinnerstein in her 1976 *The Mermaid and the Minotaur*:

What everybody correctly senses is that if women are capable of more genital pleasure than they get now, and manage to find it, they will become more willful, less easily subordinated as people; and that, conversely, if they are capable of more human willfulness than they now show, and manage to win a real share of the worldly power now monopolized by men, they will become sexually more demanding. It is hard to tell which threat—the sexual or the worldly one—defenders of our old arrangement find more basically alarming.

Certainly the women I spoke with never actually considered themselves Donna Reed raw material. They felt poorly qualified to fit such a mold of selflessness and sexlessness. Nevertheless, at marriage they each began a process of self-revision, altering or burying those parts of themselves that they perceived to exceed or violate it. Their feelings and knowledge and experience—that is, what they felt in their bodies and knew about themselves and understood about men and sex and relationships, slowly collapsed, yielding to imaginings of what they *would* feel and know and experience once they became wives. They spoke of this someone new with an irony that belied their acceptance and anticipation of her, noting often that their own *real* feelings fell appallingly short of what they thought a wife's feelings *should* be, as these three young wives, aged twenty-four, twenty-seven, and thirty-one, each said:

I mean, I'm a pretty demanding person. I was always called "bossy." So when I got married, I thought, am I going to be able to get what I need here, or is all this about giving up what I need? But I figured what the hell, I have plenty of time for figuring that out, right? I can't really change *that* much. If you're going to be a wife, you've got to trust that you'll be like one, if you know what I mean. So I thought, I'll just hang in there till I get it—other women do it all the time.

I told my husband—then my husband-to-be—Look, I'm a lousy cook, I'm horrible in the morning, and I get tired around ten at night. I can't change these things. He was great; he knows this about me. But damned if I don't feel guilty as hell about not cooking and try desperately to stay up later. It's very hard not to try to be a better, sweeter person—even when you know it's absurd.

Getting married always scared me, in this way, because I am really not, you know, the type. I've just never been very traditional. You know, very good.

And so began a process that devalued their unmarried lives and selves, as they deferred to altogether new criteria for goodness, and set about acquiring the privileged information and status deemed more commendable and more fulfilling than that which they already had. They would become as idealized as the blissful relational world they were entering: They would be well rid of the feelings they had before marriage—all those unbridled, messy, inconclusive sexual feelings in all those premarital relationships. These were emotions that once filled what Rachel Brownstein, in her 1982 book, *Becoming a Heroine*, ironically calls the "incoherent, hostile wilderness of days" in which single women wander about before perfect love comes along and "endows the aimless [life] with aim."

"TOO OVERWHELMING" FOR MARRIAGE

Becoming Donna Reed quite often began for these women with an attempt to do whatever was necessary not to feel grotesque next to her. They rarely complained of feeling "too small" by comparison; rather, they felt . . . overwhelming. They understood implicitly that the

Donna Reed model is thinner, quieter, nicer, purer, and more feminine than they were. Some felt immediately "too large" or "too fat"—others just began over time to feel "too bossy" or "too independent" or "too complicated." Or "too loud" or "too noisy" or "too emotional" or "too sexual."

Next to Donna Reed, who mainly listens and occasionally advises wisely, they felt they were "too talkative," too. They had long ago become familiar with the perceived problem of females' endlessly wagging tongues, yet they also knew the facts: that it is men, not women, who talk more in meeting halls; boys, not girls, who talk more in classrooms. When men and women talk equally in a group, people just *think* the women have talked more, Deborah Tannen reminds us in her 1990 book, *You Just Don't Understand*, and cites research concluding simply that, since most people feel on some level that women should be seen and not heard, *any* amount of talk by a woman is perceived as *too much* talk. Tannen also notes that women feel "onstage" when men are around, and are likely to curb their tongues, watch their behavior, and adjust both their style of talking and the subject matter to men's.

Aware of this perception and its wider implications, these women understood that what they were most in danger of speaking too much about was their experience and their knowledge—that is, their lives before marriage, specifically, their *sex* lives before marriage. Not wanting to be inconsiderate of their husbands, they attempted a silence that was new to them in order to achieve relatedness. Many women hid their entire sexual history from their husbands, leaving in an occasional boyfriend or two for reality's sake, but hoping not to incite jealousy; hoping not to appear, as one woman put it, "*too* experienced."

But while some women cited "politeness" and "kindness" as their reasons for staying mum about their pasts, others went beyond mere sensitivity to their husbands' feelings and proceeded to erase their pasts entirely, and without any prompting. June, for example, tells me in passing that as soon as she knew she was going to marry Russell, she burned all her old love letters.

"You burned all your letters?" I asked her. "Why did you do that?"

I don't know, really. Russell wouldn't have cared, I guess. It had to do with being ready for the real thing; a kind of preparation for getting married that I thought would ready me for all those wonderful things that were going to happen.

"Wonderful, how?" I ask.

In the sense that I would now be devoted to one man, and he would be devoted to me, and we would be true. And I guess all the other love I'd experienced wasn't the same.

"Were you aware that you were throwing out a part of yourself, or didn't it feel like that?"

Not at all. Throwing out a lot of embarrassing mush? It didn't seem like a sacrifice at all.

The majority of the women I queried about this point had decided to do what June did—to throw out letters they had received from men other than their husbands. Bettina, thirty-seven years old, told me

I pictured Ron [her husband] going through my journals one day and having a fit. I had done things with other men I hadn't done with him, and there it was, explicit sexual stuff. I was afraid he'd find out. I don't know if I thought he'd ask why I hadn't done them with him or why I *had* done them with other men, but I didn't want that confrontation to take place. It's ridiculous, of course; he knew I'd lived with other men. But I figured what he didn't know wouldn't hurt him.

Rosemarie, twenty-seven when she married a classmate in college three years before I met her, said it wasn't her sexual experience she was aware of discarding but her feelings *about* that experience, which, she felt, were "just too raw, too dramatic" to be shared with her husband, since "Oh, God, all that pain and joy and complicatedness" would have to be explained to him, "and he wouldn't even understand who that person who felt all that *was*." Her husband loved her, at least those aspects of herself that she had presented. But would he approve of those feelings she kept hidden? While all the women who had thrown out their love letters did so for seemingly innocuous reasons, the implication was that a wholesale self-cleanup was necessary as a preventive measure against some possible terrible, indicting revelation about themselves. A record of past lovers, yesterday's joy and sex and anger, proof of old passions, was dangerous, they said somewhat sheepishly, and, as June put it, "wasn't worth the trouble."

"What do you mean, 'it wasn't worth the trouble'?" I ask her. "What kind of trouble? What would happen if Russell had more than a glimpse of your past? What if you *didn't* erase your sexual history?"

I only know I read them one day and thought they were so embarrassing, so stupid, they had to go. I don't know why, really. I didn't want . . . my children to see them.

"Why do you think all of your feelings, all that experience that came before, is 'embarrassing' and 'stupid'?"

"If you could see what I wrote," she said, "you'd understand."

Burying the Sexual Past

Many women had kept some kind of journal or diary of their lives before getting married—and many had got rid of them. But they, like June, found it hard to explain why. One reason given by a forty-year-old woman named Natalie was that

> it seemed inappropriate to continue hiding something when there should be nothing to hide from my new husband.

But then, wondering about a logic that seemed to transfer the problem of what was being hidden to the object rather than to the contents, I ask Natalie: "If there is nothing to hide from your husband, why throw out the diaries? Aren't you in fact hiding nothing less than yourself?"

"I wouldn't know where to put the diaries."

"That's really it?" I ask. "There's no other reason?"

"I have a new life. I don't need these. Really. They would only cause trouble, I know it."

They were greeting a new life that would render irrelevant these old, tattered records of tumultuous feeling—an emotional history of premarital existence that was somehow no longer appropriate, was even humiliating. Janna, a thirty-three-year-old woman married four years, thought about it a long time before she called to say she still wasn't sure why she had thrown away her diaries—dating from the age of eleven—but thought perhaps it was because

> hiding my diary was something I always did, first from my mother, then from my sisters. So there was no question of that, that they must be hidden. I'd put in every feeling I had every day, all my anger toward everyone; all my petty little crimes and thoughts. Then, when it got to be about boys, I began putting in sexual thoughts and recording all of that. I don't know why I didn't decide to just go on hiding them—but I became obsessed with the silliness of that. I was a grown woman. Where would I put them? "Darling, would you empty your desk drawers so I can have room for my diaries, which you can't see?" And then I figured they weren't of any use to me anymore; that they would just take up too much room in our apartment and for what? I think I felt I couldn't justify them—as if they were old stuffed animals or something.

Wendy, a twenty-eight-year-old married two years, said, "That chapter of my life is over"; other women echoed her perception that "over" meant "canceled." Most felt, in fact, that they'd probably "destroy the evidence" again. Wendy says,

> I was *getting married*. It seemed right to get rid of them. In fact, my mother and I sat around and read them—we howled, because there were some incredibly intense letters from men I swear I can't remember—and then we—I—threw them in the fire. It was like a rite of passage, something women just do.

It was a rite of passage celebrating the occasion of becoming a bride, and of being transformed into a state worthy of marriage. It was about becoming someone new and better—and, like a baptism or any religious restoration of innocence, erasing her whole sexual history served to "cleanse" her. It was not only justified but laudable, these women felt; an acknowledgment of a husband's possessive feelings for his wife. Freud wrote, in his 1918 essay, "The Taboo of Virginity,"

> The demand that the girl shall bring with her into marriage with one man no memory of sexual relations with another is after all nothing but a logical consequence of the exclusive right of possession over a woman which is the essence of monogamy—it is but an extension of this monopoly on to the past.

How better to prepare for the marriage plot—the end of a woman's quest for love—than to jettison her memories, discard proof of her knowledge? How better to become Donna Reed than to obliterate all premarital sex—all badness—and to disdain extramarital sex, to superimpose on her psyche a model of sexual goodness that doesn't admit badness? And what else would make a woman give all this up—now, just as in Freud's day—but the promise of happily ever after?

Over the months we talked, many women slowly began to see the paradox of hiding themselves, when they had never done so before, for the sake of being in a good relationship. They began to question what such a concession signified. June, for instance, concluded that it was a disservice to herself and Russell to have thrown out all records of her sexual life. She questioned her decision and its finality, lamented that her past could never be excavated, and regretted her years-long reluctance to speak about or refer to it except in the vaguest, most dismissive way. "I really feel foolish. I would like to read those old letters to Chloe; I'd like her to know who I was before I was her mommy."

The Perfect Girl

It is not the first time these women attempted to subvert part of themselves in order to fit a more idealized version of femininity. They had done it once before, at the age of eleven or twelve, when they were right on the rim of womanhood, at that moment when girls are so often the happiest and the most themselves, the most straightforward, honest, and clearsighted, when their world is filled with complicated relationships. At the edge of adolescence, though, says Harvard psychologist Carol Gilligan, girls suddenly start a process she calls revision, when they begin to cover over what they already know and feel as if "their feelings are groundless, their thoughts are about nothing real, what they experienced never happened, or at the time they could not understand it," and their formerly keen vision of life becomes dimmed. At the same time, they begin to devalue their own familiar, chattering, nattering relationships, feeling compelled to aspire to a less prosaic and more . . . perfect life, filled up with perfect relationships. Says Gilligan,

> We speak with girls through this time and hear two things happen: What they know through experience—their own thoughts and feelings—suddenly loses authorization. And, relationships suddenly become idealized; they're suddenly won-derful, whereas up to that point girls know that relationships are intensely interesting, intensely painful, just joyous, absolutely awful . . . now, all of a sudden, relationships are won-derful. We begin to hear that breathy voice. . . .

It is at this moment that an outspoken preadolescent girl—"so resolute, so present at the age of eleven," says Gilligan, and so comfortable in her body and in the world, so able to negotiate and accept complex relationships with her parents and her friends, with boys and with her teachers, suddenly, in the space of no more than about a year, loses it all—the confidence, the deep connection with her own feelings and her simultaneous connection to her friends and family, the insistence on being straightforward and honest and outspoken, the irreverence, the humor, the firsthand knowledge that relationships are flawed and constantly in flux and that conflict and anger are as much a part of them as harmony is. She succumbs to a view of herself, of the world, and of who she should be that is unrealistic, and neither comes out of her own experience nor emerges from her own feelings: Gilligan notices that

> girls draw attention to the disparity between an insider's view of life which they are privy to in childhood and an outsider's view, intimating that the insider's knowledge is in danger of being washed out or giving way. They're subjected to a kind of voice and ear training, designed to make it clear what voices people like to listen to in girls and what girls can say without being called, in today's vernacular, "stupid" or "rude." On a daily basis, girls receive lessons on what they can let out and what they must keep in if they do not want to be spoken about by others as mad or bad—or simply told they are wrong.

The voices that people like to listen to are clearly not their real voices, girls quickly conclude, just as the characteristics of the Perfect Wife are clearly not those the women I talked with felt they possessed. The voices of girls that people want to listen to, at this moment when their sexuality is blooming, are no voices at all.

In a three-year nationwide survey of 3000 adolescent girls and boys conducted in 1990 by the American Association of University Women (AAUW)—the largest study ever undertaken on the link between gender, self-esteem, and education—it is stated that only 15 percent of the girls will argue with their teachers when they think they are right, compared with nearly a third of the boys. Teachers call on girls less frequently than boys. They tend to evaluate boys' work on its academic merits, girls' on its neatness and orderliness. Only 29 percent of girls agree with the statement, "I am happy the way I am"—compared with 46 percent of teenage boys. In fact, in the middle school years, the percentage of girls who agree with the statement, "I like most things about myself" plummets almost fifteen points. With little confidence in themselves and their abilities, they come to value their looks as the most important measure of their self-worth—and only 16 percent of white middle school girls, 10 percent of Hispanic girls and 25 percent of girls of color like the way they look. For girls, the report concludes, the loss of self-esteem is far more dramatic than it is for boys, and "has the most long-lasting effect."

Up now against what Gilligan calls the wall of "Western culture," by which she means the patriarchy, girls suddenly see before them an unfamiliar new standard by which to judge themselves: They begin to see themselves through others' eyes and, thereby perceiving themselves as objects, not subjects, begin self-consciously to hide their real feelings and observations. They become silent, because to express the truth as they see and feel it, and not as they are *supposed* to see and feel it, will be interpreted as transgressive, seditious. They fear that their knowledge, if spoken, will endanger their relationships. They are hurled into the central dilemma of relationship:

"how to speak honestly and also stay in connection with others."

In her sudden desperate effort to be what others want her to be and not what feels best to her; and in her confusion about how to stay in relationship with them but at the same time stay true to herself, a girl is likely to buckle under, to censor herself in order to become more pleasing to others—and then finally to lose her clarity and her courage. The result of girls burying their knowledge, says psychologist Lyn Mikel Brown, a member of the Harvard Project on Women's Psychology, is "self-doubt, ambivalence, panic and loss." Such a disconnection is precisely what June experienced right after marriage, when she no longer was sure of what she felt and became "unconscious" of her own sexuality.

It is a process that obliges her to become silent and inauthentic—disconnected from her feelings—and ensures that she will become profoundly unsure, unable to function honestly any longer in the real relationships she only moments before thrived in. This is the moment when parents say, *"What happened? Only yesterday she was so confident!"* She is in a crisis. She gives up relationship, says Gilligan, for the sake of a Relationship.

Simultaneously, as if sent to torture her, the embodiment of this new ideal arrives, right there in her school classroom, forcing her to witness an unfamiliar idol—the Perfect Girl—who appears right out of nowhere. Seemingly sprung from the cover of *Seventeen*, she exudes the looks, gets the grades, and extracts the admiration of everyone around her. Silent and good, she is adored by the teachers and by boys, loathed by other girls for being so pleasing and so false. Unlike the girl who is naturally good, who happens to be beautiful and studious and popular but who is also lively and genuine, the Perfect Girl clearly becomes good at her own expense. She has lost her vitality and seems out of contact. There's a lifelessness about her, as if her personality has been sapped in the interest of display. She realizes she fits an image and may even try to maintain it, but the role is as discomfiting to her as it is to her peers. She looks good but she doesn't feel good. Declared "it" as arbitrarily as if in a game of tag, she knows the honor is hers for reasons that have little to do with her real self.

With the entrance of this embodiment of a bizarre, frozen image of teenage goodness and erotic desirability, a spell is cast over the classroom: If our girl emulates it, she will lose the fluidity and authenticity of her own world and will become ever more withdrawn as she enters this stifling fake one. Her alternative is to be the kind of girl who rejects the ideal outright and refuses to believe in the reality of this saccharine creature and her false relationships and her stifled sexuality; the kind of girl who remains outspoken about what she sees and knows and feels. You know this girl: She wears a lot of makeup, maybe; she is overtly sexual; she ridicules phoniness and talks about it out loud; she dares to look and dress and speak and do precisely as she wishes. She doesn't care about the Perfect Girl. For not caring, though, and for not being pleasing; for her anger and her defiance, such a girl is called "bad."

But more than anything else, "bad" means *sexual*. The Perfect Girl, above all, is chaste. This, even more than her beauty and her compliance, is what makes her "perfect" in the first place. Virginity is the Perfect Girl's trademark. It is what allows her parents and her teachers to relax. A girl's sexuality *must* go underground if it is to be acceptable to teachers and parents, who are crucial in determining how she feels about herself. The AAUW children's study confirmed, in fact, that adults and adult institutions—parents and schools—have a far greater impact on a girl's self-perception than do her peers.

Girls' Sexuality

Yet young girls observe, just as boys do, their own and each others' sexuality. They marvel at the maturing male body, they notice the minute changes in adolescent boys' chests and voices and groins, yet nothing but a boundless silence marks this fascination. Whereas men remember and talk and write about their sexual coming-of-age—Portnoy and Holden Caulfield will continue to tell their stories to generations of young men—women, obliged to mask what they felt, to hush what they saw, to register nothing but how they themselves appear to men—are rendered mute and dumb about their own erotic development. Where are the voices of these once-outspoken, intensely observant, passionate, and articulate girls expressing the first stirrings of their own sexual selves? Where are the young women—who are so acutely observant of the most minute changes, the subtlest nuances in each of their relationships—speaking out about their own sexual yearning, their own erotic attraction to boys, or to girls? What is written to declare a woman's sexual coming-of-age from *her* point of view? Where is the discourse of *her* desire, the story of *her* sexual curiosity, the expression of *her* pleasure?

Where, for that matter, is the dialogue between mothers and daughters about sexual pleasure—a dialogue that could create, in time, a genre of literature that would equal that genre created by men? Mothers will tell daughters to be careful, to watch out, to protect themselves, to stay "nice" girls; they will talk about the mechanics of sex and about the results of careless sex. But daughters do not hear a great deal about sexual pleasure, from their mothers or anyone else—and how can silence beget anything but more silence? Girls learn no names for their sexual organs; they refer to their genitals as "down there." With no expression of girls' erotic feelings, no discourse of pleasure and desire passed from mother to daughter, no narratives of a girl's coming into sexual awareness, there exists no language for them in which to speak about their own experience. And because they do not speak, it is easy to assume girls' desire doesn't exist—for why wouldn't they say so, if it did?

We assume, then, that a girl's erotic curiosity is minimal, that her experience of her own sexuality is nonexistent, and that pleasure is the last thing on her mind—odd, given that we *know* how much sexual feeling a woman has, *know* her physical and emotional capacity for sexual pleasure is monumental, potentially limitless. Odd too, given that women talk to *each other* about how powerful their submerged girlhood sexual feelings were, recall story after story about erotic feelings they had, games they played, fantasies they were lost in. But all this is subversive; it is a knowledge that is assumed not to be there, even as we know it is; a knowledge that women are supposed to be unaware of, that they are compelled to forget.

A girl's real sexuality—that is, her own experience of it in her body—is thus replaced in the Perfect Girl by a construct, a calculation of the effect her behavior will have on boys and on her reputation. Then it is modified and presented so as to reassure others. Contrived to be neither "fast" nor "frigid," fashioned to fit a culture that demands she look one way, behave another—that she *seem* sexy, but not *be* sexy—the Perfect Girl's sexuality is airbrushed bait: It exists solely to please. Later, it will be used to catch a man, to get love, to get married.

One famous girl whose story has pleased millions of us, and whom we believed to have been boldly forthright, is Anne Frank. Few readers of *The Diary of Anne Frank* knew until recently the extent of Anne's revision—of her diary and of herself—how much even she succumbed to the image of the Perfect Girl—and how her capitulation would affect us forever after.

The diary of Anne Frank—the one we all know and love—was dramatically edited lest this extraordinary girl "who knew so much," Gilligan writes, "would appear more perfect or more acceptable or more protected in the eyes of the world by seeming to know less than she knew." Those entries in which Anne Frank originally presented what were absorbing emotional problems for her—her complicated relationship with her mother, for instance, and her engrossing sexuality—were edited out; canceled. Only in a version of Anne Frank's diary called *The Diary of Anne Frank: The Critical Edition*, prepared by The Netherlands State Institute for War Documentation and published in 1989, do we see her true, unedited feelings—right on the page, adjacent to the earlier deleted passages, so we can compare them with what she first wrote. Only here is Anne Frank "permitted" to say what she knew, to speak out about what she actually spoke out about. Only then does she become the passionate, candid, moody, difficult, and brilliant real girl she was—the girl the women I talked with remember covering over or throwing out. In one previously deleted entry she writes:

Dear Kitty,

There's no one in the world I've told more about myself and my feelings than you, so I might as well tell you something about sexual matters too. Parents and people in general are very strange when it comes to this subject. Instead of telling their daughters as well as their sons everything when they are 12 years old, they send the children out of the room during such conversations and leave them to find things out for themselves. If the parents notice later on that the children have learned things anyway, then they assume that the children know either more or less than they actually do. Why don't they then try to make good the damage and find out what the position is? Grown-ups do come against an important obstacle, although I'm sure the obstacle is no more than a very small barrier, they believe that children will stop looking on marriage as something sacred and pure when it dawns on them that in most cases the purity is nothing more than eyewash.

Anne Frank's clear-eyed resistance to the Perfect Girl, like her criticism of the Perfect Wife and her observation of adults' sexual hypocrisy, is not in evidence, leaving us with the sense that she neither resisted nor questioned the very things she in fact resisted and questioned most fiercely. We were led to believe that the Perfect Girl— docile, accepting, and unquestioning—lived inside this complex, sexual young woman. It is the lie girls every-where must contend with every day, a lie that trivializes them, silences their voices, and mutes their sexuality. It is a lie responsible for the question I asked myself again and again in this book: Why do women believe the Perfect Wife exists when they know she doesn't?

We have only to look to girls for the answer. Young girls, too, come to believe the Perfect Girl exists even when they *know* she doesn't, because adults, who have such a profound influence over them, act as though she does. Adults make it clear that it is just such a girl who will grow up to become the lucky heroine of one of many romantic love stories girls already know by heart.

Love Lessons for Girls

One after another of that beautiful silent creature, the Perfect Girl, the younger version of the Perfect Wife, fill the pages of the stories of love that in turn filled our childhood and now inhabit our unconscious. The jacket copy in front of me here calls one of them, Hans Christian Andersen's famous tale, "The Little Mermaid," a "timeless story of courage, sacrifice, and the triumph of unselfish love." Let me tell you that tale.

A beautiful fifteen-year-old mermaid spies a sixteen-year-old prince on a ship and instantly falls in love with him. A storm comes, wrecks the ship, and hurls the prince overboard. At first the Little Mermaid is overjoyed—he will be with her, in her own world; they will be together!—but she quickly realizes he can't survive in the water and that she must get him to shore, which she does.

She is miserable. How can they fall in love when he can't see her, doesn't know she rescued him, when they'll never meet again? She must be transformed into a woman, a human woman, to win his love. She consults the Sea Witch, who grants her her wish, but tells her that the division of her fish tail into human legs will feel as if a sharp sword is slashing through her (so much for even *considering* sex with the prince) and that pain will never go away. She will *look* glorious with those legs, will *appear* the essence of grace, but every step she takes from then on will be, for her, like walking on knives.

And should the Little Mermaid fail to win the love of

her prince—if he should marry someone else—her heart will break the very next morning, and she will turn immediately into seafoam. Fine, the Mermaid says. I'll do it.

As payment for her transformation, the Sea Witch exacts this price: She will cut out the mermaid's tongue. The girl will have her chance to win the prince, but in silence. And in pain. And with failure to marry him resulting in her death. But the mermaid is passionately in love, and agrees to these terms.

When she appears in human form in front of the prince, without a tongue and with those promised racking pains in her new legs, he marvels at her grace, is enchanted by this lovely girl who looks so much like the woman who saved him, the one woman he vows to love and marry. But he doesn't realize it *is* that woman. And the Little Mermaid can literally say nothing.

And so the prince meets a neighboring princess and is instantly lovestruck, believing her, not his speechless companion, to be the girl who saved his life. The Little Mermaid is enlisted to hold the bride's train at the wedding—mute, mutilated, heartbroken, and—as punishment for failing to win the prince—she must die later that evening.

It goes on. Briefly: If she will kill the prince, she can save her own life. She refuses, and therein lies the moral: Because the Little Mermaid is so good, so loving, so selfless, and so forgiving of the prince (who is living happily ever after with another woman he has mistaken for her) her life is not spared. "Of the one hundred fifty-six fairy tales Andersen wrote in his life, this story continues to be one of the most enchanting," the jacket copy concludes.

Who could be speaking that calls this tale of a heroine's muting and mutilation, of her pain and heartbreak and death "enchanting"? Whose criteria for pleasure are those qualities I just named—goodness, selflessness, and forgiveness? Little girls who read "The Little Mermaid" read only a terrifying cautionary tale, and learn what seem to me five clear lessons about love, each one progressively less enchanting:

Love Lesson 1: To be chosen by a man requires a drastic transformation. You cannot be yourself and be loved.

Love Lesson 2: After your transformation, which will be agonizing and deforming, you can only hope the man for whom you went through so much trouble will be able to see who you *really* are, unaware as he is of how much of you has been altered for his benefit.

Love Lesson 3: If he doesn't recognize who he is seeing, or if he doesn't like what he sees, you are in danger of ceasing to exist.

Love Lesson 4: No matter what happens to you, you will be without vindictiveness and vengeance. You will be gracious, silent, selfless, and forgiving. And this will be called "good."

Love Lesson 5: This goodness—that is, your willingness to be silent and be maimed in order to win a man—will qualify you for the role of the Perfect Girl—later, the Perfect Wife.

GIVE UP SEX AND YOU CAN HAVE IT ALL

Not all tales of girls awaiting discovery by the prince end so unhappily. (Walt Disney's 1989 movie version of "The Little Mermaid" was spiffed up, probably so that soft-hearted viewers would not leave the theater in tears. Although the basic premise remains, Disney's interpretation satisfies all our happily-ever-after expectations: The Little Mermaid is never in pain, her voice comes back in the end, and she, not the princess, marries the prince.) But happy ending or no, most fairy tales reinforce a similar unnatural image of the Perfect Girl. Transfixed as we are by the ordinary girl's transformation into someone worthy of being singled out by a prince, these magical tales about love confirm that what finally wins his love are her beauty and her chastity; her appropriateness and her silence; and of course her selflessness, her forgiveness of anyone who hurts her (including cruel stepsisters and wretched mothers and sea witches and other female characters whose role it usually is to introduce and enforce patriarchal laws, and to punish transgressors) and her astonishing lack of anger. While her desirability to the prince is evident, her sexuality is not: The Perfect Girl has already spent her passion in her ardor to win the prince's admiring gaze; by the time she is his, she is doomed to eternal sexlessness, unwittingly complicit in preparing for her own exit from the story just as married life begins.

The Cinderella story says much the same thing about the feminine ideal as the Little Mermaid's does: She, a chargirl, like the Mermaid, must be transformed in order to become a suitable mate for the prince, for personhood to be conferred on them as a result, and both girls await, after their transformation, the reward of male favor. The mermaid—more admirably assertive (she goes after her man, after all) loses; Cinderella wins. But both girls share one common trait: silence.

The girl who goes from rags to riches never actually *says* anything in the story about her wishes and her pleasure; rather, according to Louise Bernikow, author of *Among Women* (1980), "Cinderella stammers, unable to say what she wants—for she is passive, suffering and good . . ." and it is her fairy godmother who simply "divines Cinderella's desire . . ." to be dressed beautifully, to go to the ball, to win the prince—as we divine it too. It seems unthinkable that Cinderella might not covet this scenario.

Nor does Cinderella ever express what she feels about anything else that happens to her, bad or good. Her voice, the one that might illuminate her own aspirations for love and for life, that might inform young readers about her own experience of desire for the prince, is missing. How was the ball? Was it thrilling to be the envy of those horrible sisters? What was the prince like? Sure, he's rich and handsome, but do you *like* him? Was he fun to dance with? Do you find him sexy? And about that pumpkin threat—doesn't that home-before-midnight admonition suggest that someone doesn't want you to *have sex*? "The object of her transformation is not actually *pleasure*," writes Bernikow, "but transportation to the ball with all the right equipment for captivating the Prince." And we as readers see her through *his* eyes, content not to know what she saw and felt and said. We fill in the blanks as reflexively and as confidently as her fairy godmother did, assured that the prince's pleasure is her pleasure. We supply a missing voice—but is it hers? We supply the conclusion, but what happens to her then?

No one says outright to women, *Give up your sexuality and you can have everything*, but these women learned in adolescence as surely as did Cinderella the threat posed to a nice girl who does not get home by the stroke of midnight: She will lose everything. Her gown will turn into rags; her coach into a *vegetable*. She will no longer be desirable. And what they felt as they became silent and sexless, as they assumed the qualities of the Perfect Wife, was rage and sadness and loss—just as girls do when they assume the qualities of the Perfect Girl. Seeing the girls in the women, in fact, gave me a way of understanding something completely paradoxical, something which, on the face of it, makes no sense: Why would a vital, lively, sexual woman today give up that vitality, liveliness, and sexuality and aspire to become Donna Reed, a sexless, silent, grown-up version of the mute and mutilated Little Mermaid?

For the answer, it is back to the girls again. There are a few adolescents who say "No way," and decide to hang on to their inner authority, and to defy disconnection with themselves and others. They are determined to get what they want, not what they are led to believe they want—to hang on, in other words, to the inner voice that links them to their sexuality. Gilligan is, in fact, most interested in these girls, whom she calls resisters, because they spurn the notion of the Perfect Girl who has Perfect Relationships. These girls cannot be bought, she says, and must be supported in their courage and their resistance: They are the irrepressible, lively ones, the ones who manage to remain psychologically alive throughout adolescence—even if, as a result, they are called "bad."

Many of the wives I talked with were now-grown-up resisters, women who had made it through adolescence without succumbing to the idealized image of the Perfect Girl. They had had premarital sex at a time when it was no longer condemned. They were women who had held on to their voices, their authenticity, and their sexuality—up until marriage. Most had grown up influenced by new and overtly sexual icons like Madonna and Cher, role models that both supported them in their resistance to the Perfect Girl and in their recognition of and quest for sexual pleasure.

You would think, then, that these sexually sophisticated women, immersed in a culture that seems on the surface more decadent than puritanical, that itself appears to have liberated women from any standard of goodness that prohibits sex and reveres silence, that provides, rather, models of forthright pleasure-seeking and verbal bluntness, would feel fortified in going their own way. You might imagine that these straightforward, liberated women would approach marriage differently from the way their mothers and grandmothers did.

But a funny thing happened even to them at this juncture where women's desires and culture once again intersect: At marriage, the lure of an idyllic relationship and of happily ever after was just as beguiling as it ever was. Entranced, the prospect of becoming the Perfect Wife, enclosed within Forever's safe walls, grew simply irresistible. Marriage appears to be the moment of capitulation to this antique standard of goodness, now as much as it ever was, even for the most defiant diehards.

Chapter Four

"My Whole Sexual History—for This?"

*C*onnie and her two best friends were on a train headed for Boston in July 1975. They were twenty years old, and they had left their hometown of Chicago for a weekend of fun.

"That one," Pamela said, pointing to a young man with a guitar slung on his back. He has a terrific ass, Connie thought, as he walked by her down the aisle. The three women looked at one another approvingly. Connie got up and followed the man into the next car. "Good luck," said Meg.

Two hours later, Connie returned.

"So?" her friends wanted to know.

"So, it was . . . train sex," she answered. "The greatest thing about it is that I don't have to hear any more from the two of you about this atrocious gap in my life. My education is complete."

"How proud your parents will be. Train sex and not yet out of college," said Pamela.

"She hasn't done a threesome yet," Meg reminded them.

"And *won't*," Connie stated.

"You have to," the girls said in unison.

And by the end of that summer, she had. By the summer of 1980, at the age of twenty-five and with a decade of sexual experimentation behind her, Connie figured she had probably done everything there was to do, sexually, that wasn't just plain weird. Threesomes, anal sex, groups—and, most significantly, multiple sexual relationships, led her to the goal her crowd had insisted on: She had slept with 100 men. She had had sex on drugs, sex on planes, sex drunk, sex when she felt like it, sex when she did not. She tells me that there were no rules during those years from 1970 to 1980 except, if you discovered a rule, to break it. The only sin was refusing to try something.

"It was part of your finishing school experience to do everything in column A, column B, and column C," says Connie. "As Jimi Hendrix blared it out in the sixties, 'Are you experienced?' That was the question we asked each other. The answer had to be yes. If it was 'no,' you were the worst thing you could be: a good girl.

"My mother—the quintessential good girl—was raised to think that if she broke the rules, had sex before she got married, say, something terrible would happen to her," Connie says. "And she was right; it would have." Connie, on the other hand, didn't have to worry about getting pregnant; she didn't have to worry even if she got pregnant. It was before anyone had heard about AIDS, and as far as they knew, there was no sexually transmitted disease that could not be cured, no unwanted baby that had to be born. Nothing bad could happen; nothing irreversible. Sex could not ruin your health or your life.

In 1982, when she was twenty-seven, she married the very tall and very handsome blond thirty-one-year-old Martin, a fellow architect at her firm in New York City.

They were considered a golden couple: She—almost as tall as he at an even six feet, and with huge cornflower blue eyes, just like his—could have been his sister. I met Connie eight years later, when I found myself sitting next to her on an airplane, and, after a three-hour conversation, agreed to continue it on the ground the next week. She said would be willing to discuss with me her feelings about her marriage—and her affair. The following interview took place at my apartment in New York City in the summer of 1990.

DH: What was it that your friends and you in high school and college wanted most to gain from your extensive sexual experience?

CC: I think I was stamped to believe that sex was a creative thing. A talent—like, I don't know, painting or writing. You develop your talent, that's all. You don't let it languish—that's what our parents did. You develop it and it gets better and better. That was the myth. It would lead to something.

DH: To what?

CC: I'm not sure.

DH: To a perfect, sexually compatible partner?

CC: Not exactly. I don't think I thought so much in terms of finding one man through sex as I did in terms of finding myself. Sex would lead me to some great understanding about myself that would help me to really live. I thought of my mother as someone who had been asleep, hadn't really lived. And I still believe that. I wouldn't want to have known only one man. Imagine: How could you go through life and only know one man, or one type of sex, or one person's body?"

DH: Would this understanding of yourself, this feeling of being awake rather than asleep, lead to something specific?

cc: It would lead to happiness. We were entitled, above all else, to happiness. And sexual happiness—something we knew women in the past hadn't had—was our barometer of it. Pleasure was our God-given right. You could do everything else by yourself. You could go out and earn money, have a career, be on your own. But you couldn't be sexually happy by yourself. Not really. I mean you could masturbate, but I was very focused on connecting sexually with a man. And so that was what we were most insistent on—that a man be good in bed, in the sense that he be understanding and giving and experienced himself, and focused on making us happy.

dh: Did you find such men?

cc: Sure! In retrospect, it wasn't such a tall order, since we rarely had more than one or two encounters. Nobody's commitment phobia had much of an opportunity to dig in.

dh: Did you feel the pressure to make men happy, too?

cc: Yes and no. I wanted to please, but specifically sexually; not to be *pleasing* in some overall way. Not in the geisha sense, no. I wanted him to be as equally pleased with me as I was with him. He would get his happiness from being with a woman who wanted to have sex just as much as he did, and who wouldn't be uncomfortable with it—wouldn't hide that fact and play all those nice-girl games. Mostly, though, I was checking him out; I wasn't focused, once we were in bed, on being checked out myself.

dh: Were you checking him out so that you would find the most sexually pleasing man of all—and have him as a permanent partner?

cc: You would think so, but no. Not then. None of us really took our philosophy as far as marriage; it was too far off. Marriage was a whole other thing. The goal, at first, was just to find the best man in bed, period. It had little to do with marrying him. You found him and you fucked him. You didn't think much further ahead than that.

The emphasis at the beginning of my sex life was really specifically sexual—more like a guy's. I'll try this act with this guy. Maybe a threesome with another. I wasn't thinking, "Here's one man I can do everything with." I wasn't looking for emotional closeness, particularly. And I certainly wasn't looking for commitment.

DH: If you found a guy who was sexually magnificent, did you want to hold on to him?

CC: Maybe for another night or two. But the feeling was more like "This guy's terrific! Hope I find more like him!" It wasn't as mindless as it sounds—it was really just an understanding that we were really dating, experimenting, playing and having fun.

DH: Did you think about marriage at all?

CC: No. Only that it would happen. I would be married sometime, I knew that.

DH: Would marriage be fun, too? Would it bring sexual pleasure?

CC: Again, marriage was so far off it might as well have been a nursing home for all I really considered what it would be like.

DH: Did you imagine that marriage would bring a continuation of that sexual pleasure you were so intent on finding?

CC: Well, first I had to find sexual pleasure, and with all our talk, I wasn't finding it this way.

DH: You mean, by following a kind of Don Juan script—lots of variety?

CC: Yeah. I had to do that a few years before I understood what it was I was really looking for.

DH: And what was that?

CC: I wanted really great sex, still, but I wanted it in a relationship. I wanted a deeper connection, more of a spiritual one. I wanted to create my own model, not follow anyone else's—my friends' model or a male model, which was more sex-for-sex's sake. By the time I was twenty-two or twenty-three, I was looking for more closeness with a guy.

DH: So your attitude about sex did change, quite fundamentally.

CC: Yes, I had long-term good sex, and real boyfriends, men I got close to, and men I lived with. And that was much closer to what I really wanted out of all this sex, and *that's* when I started thinking about marriage.

DH: When you started thinking about it, did you think you'd find someone with whom you had terrific sex, and that that would be one of the criteria for marrying him?

CC: Well, I married a man with whom the sex was not wonderful—so there's your answer. It wasn't bad, it just wasn't something I would have chosen him for. I didn't think of choosing a husband on the basis of good sex. It's like sex suddenly wasn't a priority anymore, and I'm not sure I can explain why. And the thing is, because of my upbringing—which is that sexual happiness is my God-given *right*—I feel really gypped. And yet whose fault was it? I was the one who made the choice to marry him; I wasn't forced. I knew that the sex wasn't great when I married him.

DH: Do you have any idea why you did that, given your priorities?

CC: Well, I loved him. And you won't believe this, but I think the sex was the way I wanted it. Because I knew what all that sexual wildness meant, and it meant being out of control. And it meant leaving. It meant temporary, and I thought in a perverse kind of way that if I married someone who wasn't, I don't know, wild in bed, we wouldn't go to the limit—we wouldn't keep pushing it. And it wouldn't be temporary. I didn't want sex to be a major deal in the marriage, because I was a little afraid of what that meant, if it were a big deal. I thought that as sex took on less importance, my life would be more . . . normal. A traditional marriage like *parents* have, where sex isn't a big deal, *that's* the way to be married, I thought, and the way to stay together! Because how could you stay together when you were fucking each other's brains out—I mean how long could *that* last? How long had it lasted for any of us—a night, two, three weeks? If I married someone who wasn't that into sex, then I was safe. He would be my partner, he would be faithful to me.

DH: And you to him?

CC: Yes.

DH: But your model was specifically *not* your parents' model; how come you managed to switch into their gear?

CC: Marriage was not dating. Marriage was different. We were talking about monogamy here, and staying together.

DH: Was monogamy important to you as a moral ideal or did you just automatically link it with marriage?

CC: Both. I don't think I thought much about whether it was important to me, really, but it was, and it was part of the package. And it wasn't really a moral ideal, just an ideal. Being married meant being faithful.

DH: Why? Wasn't the whole point to break the rules about sexual behavior?

CC: Not once you got married. This was unwritten of course; no one ever articulated it. But somewhere in the great beyond, once you were married, you arrived at this mythical place.

DH: Where everyone is faithful and everyone is sexually happy and where you are contented?

cc: Yes. We didn't try to change *that* script because it was so far away and it promised so much; it was what you would do way, way in the future, when you had already lived your life. Although when you think it through it doesn't make any sense. At twenty-two, you haven't really lived your life. After years of having sex and playing around and loving anyone you wanted to, you're not suddenly going to be able to have a real relationship. *One* real relationship.

dh: But what you're telling me is that you *were* experiencing real relationships, as soon as you shifted away from your early model of sex—what experts call the "male model" because it stresses casual sex and a variety of partners—and started having more expressive, longer-term relationships with men. These were the real relationships—while this far-off thing you'd have when you'd already lived your life, as you put it, was in fact *not* real. How does the fantasy flip-flop, so what's real becomes unsatisfactory and what's idealized is what's in fact *not* real?

cc: Because if you see something as the goal, and you've seen it that way all your life, then that goal is what is most real to you, I guess.

dh: But your premarital goal was to have pleasure with men, and now you're saying your marital goal didn't factor in that pleasure. I guess what I'm asking is how, when you were living this life that was oriented toward your own pleasure, according to your own terms of the word, that life and that orientation came to have so little value to you when you chose a husband. Why what was so real became so unimportant.

cc: I guess I just thought marriage would be the realest relationship of my life.

dh: And you never thought, Hmmm. I've had a hundred guys in ten years—ten men a year, that is what's real to me. What will it mean to me, what will it require of me, to trade this reality in for that other model of relationships, and stay with one man forever?

CC: If I thought about it at all, and I don't think I did, it was that marriage would be just great. See, marriage wasn't the same thing as the life I was leading. It would be different. *Good* different; up *here* on the scale of good things. So you didn't apply the same criteria to it.

DH: So here you were, a sexual outlaw planning the most traditional marriage for yourself all along. A calm, loving, sexually exclusive marriage just like your parents had.

CC: Yes. I thought I wasn't really planning like that, because I was working so hard to have something different before marriage. I *did* have something different before marriage, at least, different from my parents.

DH: But it didn't make you happy?

CC: No, in fact it did. It was just . . . time to get married.

DH: Why do you think you didn't want to make a different arrangement for yourself *after* marriage—you know, reinvent the institution to include what you were trying so hard to have before marriage—your sexuality, your badness?

CC: Because I didn't think that would be necessary. Look, I knew it was bullshit in a way, and that I was buying into something unreal—but, don't you see, I wanted to believe it. One thing I really knew about was relationships with men—but I couldn't wait, somehow, to replace them with marriage because it promised the greatest relationship *in the world.* Marriage was held up as this wonderful thing that you'll have someday that will include whatever you need it to. It's already wonderful, right? So why would anyone want to fool with it? It's fixed. All you want to do is live and then wait for its wonderfulness to happen to you.

DH: Tell me about its wonderfulness. What it meant to you.

CC: Oh, you know. Perfect love. For me, it meant someone who would *get* me. We'd be very close. Really good friends. We'd talk and laugh and have sex and it would all be of a piece, and marriage would seem totally natural and unavoidable. The thing is, it gets so hard to keep that idea of really close friendship and exclusive intimate sex when you actually get married.

DH: Why? How so?

CC: Like, I got what I wanted. My husband was faithful, is faithful. I, on the other hand, climbed the walls from almost the beginning. It makes sense in a way—a year into my marriage I thought, "There's something funny here. Sex is so . . . bland. We're not laughing a lot. We're not closest of friends." I mean where did I go wrong? And I remember thinking, Okay, I just will do it. I just . . . I made my bed . . . (*she laughs*) . . . this is *my fault*."

DH: Why your fault?

CC: Because I was so naive. Even sexually—which God knows I shouldn't have been. I thought at first, well, since *I'm* good in bed, any sex will be good with anyone I want it to be, because I can make it good. "I don't really need a man who's good in bed, because I'm good." I have orgasms most all the time, so everything will be fine. . . .

DH: What did you do?

CC: I did what all my friends are doing. I thought, I'm good; I'll make him good. But if someone is not sexual, you don't teach him how to be. And Martin isn't. At least not with me. Not really. He's incredibly sexy *looking*—perfect, really, that ideal body and gorgeous skin—and he's macho and you know, *male*. He looked the part. But he doesn't really like sex that much, I think. He has a lot of WASPy inhibitions about it, and anxieties, and expectations. He used to insist that we have sex every night, like a test—a test of his manhood. "That's what married people do," was how he thought. It didn't matter whether he felt like it or I felt like it, it was a test of the marriage. And I never have the feeling that it had anything to do with pleasure.

DH: More like a release from anxiety?

CC: Yes. And I'm the receptacle. It's never relaxed in bed—he actually pays attention to how loud I breathe, and if I don't breathe loud enough he complains about it. "Er . . . Connie," he announces disapprovingly, "you're not aroused." Like it's my fault? There are these invisible meters all over the place by which he assesses my response.

DH: Have you stopped responding?

CC: Yes, pretty much. It's too much like a performance—I feel like it's supposed to be like . . . movie sex, or it isn't "right." It causes a lot of tension between us. I've gotten—and this is really weird—so that not only can I not breathe the way he wants me to but I have trouble breathing at all. I feel comatose. Deadened. I'm supposed to have orgasms every time, but on my own, somehow. He does very little to support that expectation. I'm just supposed to *do it*, to make it all happen for myself. And if I don't come up with the response he expects, then I feel I've failed. I've failed *and I've made him fail*. It's a Catch-22: I should be a totally responsive, orgasmic, passionate woman, somehow. And on the other hand, if I'm a totally responsive, orgasmic, passionate woman, he's terrified of me.

I used to try masturbating for him, thinking that what he really wanted was to watch me do it alone—with no pressure on him. But he wants the illusion of being involved in it; he wants to be seduced. So the masturbation routine kind of annoyed him—what was I doing for *him*, he wondered. That's what I mean about there being very little pleasure in this, for him or for me.

DH: What happened when you tried to show him what feels good to you?

CC: He couldn't stand that I was showing him something he was supposed to know. It didn't work. Maybe I was too aggressive. I don't know.

DH: You blame yourself for being sure what you needed sexually was within you, and for hoping you could bring that to your husband. But why is that your fault?

CC: Because, I was so . . . off. I was so wrong about the way things are, even the way things are sexually in marriage, or in this marriage, anyway, and sex was something I thought I really understood. I'm the one who had such a different picture of how marriage would be, so I guess I blame myself for how wrong that picture was. I think he kept wanting me to be more like a traditional woman—to become emotionally dependent through sex—I think he wanted that clinginess, saw it as feminine—and hated it that I was able to have sex and be independent, too; to own my sexuality, you know, and not give it up to him.

DH: So you're not talking about familiarity or time cooling off your sex life.

CC: No. I think my sexual independence was a terrible threat to Martin.

DH: There's a theory that some men are what sociologists call "situationally expressive"—loving and forthcoming during courtship, when they are eager to win a woman, but inclined to withdraw expressiveness once they win her.

CC: That might be. It all happened so soon, to me and

my friends. I mean I think something slipped away incredibly fast. It was almost before I knew it, I wasn't myself, really—like you keep trying to fill some bill, both of you, that the other person isn't even hip to. Me trying to win him sexually, but by being in what some way I had never really been: unsexual. Pretending not to be sexy, in order to make him find me sexual. I don't know. It takes place before you even get married, when both of you make all these choices in preparation for marriage that have nothing to do with your real desires.

DH: Like choosing a man you don't have great sex with?

CC: Yes. You used to hear about men having great sex before marriage with "bad" girls who they would refuse to marry. And then they would marry a cheerleader and forever wish they had better sex with her, forever long for the girls they didn't marry.

DH: Maybe all that objectifying did leave you with your own intimacy problems, is that what you're worrying about?

CC: Well, I wonder if I didn't do a bit what those men do—alter my real needs and desires because they're "bad." Which sort of guarantees frustration. And I do feel frustrated and constrained. Like I should be polite and giving. Quiet in my search for love, properly noisy in my expression of it. It's choking. It's hard to explain.

DH: Like a "good girl" has sex?

CC: Yes.

DH: But do good girls even have sex?

CC: Of course not!

DH: And you were not that, before.

CC: I was a bad girl! You know, a cool crusader; and the girls who fueled the image of myself that I wanted to have were all outlaws. Patti Hanson married Keith Richards; Jerry Hall married Mick Jagger. They were our heroines. They had tons of sex and they got everything else too—they were top models, so they made their own money. They were bohemian, but also these "Be all that you can be" people. A latter-day Bohemian Image. Boho meets Cosmo. They seemed to defy the "feminine" way of things, which was great by me. Not operating by the rules but still getting it all.

DH: But didn't they get their glamorous lives by old rules—through being beautiful as well as hooking up with powerful men?

CC: Yes, but they chose men who were outlaws, too; men who wouldn't require them to be good girls. They were too outrageous and sexy and *bad* to suddenly become "a wife" in the traditional sense—in effect chaste, virginal. That was what I was relying on for myself. That no one would ask me to be good, either. And the thing that kills me is that I asked *myself* to be a good girl. And I didn't even know I was doing it.

DH: So when did you start your affair?

CC: A year ago. To tell you the truth, I'm amazed I was monogamous for so long.

Chapter Five

THE LANGUAGE OF LOSS

"Ah yes!" returned Félicité. "You're like old Guérin's daughter, the fisherman at Le Pollet, that I knew at Dieppe before I came to you. . . . It seems she'd got a sort of fog in her head, the doctors couldn't do a thing with her, and no more could the *curé*. When she got it real bad she'd go off by herself long the beach, and the coastguard often used to find her there on his rounds. Stretched flat out on the shingle she'd be, crying her eyes out. . . . They say it went when she got married, though."

"But with me," replied Emma, "it didn't come on till I was married."

—Gustave Flaubert, *Madame Bovary*

*O*ne decade after Connie spat in the face of the character called the Perfect Girl, choosing to emulate instead a model of girlhood that kept her confidence and sexuality intact, our once-outrageous outlaw, the most flagrant of the bad girls, greets her new nemesis: The Perfect Wife. She enters a relational world as foreign to her rock-'n'-roll soul as the pristine universe of a Carmelite nun. She rambles about in it wondering not only where sex and laughter and fun and pleasure have gone, but "Where have *I* gone?" and becomes as mute and deflated as she did when she was eleven, before she summoned up her resistance to having her sexuality thwarted.

In what she hopes will be "the real-est relationship" of her life, Connie senses confusion over the two interwoven issues of sex and idealization that once again heave her into that old, familiar crisis: What can she say? What voice does Martin want to hear? How much of her expert knowledge of love and life and relationships can she hold on to now that what she once felt as pleasurable is seen as "bad"—now that her whole past suddenly feels "embarrassing"? How much of her sexuality, which she owned outright and was proud of and explored intensely in relationships for twelve years, can accompany her? How should she *be* now that she is reluctant to remind her husband of her wild days, or to appear the "cool crusader," or in any way call attention to her life before him?

And this is how Connie's extensive sexual education ended, how all those difficult, passionate, crazy, complicated relationships and her own tumultuous feelings within them became just a shameful secret. And so began the marriage plot, the sexual requirements for which were something Connie could never have prepared, because there are none. So she watches as a new "good" and orderly scene is painstakingly sketched onto the newly whitewashed mural of her life, all but obscuring the bold colors that once were there.

Like Connie, none of the other women detected those vibrant hues and shadings of their histories fading from view as their pasts were concealed and their futures were painted on, certainly not while it was happening. They believed the superimposition process a benign ritual, something potentially exciting and joyful that they were entitled to as brides—they felt immune to its treachery. But one woman does remember the writing on the wall,

> . . . How weird I felt at my bridal shower, how all my friends seemed so different there. We all did a lot of, I don't know, squealing—little bursts of fake laughter that sounded like we were women from some other planet getting together to giggle over the wondrousness of my new life. Women being *wives*.

Connie never told a single one of her friends about feeling as if she were living in a cathedral rather than in a relationship, out of shame at seeming a misfit in marriage. Many of them, she learned later, felt the same way, but had systematically withheld from each other the truth about their uncertainty and isolation and disorientation, afraid of confirming their inadequacy or, even more damning, their unhappiness. They had become complicit in perpetuating the myth of their success and contentment as wives; colluding, in other words, in their collective silence about what they really felt and thought and knew.

It came as a shock to Connie when she finally asked her friends pointedly, "What's going on here?" and discovered that all but one or two of them were as baffled as she, had sex lives as pallid as her own, and were equally filled with guilt and self-blame.

"We finally had it out. And we would sit there at lunch saying to each other, 'What's happened to us? We used to be such fun! We used to *laugh*! We promised each other we'd never be reduced to talking about *drapes*! Why are we now so *matronly*?'" In severing their connection with one another, the bond that once held together their universe, they became even more estranged, falling ever more silent and ever shorter of that elusive Perfect Woman they assumed each other to be.

Connie experienced her own silence as a division not only between herself and her friends, but more centrally, between how she really felt and how she felt she was *doing*—that is, turning from subject to object in a flash, she began to separate from her own true vision of things and focus on how others saw her. "You've got what every woman wants," this little voice inside her announced. "What more could you possibly want?"

"This little voice" within her, the voice reminding her not only who she "should" be and how she "should" behave, but also how she "should" feel, confuses her, because it is not her own voice, the one that speaks from her own experience and says, "I want, I feel, I know, I think." It is a voice belonging to someone who objectifies and judges her and silences her own real voice. This strange critical voice does not merely question her about her feelings; rather it "knows" how she should feel, how she should maintain a relationship, how she should *be* in order to get the love she wants—and it demands that she obey or else forfeit that love and fail at the all-important task of maintaining a good relationship.

The model of goodness and relationships dictated by this disembodied voice has little to do with her real desires, but she finds herself losing track of what they are in her new effort to be "good enough" to be loved. She senses that whatever it is she really wants is irrelevant now, less important than holding on to her marriage and to her sense of herself as a good and moral and loving woman. She is thrown further into crisis: She suddenly feels not only the frustration but the criticism behind Freud's famous question, which now, uttered by this same voice, interrogates her: Well then, if this *isn't* what you want, then what on earth *is*?

THE "SHOULD" VOICE

In classical psychoanalytic terms, this voice that speaks to the self in such a condemning tone—speaking over the authentic "I" with such moral authority—is called the superego; in object-relations theory it is called the "false self"; recently, Dana Crowley Jack, author of *Silencing the Self: Depression and Women* (1991), dubbed it "the Over-Eye" because it watches and speaks over the "I" of the woman's authentic voice. But whereas the judgmental, moralist tone of this voice has been loosely ascribed to the conscience—as if it spoke some of the woman's own true feelings—Jack reminds us that it is not at all her own voice:

> The Over-Eye carries a decidedly patriarchal flavor, both in its collective viewpoint about what is "good" and "right" for a woman and in its willingness to condemn her feelings when they depart from expected "shoulds." The Over-Eye remorselessly pronounces harsh judgment on most aspects of a woman's authentic strivings, including her wish to express herself freely in relationship, her creativity, and her spirituality. Because the judgments of the Over-Eye include a cultural consensus about feminine goodness, truth, and value, they have the power to override the authentic self's viewpoint.

Since the voice demands behavior as prescribed by the culture, not natural to the woman herself,

> when relationships are troubled or fail, the voice of the Over-Eye becomes even louder, pointing out how a

woman's own shortcomings caused the problems, and blaming her for whatever went wrong. Rather than being undermined because it did not work, the theory of how to secure love held by the Over-Eye can gain in strength at this point, since the convictions of the authentic self carry less authority than those imposed by the culture and personal history.

The world of meaning and capacity for control contained in that little word "should" cannot be overemphasized. Its power to effect loss for women—to encourage them to follow it, rather than their own authentic voice, into stifling and self-destructive selflessness, has been cited by scholars and writers, by psychologists and sociologists, many of whom have pointed out the culturally induced moral imperative women feel throughout their lives to do the work of making and maintaining relationships. Because women's sense of self has become integrally bound to how well they do this work, "events in the domain of relationships are most relevant to their definition and evaluation of self," says Dana Crowley Jack, and adds that the moral meanings a woman ascribes to interpersonal events "profoundly affect her self-esteem."

In yielding to an image of "goodness" that splits them off from themselves and from others, in taking to heart a condemning inner voice that threatens them with loss of love at every turn, all the women I talked with felt psychically bound, caught between what they really feel and what they're supposed to feel, between who they are and who they should be. The authenticity they sacrificed, the visceral, honest, unshaped, and uncontrolled responses that went underground, are precisely the attributes that once comprised the vital self they loved being and that I am calling their sexuality: the playful, creative, uninhibited self that spoke out freely without censoring anger, hostility, and conflict, that experienced pleasure, that thrived in relationships.

Novelist Margaret Drabble, rewriting George Eliot's masterpiece *The Mill on the Floss* in her 1976 *The Waterfall*, has her heroine, Jane Gray, speak directly to this division between what she wants to do and what she should do, in an effort to dispel the power of the latter. Unlike her 1860 fictional counterpart, Maggie Tulliver, Jane Gray chooses not to operate out of the old framework at all, insisting that the existing sexual morality is punitive to women and that "if I need a morality I will create one." By creating a morality that embraces her, she finds the adventure and joy prohibited Maggie: Her own passion for her cousin's husband, rather than punishing her as it did Maggie, "releases [her] from enclosure"; "delivers" her to a new life in which she experiences a "rebirth."

THE NEUTERED AND NEUTRALIZED WIFE

In 1976, sociologist Jessie Bernard lamented in her book *The Future of Marriage* the complicated process by which women come to blame themselves for feelings that don't jibe with feelings they "should" have. Calling marriage "pathogenic" for women, she said they nevertheless so desire it that they do not notice that they become "deformed." Even though "women accustomed to expressing themselves freely could not be happy in such a relationship; it would be too confining and too punitive," wives nevertheless conform silently, a fact she attributed to brilliant socialization. "We do our socializing of girls so well, in fact, that many wives, perhaps most, not only feel that they are fulfilled by marriage but even hotly resent anyone who raises questions about their marital happiness."

Trying to account for why so many wives called their marriages "happy" when they revealed signs of feeling deeply alienated in them, Bernard found that researchers tended to ignore what a woman said unless certain arbitrary criteria were met. They measured the success of a woman's marriage not according to her honest appraisal of it, but rather to their interpretation of her *adjustment* to it. If in their eyes she had adjusted to marriage well, she was declared "happy." Bernard concluded that if researchers measure a woman's happiness in marriage by her adjustment to it, it is understandable why a wife would do the same, since she then "interprets reconciliation as happiness no matter how much she is paying for it in terms of psychological distress."

Bernard had years ago introduced what she called the "shock theory of marriage," stating that "marriage introduced such profound discontinuities into the lives of women as to constitute genuine emotional health hazards." She cited some of the "standardized" shocks: the conflict the bride experiences between her attachment to her parental family and her attachment to her husband; the disenchantment that occurs after the honeymoon; the lack of privacy in marriage; the change that occurs when the wife ceases to be the catered-to, as she is during courtship, and becomes the caterer-to; the lowering of status that marriage confers on women, despite "all of the clichés about the high status of marriage."

Responding to Bernard's warning in 1972 that "marriage may be hazardous to women's health," Susan Faludi, author of the 1991 *Backlash*, finds evidence to support it in psychological data today, almost twenty years later:

Married women in these studies report about 20 percent more depression than single women and three times the rate of severe neurosis. Married women have more nervous breakdowns, nervousness, heart palpitations, and inertia. Still other afflictions disproportionately plague married women: insomnia, trembling hands, dizzy spells, nightmares, hypochondria, passivity, agoraphobia and other phobias, unhappiness with their physical appearance, and overwhelming feelings of guilt and shame. A twenty-five-year longitudinal study of college-educated women found that wives had the lowest self-esteem, felt the least attractive, reported the most loneliness, and considered themselves the least competent at almost every task—even child care. . . . The Mills Longitudinal Study, which tracked women for more than three decades, reported in 1990 that "traditional" married women ran a higher risk of developing mental and physical ailments in their lifetime than single women—from depression to migraines, from high blood pressure to colitis. A *Cosmopolitan* survey of 106,000 women found that not only do single women make more money than their married counterparts, they have better health and are more likely to have regular sex. Finally, when noted mental health researchers Gerald Klerman and Myrna Weissman reviewed all the depression literature on women and tested for factors ranging from genetics to PMS to birth control pills, they could find only two prime causes for female depression: low social status and marriage.

Among the subtlest changes women experience when they get married, Bernard also observed, is moving "from the status of female to that of neuter being. . . . Much of the alleged decline in sexual attractiveness of women which is attributed to age is really attributable to the prescriptions for the role of wife." Adding to this idea that by trading up to the status of married woman you trade in your sexuality, Philip Slater wrote in his 1970 book, *The Pursuit of Loneliness*, that in matters of style, "it is only young unmarried girls who are allowed to be entirely female . . . as soon as they are married they are expected to mute their sexuality somewhat, and when they become mothers this neutralization is carried even further. This means that whatever sexual appeal exists in a malnourished nymphet is made highly explicit, while the kind of mature and full-blown femininity that has excited Europeans for centuries is masked almost beyond recognition."

Certainly these women had not obviously been neutered or neutralized; nor did they feel that anyone specific expected them to "mute their sexuality somewhat." They hardly resembled what Bernard called "the sad picture of the mental health of married women." Yet when I listened carefully to their words, when I paid close attention to the language, it was eerie how many of these vibrant women talked about their own "fragmented" bodies, "colorless" dreams, "dulled" vision, and weakened libidos. They spoke of a profound awareness that they were somehow no longer themselves, that they weren't *in* a relationship but *playing a role* in one, that parts of them had been buried, for some inexplicable reason, and that pieces of their bodies or their psyches had been shattered and scattered as if by exploding missiles—all of this happening during the years they'd been married.

Someone "vital" had existed before—the woman their husbands had fallen in love with—but that someone had become "less big" or "muted" or "desiccated" or "frozen" or "dead" or "half alive" or had gone "under wraps" or had begun "living in a dream." Or that someone had become, as Connie dreamed at least once a month for eight years, a zombie.

Marcie, a thirty-two-year-old woman, said she had spent years feeling her brain had gotten "fuzzy," tracing it to a year or so after her marriage ten years before. Estelle, fifty-seven, said her heart hurt, but she had had it checked and there was nothing wrong. Carolyn, a twenty-five-year-old art dealer, said she kept getting mysterious bouts of laryngitis soon after marriage. Alison, thirty-nine, spoke of being cold all the time, and her words conveyed the chill she was always feeling: She described herself as having been "on ice" for many years and, aware of her own powerful imagery, observed after my remarking on it that her phrase not only described a profound sexual chill, "but also a dead body." Karen, twenty-seven, had begun to interrupt her own sentences; she would stop sentences by trailing off, as if ending them didn't matter to anyone. Forty-five-year-old Virginia, a college history professor, tells me that she was able to construct what she calls "a wax doll" for eighteen years of marriage—an ideal self as perceived by both her husband and herself.

> It's a wax doll with no feelings; she's simply whatever he wants her to be. I was really his creation—learning opera and Chinese cooking, teaching the kids about Mozart. When he's out I play Fleetwood Mac and eat ice cream. When the wax doll became suffocating and I wanted out—began doing all sorts of things he didn't approve of—not cooking at all, for example, taking courses in tap dancing, which he thought was dumb—he felt betrayed. When I realized how many parts of myself had to be lopped off to fit inside the doll mold, I panicked: if I burn through it, become myself, I'll lose the relationship.

Peter, her husband, didn't quite understand what was going on, didn't understand that Virginia had lost anything in the first place, never mind why she felt it now, eighteen years later. He experienced her confusion and her rage, she says, as a childish rebellion misdirected at him.

He felt as if he were the villain because I was altering the contract. He was right; he wasn't the villain, and my anger must have seemed directed at him. But I didn't blame him; I helped create this "me" we *both* expected me to be. I was as responsible for what I'd become as he, and you know what? I don't even think he liked me that way; how could he, really? It wasn't the person he married! He really liked me in the early days, and this . . . person . . . wasn't half the person he married! It wasn't a person at all. But neither of us saw it, saw this. And we just were locked in battle, him wondering why I had gone crazy, me wondering how to make him see why I had without getting defensive.

Like Virginia Woolf's powerful description of her childhood depression, "the feeling . . . of lying in a grape and seeing through a film of semi-transparent yellow," wistful references to muted voices and clouded vision and diminished vitality and half selves or substitute selves were threaded through every woman's story. Their words, graphic in depicting physical discomfort, alienation or fragmentation, led me through the murky film to the well of longing and sadness beneath it. Their language of physical sensation—a body language of the self as it is felt when it is out of connection, detached from the body—told a tale of unspeakable loss and unearthed a soul seriously out of sorts, albeit covered amiably with self-deprecating humor, acceptance, and general good cheer. But it is a good cheer that is suspect, like the good cheer with which women observe the sign greeting customers of the English restaurant chain, "The

Silent Woman," or who note the label on the wine called "The Quiet Woman"—both of which depict the female form duly decapitated to ensure their silence. They take it in, they may even smile, but they know something is amiss. And they feel vague, inexplicable shame.

The women struggled, as they wallowed in this other language of prohibition and restraint and goodness, to find words that might express what those diminished, fragmented remains of self felt like. How were they to describe what it felt like to lose their sexuality, when they spoke a language that has no concept for such a deplorable thing, no words for it?

Wendy, forty years old, remembers feeling about her marriage eighteen years ago that

> It was all so just right. So comfortingly by the books. But I remember the double-edged feeling I had, how I began to feel dread in the pit of my stomach, the way you get at the beginning of a murder mystery, and how I was always thinking, Okay, this is nice, but when do I get to get on with my life? When do we get real? When does Ben [her husband] start talking to me a lot, the way all the men I've ever known always did? And when do I start being myself, as well? I felt I was losing something and I hadn't had it yet, and I thought, When does this relationship start to be as intimate and easy and happy as I imagined it to be—and as it promised to be before we got married? Who's going to do that for it? It took a year for me to get it through my head that this was *it*.

She described that feeling of impending doom in the pit of her stomach as the dread of "losing something." Kay, twenty-three and married a year and a half, felt she was undergoing a relentless "editing" process, and was not even aware that she herself was the editor.

Like I didn't want to become different. I just did. I started forgetting things. All kinds of stupid things. I sort of just . . . lost my memory. My memory felt substituted by, I don't know, air. I shut down. I felt like an addled old lady. That became my . . . style.

She blamed herself for this new "style" of hers—describing herself, in effect, as an airhead—a self-denigration that helped to prevent her from experiencing whatever it was that was making her feel so "shut down" and for expressing that feeling out loud. It was as if she had come up against some intangible force that obliged her to be less herself, that forced her to forget what she in fact remembered. Judyann, thirty-seven, describes it this way:

I felt less big, as a personality. Smaller. Contained. And I kept trying to stretch myself out. It was a war I was having within me, not with my husband, really—although it's complicated, because I don't think he had any understanding whatever of what I felt, even though I tried to tell him, which made me mad at him. See, he didn't really notice any change in me; I mean, he was happy with me. But since I was like a shadow, I wondered, How could he like this? This wasn't the woman he knew—why doesn't he notice that? How can he be pleased with this shadow when I hate it so? Why doesn't he help me?

Joyce, just twenty-seven, says,

I began doing those little things that wives do. My skirts got longer; my blouses higher. My hair shorter. I swear to God this was the way it started, even as I joked about becoming more wifelike. But I suddenly felt not so much just older, but *matronly*. Inside my marriage, too.

And forty-year-old Suzy says:

Do you know what I do? I don't tell my husband what
things cost—things for me, that is. I act like my job in
life is to protect him from the price of women's clothes,
lest I be blamed for them. I behave with him as if everything I buy is on sale, you know, *a good bargain*, and
have even stopped going where I used to go to get my
hair done. It's insane. I mean, he would never say,
"You're spending too much on your *hair!*" But he
doesn't need to. A little voice inside me does it for him.
I sneak in clothes, pretend things cost less than they do,
talk a lot about half-price deals and sample sales. All my
friends do this, even though it's often our own money
we're spending. Have you ever heard a man say, "Er,
well, honey, this tennis racquet was a *fabulous bargain*
and *I just had to get it because it was so cheap*!

Zombie Dreams

They experienced their edited selves, whether as a
shadow or a zombie or a wax doll, judgmentally. After
all that work to become good wives, they didn't feel as
if they had succeeded. They just felt worse, more defective, more deformed, more at fault. They were "too
withholding," or "too demanding," "too awkward"
about expressing what they wanted in their marriages, or
not "energetic" or "persistent" enough to clarify it.
They felt unsure of themselves. One after another complained of feeling as if they were "not the real me" with
their husbands; as if their substance had been altered,
their essence converted, "like the way those mytholog-
ical gods changed women they were mad at," twenty-
six-year-old Gloria explained, "into a tree, or
something."

. . .

Marriage, Gloria said, seemed to be a different category
of *being* for a woman, not just a different style of living,

> and yet it isn't for a man. A man's *substance* doesn't
> change, does it? He doesn't hand over some part of his
> deepest self and then never see it again, right? Does a
> man *give up* anything deep within himself when he gets
> married? I don't think so.

Other women reported a similar feeling—that while a
man may choose sexual exclusivity just as a woman does
when he enters a marriage, he does not alter himself
inwardly in doing so. He obeys the same rules of fidelity
as she, but he is not asked to pretend that his choice
reflects his basic nature. He owns his sexuality. He is
not asked to renounce it, ever, or to disown it. A married man keeps his sexuality while opting for sexual exclusivity; a married woman is supposed to become
inherently monogamous, as though her sexuality were
easily transferred elsewhere because it is not really her
own; and as though sexual exclusivity were a deeply
ingrained, biological female personality trait. His choice
of fidelity clearly comes from without; hers is supposed
to come from within.

Overwhelmed by this sense of having been altered,
mysteriously and yet concretely—the women found
themselves withdrawing, said they stopped trying to explore themselves and their husbands sexually—they began to "work" on their relationships. Several women
explained they had got sick of "trying to communicate"
and tired of "talking about what might be wrong" because they had the distinct sense that working on the
relationship was somehow beside the point, and that

their husbands knew it. Ellen, forty-eight and married twenty years, and Betty—also forty-eight and married twenty-one years—said much the same thing.

Ellen:

I'm not sure Jim ever really tried. The relationship, when we discussed it, was something he called the re-*la*-tionship, like, here we go again, what now, and I thought in a way he was right, and I just got sick of it myself. I got sick of always wanting to make things better—like the relationship was totally my thing, my responsibility, and I had to drag him into this torture. I wasn't so crazy about working it out, either, frankly. I just wanted to do something.

Betty:

I was really a hot ticket once. I only say that because it's almost impossible for me to remember it. I don't say it to brag, like I was really a knockout and should be congratulated, but because the someone my husband had fallen in love with was so different and it seems so *amazing* that I'm so different now and I don't know why I am. In a way I want to talk about it, you know, what happened; but in another way I don't think I even know what to say. And [her husband] doesn't think there's anything to talk about. He thinks I'm fine.

Connie marks the moment when her sex life seemed to deteriorate:

I was definitely the aggressor for the first few years, and I remember Martin's saying he wasn't sure he could keep up with me sexually. He needn't have worried. By the second year or so, our roles had so subtly switched that I couldn't believe that earlier I had been so aggressive. I was somehow, now, in this position of being the reluctant wife.

He would approach me as if he expected to be rebuffed; as if I had a headache or something. Apologetically. It irritated me. And you know . . . I had this feeling that that was the way he liked things. That it was the way he thought it was *supposed* to be—the wife with the headache, the husband wanting more. But in my heart it was I who wanted more; it was he, I felt, who was rebuffing me. I think the real truth is that the me *I* thought I was—sexual and hungry—was just too threatening to him. So we did this whole dance of images to make it look different. He could control *his* image by acting as if he was the one who wanted sex; I controlled *mine* by pretending to be the one who didn't.

Sandra, thirty-three, echoed Connie's feeling that maybe her sexuality was threatening to her husband.

I think Dan would be shocked to know how wild I was before we got married. I never told him—I admit to playing into the old, "Why, let me *see*, well, yes, I did have *some* sexual experience but not a whole lot," bit. In fact, I had wanted sex constantly. When I got married, I felt differently. I wanted sex, but I also felt like I should cool it; that this was different. It didn't happen at first, this feeling that "Whoa, this is different," but it did in time. I started feeling awkward.

I asked whether it could be that working on the marriage was a way of contending with boredom, with the dailiness of marriage.

No. No. I like that about marriage, being with someone all the time. I don't have a problem with that. I think I did something to myself. I can't explain it otherwise. I began losing something about myself; I began editing myself; asking for approval of behavior I had never needed approval for, of my habits, my daily life. Checking myself. I'd shop more judiciously. Buy different foods. I just put myself up for approval. He didn't ask me to do that; I did it. I did it even when I didn't want to do it.

Bored? No. I think I felt bor*ing*.

Newlywed Maryann and her husband found themselves earnestly "working on the relationship" almost all the time.

We worked and worked and talked and talked. But we both knew that something else was going on. It wasn't an affair, at this point, and it wasn't dissatisfaction with each other. It was something we couldn't quite get at.

Constance, sixty-four, describes the way she experienced it:

My husband started to sense that I was acting different, and that something was wrong. His response was "I'm losing you, aren't I?" and he got furious, frightened, really. So here he's running around feeling "I'm losing her" and I'm running around feeling "I'm suffocating; I'm being squashed" and he only makes me feel more suffocated and I only make him feel more like he's right, he *is* losing me. So I run after him to prove he's not losing me, and he runs away from me to prove he's not scared. It's nuts.

Missing: Pleasure

Even the most assertive women I interviewed—the ones in the most high-powered jobs who, sociologists say, feel more entitled than other women to make demands in their relationships—said that they felt slightly clumsy when it came to voicing and getting pleasure in their marriages. They began to fear that pleasure was not available to them—as though it was there for unmarried women, but not for wives. They perceived the role of wife as a pointed renunciation of pleasure, a fact for which they didn't blame anyone. It was what one adopted when one married, this position of being less needy emotionally and sexually. "Someone's got to be the wife, it's just too bad it has to be me," was what one woman said.

Painfully, they described having fallen into a sexual role that felt foreign and undesirable. The uniformity of their response—an overwhelming bafflement—convinced me that something had happened that stifled as well as stymied them. What was really needed was an elaborate excavation process—exhuming a lost sense of pleasure and play and fun, dredging up a lost sexuality that had early in the relationship been buried alive.

THE PHYSICALLY PERFECT WOMAN

It was not the first time I had interviewed women whose disconnection from their deeper selves is expressed as an alienation from their bodies, as a detached body part, or as a temperature anomaly within the body. Adolescent girls, with whom I've also talked, often reveal conflicts about growing up and becoming women by battling their natural physicality, suddenly experiencing the emergence of the most female, most sexual parts of their bodies—their thighs and breasts and stomachs—not as new and wonderful and exciting but as disgusting, undesirable, and terrifying. They greet their burgeoning femaleness and sexuality with loathing, as their bodies inexorably fall shorter and shorter of society's physical ideal of womanly perfection—that preposterous compilation of adolescent boys' legs, prepubescent girls' bellies, and teenage girls' breasts—that has nothing womanly about it at all.

This phenomenon among normal adolescent girls—which I described in *Mademoiselle* in 1986 as BIDS, for Body Image Distortion Syndrome—was once the sole province of young women with eating disorders, often anorexics or bulimics who look in the mirror and see "fat" stomachs, "revolting" thighs, "huge" breasts, when in fact they weigh somewhere around seventy-nine pounds and may have concave stomachs, thighs the size of their calves, and no breasts at all. But BIDS was beginning to crop up increasingly among young women of normal weight, women who had no eating problems, who weren't binging and purging—girls whose bodies would be assessed as lovely by an outsider. *Psychology Today*'s respondents to the magazine's 1985 body-image survey were "considerably more dissatisfied with their bodies" than were the respondents to a similar survey taken in 1972. Looking into the mirror and "seeing" loathsome bodies that have nothing to do with their reality is a phenomenon no longer limited to young women with eating problems: It afflicts the majority of healthy young middle-class women in this country.

In one study at the University of South Florida in Tampa, for instance, 100 normal women with no eating disorder symptoms were asked to approximate the size of at least four parts of their own bodies: waist, hips and thighs, and even their cheeks—their answers were then compared with the subjects' actual measurements. More than 95 percent of the women overestimated their body size by 25 percent, on average (so that her actual twenty-four-inch waist would loom as large as thirty inches).

Two women in five overestimated by a large margin, perceiving at least one body part to be at least 50 percent larger than it really was.

In a study of 33,000 women conducted by *Glamour* and published in February 1984, 75 percent of those aged eighteen to thirty-five thought they were too fat (only 25 percent were overweight) and 45 percent of those who were underweight also thought they were too fat.

It seems that what most young women are able to do when faced with a literally impossible physical ideal is this: Instead of rejecting the *ideal* for what it is—unwomanly, ludicrous, destructive, ugly—they reject *themselves*, literally adjusting their vision so that it is they who are ludicrous, ugly, and unwomanly. Doctors O. Wayne Wooley and Susan Wooley, who conducted the *Glamour* survey as well as a body-image study in *Psychology Today*, concluded simply, "To the extent that women internalize a relentlessly thin standard to determine their attractiveness, they are left with two chances for a good body image: slim and none." They are left, more precisely, with no chance of recognizing what a female body really looks like; and only a slim chance of ever wanting to inhabit such a body.

Imprisoned in a fantasy of their own obesity, they turn their own reflection into the single most revolting image of their gender. They look in the mirror and see formless, faceless, grotesque blobs—female loathing incarnate.

With this ideal of female perfection in mind, some, when they get older, will prefer to alter their entire body surgically than readjust the ideal, literally attempting to cut out all evidence of natural womanliness, to excise the raging anxiety that plagues them and to which they attribute their "hideous" selves.

Greeting the grim promise of womanhood this way will be called a body-image problem, as though the problem lay in their perception of their bodies. Steven Levenkron, a Manhattan psychotherapist and eating disorders specialist, says it is not a body-image problem at all but an appropriate response to our culture's "antifemale ethic." Author Naomi Wolf calls it, in *The Beauty Myth* (1991) "not an obsession about female beauty but an obsession about female obedience," and says that the thin "ideal" is beautiful not as an aesthetic but "as a political solution." A hungry woman becomes weak, silent, unsure, confused, and unsexual, she adds, so how much of a threat could such a person be to anyone?

Women's body language, like adolescents' body image, speaks of a loss so profound and an anger so vast that it can only be turned further inward into more ineffable self-loathing, more hatred of femaleness. These idealized images—of the perfect body and of the Perfect Wife—ensure that women will continue to be hard pressed not to hate their real selves. Their loss of humor and vision and voice are just the beginning of what they lose in adjusting to this falseness.

So Wendy's loss of memory is no surprise, since she had been asked to "forget" most of her relationships with men and leave behind all the sexual experiences of her lifetime. Carolyn's laryngitis surely had something to do with her feelings of being silenced, as did Karen's tendency to end her sentences in midair. Alison's icy limbs make sense, given that the emotional waters she and her husband were swimming in seemed to have been cooling imperceptibly all around her for years, with neither one noticing the fact that they had finally frozen. And Connie's recurring zombie dreams don't seem too difficult to understand: A zombie is, after all, nothing more than a disembodied thing, a soulless human corpse, still dead but infused with a foreign energy that enables it to walk and act and move just as if it were alive.

DEPRESSION AND DESEXUALIZATION

In her 1980 book on depression among women, *Unfinished Business*, Maggie Scarf writes about encountering what she first thought were "bizarre" statistics that showed, in all the literature and in all the studies she could find, that "for every male diagnosed as suffering from depression, the head count was anywhere from *two to six times as many females*" (italics hers)—and rising. The context for this staggering figure, she found, is almost always "the loss of emotional relatedness"; that "it is around *attachment issues*, more than any other sorts of issues, that depressive episodes in women tend to emerge."

Delving further into the connection between depressed women and loss, Scarf got one clue from the work done by the late Professor Marcia Guttentag, then directing the Harvard Project on Women and Mental Health, who called the degree of women's depression "epidemic." Guttentag and her colleagues were trying to ascertain underlying differences in the themes of stories and articles in popular magazines aimed at women and those aimed at men. In the fiction and essays directed toward men, the material tended to concern adventure, the overcoming of obstacles; the preoccupations were with mastery and triumph.

But "the magazines being written *for women* [italics hers] had a very different orientation," Guttentag observed. "The clear preoccupation, in these materials, was with the problem of Loss. While many women's articles and women's stories did have to do with relating to others emotionally and with pleasing others—especially," said Guttentag ironically, "with pleasing *men* [again italics are hers]—the theme of Losses, and how to handle losses, was omnipresent." In all these materials aimed at women, the threat of possible disruption of crucial emotional bonds was, finally, the "huge concern" and the inescapable theme. Psychiatrist Jean Baker Miller, emphasizing this, has said, "Eventually, for many women, the threat of a disruption of an affiliation is perceived not just as a loss of a relationship but as something closer to a total loss of self."

Reading this tendency to be an indication of women's overdependence on their relationships is to read it all wrong, observes Dana Crowley Jack in *Silencing the Self*, since "if depression stemmed from women's being excessively dependent on their relationships, then the loss of those relationships should precipitate depression and we should find widows more often depressed than widowers." But the opposite is true.

Yet within unhappy marriages, studies show, women are three times as likely to become depressed as men. And in happy marriages, where the incidence of depression is lower for both men and women, women nevertheless are almost five times as likely as men to experience depression.

It is known that depression peaks twice in a woman's life—first at adolescence, and then sometime between the ages of twenty-one and forty-four (with the age of onset getting even lower). At both these junctures, women face a relational crisis that revolves specifically around their sexuality: Both at adolescence and in marriage, they are obliged to restrict and reshape their erotic selves into a more pleasing, contained, and selfless form.

I think of the simultaneous adulation of and anger at the Perfect Girl on the brink of adolescence and, later, of women's adulation of and anger at the Perfect Wife. I think of the silencing of that anger in a society which still maintains these rigid models of goodness. ("Even today," notes Carolyn Heilbrun, "after two decades of feminism, young women shy away from an emphatic statement of anger at the patriarchy. Perhaps only women who have played the patriarchal game and won a self despite it can find the courage to consider facing the pain that the outright expression of feminism inevitably entails.") And I think that the depression common to these two groups is neither coincidental nor inexplicable. At both those junctures women are specifically asked to reinvent themselves to more perfectly fit what they "should" be and into what they "should" want; to trade in their existing relationships and life stories for idealized, calcified versions of both. It is a requirement that alters their feelings, devalues their knowledge, prohibits their experience, severs their connections, and hobbles their sexuality.

"Depression resembles grief," Dana Crowley Jack reminds us, "because, in both, feelings of loss and sadness dominate the emotions." The women I talked to were experiencing grief over their missing sexual selves. The loss they talked about was not a potential loss, not a threat of a severed emotional attachment, but a fact; not an inchoate fear about a future loss, but an insistent echo of a past one—aching, aching throughout the terrain of their bodies like phantom limbs. They were not anxious about a connection that might soon end, but mourning a capacity for pleasure that had already ended. Where it ended—where they lost their sexuality—was not in marriage per se, but in goodness. Marriage was merely the occasion for capitulation to this goodness, and the vehicle for supporting and sustaining it (later, motherhood only adds fuel).

However frightened these women were about staying in relationships in which they had stifled their sexuality, they also feared attempting to reclaim it. That would leave them with nothing, they feared, but the total loss of relationship and self to which Jean Baker Miller and Maggie Scarf and Dana Crowley Jack refer, and the magazines respond. Here is where each woman faced not a depressing choice, but a paralyzing one: She could continue to become the "female impersonator" Gloria Steinem has said we are all trained to be, or she could attempt to reclaim her sexuality and follow the passionate, doomed heroine of the romantic novel straight to her fate under a train.

Over three hundred years ago, in Boston, there lived the most famous and beautiful adulteress in American fiction, Hester Prynne. As Prynne's creator, Nathaniel Hawthorne, described her, she was tall—"with a figure of perfect elegance on a large scale," and she had "dark and abundant hair, so glossy that it threw off the sunshine with a gleam," and a face "which, besides being beautiful from regularity of feature and richness of complexion, had the impressiveness belonging to a marked brow and deep black eyes."

Exotic, majestic—gorgeous—her lush sexuality and shining womanliness stood out against the backdrop of plainness and repression that was Puritan New England; the townspeople revealed, with every drab garment on their bodies and every pinched expression on their "hard-featured" faces, their religious and moral severity, their condemnation of pleasure and compassion, their revulsion of sexuality, and their unwavering belief in the basic sinfulness of men and women.

In starkest contrast to Hester's dramatic sexuality were the others of her gender in this sober, pleasureless community—all of whom Hawthorne calls "dames" and "females" and "goodwives" and "matrons" but never "women" because they bore such an amazing resemblance to the stern, ruling "iron" men. We see them, first, awaiting Hester outside her prison door, calling for a hot-iron branding on her forehead, or, as one goodwife pleaded, death—and Hawthorne observes that they resembled the "man-like [Queen] Elizabeth" who reigned in England almost a hundred years before. Trying to account for their mannishness both in looks and in judgment, Hawthorne explains, "the beef and ale of their native land, with a moral diet not a whit more refined, entered largely into their composition," and calls attention to "a boldness and rotundity of speech among these

matrons . . . that would startle us at the present day. . . ."
They were as loud, coarse, beefy, and severe as the men,
not only because they ate and drank and thought just
what the men did, but because, psychologically, they were
locked inside the very same impenetrable "iron framework of reasoning" the men were.

It is as if Hawthorne wanted Hester's exotic beauty
and exultant womanliness to bedazzle this sin-spooked
community; to force the townspeople to witness not only
what a sinner but what a real woman looks like. For
Hester's extraordinary qualities endowed her with such a
unique understanding of human relationships, he tells us,
that she alone might become a kind of prophetess to the
Puritans—and her mission would be to reveal to them all
"the new truth that could establish men's and women's
relations on a surer ground of mutual happiness." She
alone could bring in a new age of love and compassion,
an understanding and a harmony between men and
women, and the scarlet A on her breast was "the symbol
of her calling."

Hawthorne slyly calls attention to the scarlet letter's
luxuriance, to its "elaborate embroidery and fantastic
flourishes of gold thread," as if the love and passion and
vitality sewn in with the threads of sin might reveal to
the womenfolk who reviled it something pleasurable,
magnificent—if only they could discern it. Look! it said.
Here lies the secret of Hester's character! Listen to her!
Learn from her! If they were able, they could see in the
embroidery not only the sin but the love, a woman's
knowledge and experience they had never known and
could not even imagine otherwise—just as Hester could
envision the possibility of a "mutual happiness" between
men and women that they were blind to.

It was her sexuality that made Hester Prynne the only
woman among all these "goodwives"; her passion that

had propelled her out of the iron framework; both qual-
ities together that made her so sinful but so effectual,
too—"so strong . . . with a woman's strength." It was
precisely these, her sexuality and her passion, that gave
Hester alone "so much power to do, and power to sym-
pathize" that "many said the letter A meant not Adultery *but* Able."

Part

TWO

Chapter Six

"SHOPPING WAS MY SEXUAL RELEASE"

*P*aula is depressed, both because her daughter, Melissa, has just gone off to college and because her hairdresser bleached her hair the color of peas. Paula is thinking about these two dismal facts on the Designer floor of Bergdorf Goodman in New York City. She has no recollection of how she got there, or why.

A mustard-and-black-striped Gaultier jacket on sale for $779 makes her remember, sending waves of welcome energy through her for the first time in weeks. Red suede Joan & David shoes dispel her depression; a medley of little Romeo Gigli wrap tops and skirts convince her she can bear the fact of Melissa's departure—God knows a mother-daughter relationship like theirs can withstand higher education. Come to think of it, it will be good for her to function without the constant thought and presence of her daughter; she will get a lot of work done and see more friends. She feels a little wave of anxiety.

Viewing the freshly stocked Young Designer floor

with the bright eyes of a child beholding a roomful of Christmas presents, her anxiety dissolves and happiness is hers again. Looking stunning this fall and having a rich, fulfilling life from this moment on is a possibility that suddenly seems as clear and bright to Paula as the colors in four fabulous Vittadini sweaters, as sure as the unique simplicity of three little Calvin Klein skirts and jackets; as unavoidable as Chanel's basic black dress and pearl choker—all being wrapped for her on different floors.

On the way down on the escalator, she feels hot, thermally and spiritually. She's in a frenzy now. She knows one thing: She should leave the store immediately. She hits the escalator, pretends she's a mannequin glued to the steps, but comes unglued at the Donna Karan boutique, where she finds herself charging up cashmere body suits with adorable matching cashmere sarong skirts. Images of going to jail fill the right side of her brain; visions of owning Karan's sequined tank dress fill the left. Everything, she suddenly figures triumphantly, with no brain at all, is so *packable*.

Faded but still feverish, she continues down the escalator, her pea-colored hair sitting flat atop her head at an angle, like a greasy beret, from having tried on scores of pull-on tops. She stops off at Cosmetics and slaps on some blusher and also acquires, in a magical three minutes, a whole new hair-care regimen and four new lipsticks—one for the Romeo Gigli stuff, sort of flat and matte and no-color, two reds for the creamy cashmeres, and a frosted gloss—good over everything.

Exhausted, she's almost made it out of the store now, but not before the whopping price of a faux-crocodile handbag makes its way onto her charge card. And a matching belt. Only a few feet from the doorway, she smiles wanly at the handbag salespeople. With one last gasp, she snatches a huge gray bag—too big and shapeless and absurdly expensive, but with a backpack option—and has it sent home.

The $8,096 bill for the day keeps Paula up all night, putting her in a state that makes her earlier depression seem almost manic by comparison. She turns to George, who is breathing deeply, guiltlessly, and watches him for a while; then, guilty to the point of nausea, she vows to return everything the minute Bergdorf's opens, four hours from now.

For Paula to pay what is on her two American Express cards (one gold, one green) and her Visa, she would have to go into insider trading; certainly she goes through the pathetic amount of money she makes as a children's book editor in seconds. Increasingly, shopping is less fun than it used to be.

Paula's relationship with her husband, George, is friendly, she says, but not particularly close.

"Is 'estranged' the right word?" I ask.

"No. Not estranged. It's the relationship of old-fashioned couples. Not like new couples who are in therapy and are working on their relationships. Ours is the kind of relationship young girls swear they'll never have."

"You mean unexamined; parental?" I ask. "Where the husband and wife call each other 'Mother' and 'Father'?

"Exactly. George and I have been known to do that. We have always rather liked doing that. Melissa wants to kill us when we do. It's not cool. In any case, George is a good husband, and we've been married forever, and we'll stay married, and he's a traditional male, I think that's what they call them—men who don't engage all that easily. And our sex life is nowhere particularly. And I imagine George has had an affair over the years, but I'm not sure."

"If you were sure, would you feel terrible?" I ask.

"I've thought of it, and this is really not the answer you're looking for, but I don't think I'd mind. In fact, my fantasy is that—since the happier he is around the house, the happier I am—it would be workable. This assumes that George would handle it well, and not hurt me with it. My fantasy also is that a girlfriend might make his demands fewer. Like I'd call her and say, 'Why don't *you* take care of all his clothing requests—the shoe-maker, cleaners, and shirt-and-tie replenishments—and *I'll* make sure his food preferences appear in the refrig-erator! Okay? I mean, let's work this thing out so our lives are easier!' "

"Did you ever consider having a relationship with another man?" I ask.

She did, she said, "but only in the abstract. I don't feel appealing enough to attract anyone, or even remotely sexual enough to want someone; I feel a little desiccated, sort of like I was a woman once, and now I'm something else, something slightly less. A little defective. It's strange, but a man is the last thing on my mind. In fact, I wish I *were* out to prove my attractiveness to someone. Someone besides myself. I feel like I'm in a tower, re-moved, like a princess, outside of reality yet functioning in it. Also, you have to remember, I'm a shopper. Shop-pers are good girls. I'm a good girl. A nice girl from a nice, Jewish family. I don't do anything wrong. I just could go to jail for my shopping bills."

"*Should* go to jail for your shopping bills?"

"Right. *Should*. I barely go a full morning without getting an 'I should' in somehow, to motivate myself. I should make a healthier breakfast for George, even though he hates breakfast; I should get up when he does and have this mythical breakfast *with* him; I should ask him more about his work, talk to him more about my feelings. I should confront him: that's the usual family-therapy way to a better marriage. Talk about the marriage. I should be more ambitious, like my friend Jenny. I should *call* my friend Jenny. I don't nurture my friendships enough. Maybe I'll have a party. I should be more social. I should diet. I should cook more. I should cook low-cholesterol foods. No, I should have more things catered. I should work out. Maybe I should seduce George. No, dammit, George should seduce me. And so forth."

Among Paula's "shoulds" is her commitment to fidelity, although she's no longer quite sure whether it is morality that fuels that commitment or terror. Or sexual malaise. Or going along with something she never felt was a negotiable issue anyway. She feels that the fact that she was a virgin when, at twenty-four, she married George some twenty-three years ago, affects her ambivalence about exploring extramarital sex. Most of her married friends who have had extramarital sex also had premarital sex, which has convinced her that an affair is kind of like riding a bicycle, easier to do in later life if you learned how when you were young. She has decided that once sex is an option in a person's life, it continues to be, married or not. And for her, monogamy is a condition, not an option.

"Sleeping with someone else is not something I think much about—honestly—or even fantasize about," she says. "I don't think, 'Well, George may well be having an affair, so I will, too,' any more than I feel that because George barks orders at me, I'll bark orders at him. We're different people with different styles. I don't necessarily want what he wants, nor do I want to be what he wants to be.

"You know when I can really imagine the possibility of a man?" she asks, as if thinking about it for the first time. "Right after I shop, when the desiccated feeling goes away and I feel like . . . a ripe plum. I feel so good, so *hopeful*, so . . . hot. Sometimes I feel if I could shop enough, really enough to keep that feeling of hopefulness and excitement there for a week or so, I'd be out of the mood for shopping and in the mood for an affair. But the feeling never lasts, and once I leave the store I can barely think about dinner, let alone sex."

"Tell me more about your marriage," I say. "More about you in it."

"I've struggled to be the *real* me in my marriage and I just am not, either in or out of bed, and I don't know why. It's a strange thing. Something happened, early on; nothing dramatic, mind you. Just . . . it got a little less cozy, somehow. More professional, like we were running a business together. But I figure, well, marriage is . . . marriage. That if you're provided for, and if you're friendly to each other, then it's a successful partnership and what's the point of divorce? Marriage *is* a business. No one in my family was ever divorced. In my family, divorce is out of the question. And it's an old-fashioned idea, but when I think of all those women in the seventies with those consciousness-raising groups—they ditched their husbands, got tremendous support from the groups for doing so, and were promptly hurled into poverty for the rest of their lives, since they then comprised an unprecedented number of American forty-six-year-olds running around in broken-down station wagons, pissed off at men, never to remarry. We're a little more realistic."

She doesn't dislike her husband, George; she thinks he is coping with the pallor of their twenty-three-year-long relational life and their years-long, respectful sexual distance from each other the only way he knows how—and that she is, too. Only four or five of their years together were sexually involving for her, and she has concluded that she doesn't have a particularly strong libido—not like George's, anyway, or what George's used to be. She is happy being married to George and figures, after all these years together, he has a right to do whatever he needs to do and so does she.

And what she needs to do is shop. It makes her as happy as she can remember being in years, if only temporarily. "It's strange to admit," says Paula, "but that euphoria beats sex any day. Or maybe it's exactly what great sex is like; I'm not sure I even remember.

"But I do remember my physical response to shopping. Immediately, my mind clears. I get a surge of energy that makes everything—even my vision—slightly sharper. Colors look brighter, feelings edgier. I'm on top of things, I'm not just dragging around. I joke around with the salespeople. I'm funny. I'm clever. I'm *darling*. I solve, believe it or not, heretofore insurmountable problems—about work, about my family—suddenly, magically.

"And I'm special. I can have anything that any other woman in the world can have. I'm Ivana Trump. And of course salespeople are always impressed, always treat me well because I buy so much. They think I'm rich. *I* think I'm rich."

On days when the rendezvous at a store isn't completely frenzied, a quick shop—"a nooner," Paula calls it—is a leisurely seduction. When she arrives on the fourth floor of Bergdorf's, for instance, she finds her favorite salesperson—a man named Jimmy. She is relieved to see him; he is thrilled to see her. He says he has a surprise for her, something fabulous that just came in, something exactly right for her. He takes her to "their" dressing room—the biggest on the floor—and sits her down.

The "surprise" is on another floor; it's so fabulously beautiful, Jimmy tells her, that it was grabbed for the day by a young model who wanted to wear it while handing out perfume samples on the main floor. But, he assures her, he'll retrieve it from her right now. Paula feels suddenly panicky, jealous. She wants it. She doesn't even know what "it" is, but she's nervous she won't get it. Jimmy reassures her. "I'll get it away from her," he says with steely calm, "even if it's on her back."

When Jimmy returns, Paula is waiting, wearing only her black lace teddy, pantyhose, and shoes. "Well, gorgeous, I've got it," Jimmy announces proudly, then, noticing her undressed body, sighs. "That is unbelievable," he says, eyeing her teddy. "Sant' Angelo?" he asks, touching the lace panel down the side of her hip. "Nope. Olga," says Paula. "Well, well, well," Jimmy says drily. "She's found the way to save pennies. She buys Olga underwear." They both laugh. "Gimme," she says, grabbing at the silk charmeuse confection he's holding. "Not so fast," he says, yanking it away from her while he adjusts the dressing room lights. "I want to see you in it the way you'll look in the evening . . ."

He puts on a special lamp that alters the store's daylight-imitating fluorescent glare, making Paula's skin look suddenly peachier. "*Now* gimme," she says. "C'mon, Jimmy, what is it?"

"It is to die," he says, holding up in front of him a slinky, spaghetti-strapped, empire-waisted, floor-length dress the color of Devonshire cream. "What you do with this," Jimmy announces softly, conspiratorially, "is . . . nothing. Absolutely nothing. No pearls, no earrings, no bra, no pantyhose. Skin and silk.

"Now. Take off the teddy. I want to see the dress

with nothing underneath. No jewelry. Not even your watch. Not even your *wedding ring*, do you hear? I'll be back in five minutes. And Paula, pull your hair back. Severe. In a knot."

Paula does as she's told. Takes off everything. The earrings. The wedding ring. Against her skin the dress feels like something angels would weave, some celestial fabric she's never felt before, a kind of satin-finished silk, but finer, more fluid. Her heart pounding, she carefully closes the side zipper. She pulls her hair back. Quickly sneaks on some blusher and lip gloss, to impress Jimmy with her high color. She looks at herself gravely. She approves. She waits.

He takes a deep breath when he sees her. "That," he says softly, reverently, "is just the way I pictured you in that dress. You're perfect. Do you have any gel?" he asks, pushing some wisps of hair back from her forehead. "Yes," Paula says, "but I only use it in summer, when my hair is wet." "Use it," Jimmy orders. "Your hair must be slicked back. You must look just this undone, just this simple. The effect is you—nude—and that dress. Nothing frou-frou; none of that red lipstick you love—nude, right?—beautiful skin."

"Okay," Paula says, thrilled at his approval; stunned by the effect of her new "nude" look on Jimmy.

"And we're doing something about that hair color, right? I mean who *did* that to you?"

"Oh. You mean the greenish tinge?" Paula asks. "The Le Sueur look? You don't like canned peas?"

"I want it darker. Less ash. Go to Constance. Tell her you know me. Tell her I want honey blond. Okay?"

"Okay."

"Now," Jimmy announces. "We get for this a sandal. Not fancy. Not too high. A two-inch heel. Silver, I think. Come. Get dressed. We'll go to four." Paula, sweating now, infused with the pleasure of her—their—victory, hurries to get ready.

Once outside Bergdorf's, flushed with satisfaction, armed with the charmeuse gown and silver slippers, the people pressing each other along Fifty-seventh Street look wonderful, colorful, lit up from within. The scene is an animated film, a charming Chaplin film, all going a little too fast, all adorable. Her what-a-great-city feeling lasts till she gets through the park on the Sixty-seventh Street crosstown bus.

And then it happens fast: that morose, motionless, stop-time feeling. The realization that that utterly dreamy silk-satin-whatever-it-is dress has no place to go. It will never be worn. This bus is as far as it will go. Jimmy's intensity, his obsessional interest in her, has awakened a responsiveness she can express on the fourth floor of Bergdorf's, in a dressing room. All that excitement and pleasure, all that mock intimacy, Jimmy's hovering attention—for a dress. And shoes. She is overcome with shame.

She goes home, taking a sudden hate for her packages. The cleaning woman is there. She can't bear to have Flora see her bring in another batch of packages from Bergdorf's. She used to hide purchases from George; now she hides them from Flora, too. She unlocks the door and walks in, leaving the celestial dress and silver slippers outside. Her cleaning woman not in sight, she grabs the packages and sticks them in the front hall closet. She feels ridiculous. Her heart is pounding from fear of being found out. "I am afraid," she says to herself soberly, steadying herself to walk into her living room, "of my cleaning woman. I am afraid she will find out. That I've come back from a hotel? No. That I've shoplifted? No. That a man is coming to my home? No. I'm afraid that my cleaning woman will see that I've bought new clothes. Good Lord."

Paula knows by now that her guilt, and the depression that follows, add the fuel necessary for the whole process to repeat itself. They're the down side of the high, the purge part of the splurge; the hangover. They are what make her regain control, and keep her out of trouble.

Trouble came seven months after I first interviewed Paula, in the form, she told me on the phone one summer day, of a man in his early fifties named Harry.

He was an illustrator. She met him at his publisher's, who had given her a book to edit with his illustrations in it. Long before she had finished working on it, he called with a new illustration. Then, when she was done, he called again to thank her, and suggested they go for lunch. They ended up at a Chinese restaurant in midtown, had such a good time that they decided to meet again the following week, same time, same place.

Once she'd decided—somewhere around the third lunch—that she really liked seeing him, she found herself hyperventilating a lot. And shopping. "The idea of buying clothes I would actually *wear*, in front of someone other than Jimmy at Bergdorf's, added a whole new dimension to my purchasing: Reality. 'Get serious,' I said to myself. 'The frock you need isn't for a mythical inaugural ball or something that would look cute on Geena Davis on Rodeo Drive. You've got *lunch at the Chinese restaurant with Harry* to think about.' So I wound up with six or seven lovely little 'Daytime Dresses,' as Jimmy calls them. Lots of hats and gloves. Matinee clothes your mother would wear.

Tea dresses. Oh, hell, it didn't matter; Harry thought I was swell."

She also began thinking about that fact of her life, monogamy, about what it would mean to her to break it after all these years. "I mean, clearly this was between me and me—at this point it wasn't at all about George and me, since, given our sex life, he had no right to expect anything of me by way of fidelity. But my sense of myself as a faithful wife was so closely linked to my sense of myself altogether.

"Who would I *be* if I were unfaithful?" I wondered. "I am almost fifty years old! I am a moral person! I was flooded with all that *stuff* about monogamy—old feelings, old beliefs, I guess—about how it meant that this one person you gave your body to for your lifetime would be yours, you his, and you would take care of each other, body and soul. I thought about how stupid it was that I'd given up my expectations of George, but never gave up the same expectations of myself. I thought about what I'd feel like breaking that, would I feel hurled into space? As if, suddenly, I wouldn't be taken care of in any way? Would I just be out there, uncared for, on my own?

"And of course I'd always thought that dividing yourself in two was tantamount to taking on a playgroup of six-year-olds—how does a woman *deal* with two men, let alone sleep with them and love them and give them any time at all? How can she think? What does she say to one—the same thing she says to the other? Would I greet Harry in the afternoons and talk about the children's books I'd acquired? The new flooring I bought? The bills? Was it like taking on another husband?"

Chapter Seven

THE MURDER OF DONNA REED

It is widely believed that with a truly happy relationship, partners would not be "driven" to non-monogamy. Another piece of folk wisdom is that partners go outside for sex when there is too little of it at home. We find that heterosexual couples who are monogamous have neither more nor less sex than those who are not. Some might say that it is not the amount of sex, but its quality that keeps partners from straying. This also turns out to be untrue. Monogamous and non-monogamous heterosexual couples are on average equally pleased with their sex lives together. Another possibility exists: that partners are non-monogamous because they are fundamentally unhappy with the relationship. There is no evidence for this contention. . . . Heterosexuals who have non-monogamous sex are on average as happy with their relationships as monogamous people. But they are *not* as certain that their relationships will last. These facts tell us two important things: First, most heterosexuals are not propelled into non-monogamy by bad feelings about their relationships. Second, for most heterosexuals, non-monogamy is associated with less commitment to a future together.
—Pepper Schwartz and Philip Blumstein,
American Couples

$\mathcal{C}$linging to the most treasured of her traditional values while on the brink of giving them up, Paula confronts her dilemma the same way June did, by struggling with questions that are, at heart, moral questions. The "shoulds" that governed her life, the "oughts" and "musts"—words she has lived by and that control the idealized self she has tried to cultivate, now attempt to insert themselves in that unbridled part of her that feels desire. But it doesn't work. That self does not speak this language. It does not respond to "should." With one man beckoning her outside the framework, another man inside it, she is at the core of the selfless-selfish quandary, wondering how to stay responsible to her marriage and to herself as well. Her decision is momentous and she knows it: what is at stake is the very essence of the ideal and the linchpin of the myth: her sexual goodness. If she gives it up, she is not sure what she will have left.

After three months of lunches with Harry and six new tea dresses to have them in, Paula can no longer avoid confronting the thorniest issue head-on: whether she can have Harry on any basis, let alone a sexual one. The possibility that she might put herself first, before George, before her twenty-three-year marriage, before even her child, throws her into despair: She cannot do it. Someone she loves might get hurt. But what about her? What about what might be good for her? Feelings of desire warring with feelings of responsibility now, she examines the pertinent questions like a jeweler looking for flaws in a diamond: What *is* infidelity, anyway? Is it when you exchange secrets with a man—secrets maybe even your husband doesn't know, or is it when you have lunch with him without telling your husband? Is infidelity the fact of the friendship or the secret about it? Is it specifically when you have sex with him?

And then, does "sex" mean sexual intercourse—or

does an affair, in its essence, really have nothing to do with sex, per se? Isn't the betrayal an emotional one? Testing the boundaries of good and bad, she considers her one last chance at innocence: the possibility of keeping her new friendship but declaring it openly—she will incorporate Harry into her life, introduce him to George, end the secret, avoid the question of sexual infidelity altogether. She will have the pleasure of this friendship, but without the sex. She will be good.

THE VOICE OF GOODNESS

After all, she reminds herself, relieved at her decision, she is not unhappy in her marriage.

But then why is she so driven to go outside it? she wonders. Why can't she just say something to George— like, Hey, this isn't working!

Because, she answers herself, it *is* working. She *has* a good marriage.

Then what, this strict, agitated little voice chimes in, *are you doing?*

And her only reply is, I don't know, I don't know, I don't know.

Why would you risk it all? it demands.

Because I must have something that is not here, a set of feelings that I have given up; because I've become muted and frozen and the real me is living somewhere else, up in a tower, and it's not George's fault, but if I told him how I felt, he wouldn't understand. He might tell me to get a different job. To get some exercise. To get some help. Maybe I should, in fact, get a different job. God knows I need more exercise. But who can help? And what will I be helped to do? George would definitely ask me why I'm talking about living in a tower. . . .

And then what would you say? And then I would say . . . I don't know, I don't know, I don't know.

Scarcely able to articulate what she is feeling, let alone utter it aloud, she feels only that it is all her fault, not her husband's; that wantonness is creeping in like a virus.

Tell him! Talk to him!

Tell him what? Say what?

Stymied by the recognition that her words would necessarily be expressed in some language other than the one they speak together, and that he might try to respond in the language of shoulds and oughts, she remembers her old recurring nightmare: She is running down a hotel corridor, holding the key to her room in her hand, but no matter how many doors she stops at, the key doesn't fit any of the locks.

Suddenly she is thrown back to her adolescence, immersed in memories of an almost identical experience: She is trying to reconcile her true sexual feelings with her good intentions. Then, as now, the question is *whether to have sex*. Then, as now, she weighed and measured her actions, warily pondering the conflicting rules that pit goodness against badness, abstinence against "going all the way."

Like Paula, the other women were flooded with insistent teenage reminiscences: Dana, twenty-eight years old and married three years, tells me that her confusion about "how far you can go and still be faithful" to her husband sounded identical to the earlier problem of "how far she could go" and still be a virgin. It plagued her.

Dana said that three years after she wed she had had oral sex with a man other than her husband, but nevertheless now considered herself "still faithful" because "we never actually *did it*." She knew how disingenuous her definition of "still faithful" was, but grappling with the choice between losing her virginity and being called "bad" or rejecting sexual opportunity and being called "good," she decided simply to work around it: If what was "bad" about sex was sexual intercourse, then maybe anything short of sexual intercourse was *not* bad. It sounded good. She recalls how she deftly pushed the permissible to its limits:

> You are a virgin until you have sexual intercourse, right? I figure it's the same for a wife: You're faithful until you have sexual intercourse with someone. So for six months, Jeremy didn't penetrate me. We used vibrators. We tried Chinese balls—I'd sit on a chair and, in effect, masturbate with these two little silver balls. We would swing from the goddamned rafters—but in my mind I was still a good wife because we never had sexual intercourse. If those were the rules, I was playing by them, damnit.

Frances, sixty years old and married thirty-six years, recalls with irony her attempt to reconcile her decision five years ago to have extramarital sex with her desire to be good—"I mean really, after all these years!"—and to stay inside the framework. Like Dana, she too had found the way to extend the thin line of what was allowable— she would simply avoid actual intercourse.

> It occurred to me that Fred might not go for the idea that I was giving extensive and excellent blow jobs to the chief accounting officer of my firm, but somehow I had learned earlier not to take heavy petting too seriously: When I was young, you could be a *virgin* and still give and get oral sex, so couldn't you now still be a *wife* and do the same?

Even women in their twenties and thirties, who all had had premarital sex, found themselves recalling the "good girl/bad girl" conflict they had experienced then. Extramarital sex, they found, is far more disapproved of than premarital sex. Said Ingrid, thirty-five:

> I was proud of myself for not being "easy" when I was sixteen, but I also felt this cumbersome virginity upon me—I was, after all, already older than the other girls who had gone all the way. It was an odd sense of feeling virtuous but also weighted down by a kind of marital purity. It began to feel like virginity at too old an age— like, who needs this? Who am I doing this for—certainly not me! And I had this need to shed it.

And thirty-two-year-old Julia, married one year, said:

> I felt very moralistic about infidelity—very sure it was wrong. Yet I also felt heavy in my heart, like this attitude wasn't really my own. I had adopted it and it was my job to defend it. I felt hypocritical. The kind of woman who wears sensible shoes but constantly eyes the spiked heels in the windows. Her husband relies on her and respects her but doesn't particularly want to sleep with her. People call her a really good person because she's so fucking unsexy. The adult version of the high-school girl with the great personality—that euphemism for an unattractive creature with high morals, sensible shoes. I was that woman, and I didn't know quite how I got to be.

Martina, thirty, felt the same "hypocritical" feeling:

> There was this same good girl/bad girl conflict inside me that I hadn't felt since I was in love with Tommy Thomasson in ninth grade. Yet dimly I remembered that replacing the good girl with my bad self, traumatic as it was, had served me well. I had felt much, *much* better. It would probably serve me well this time, too, maybe.

Alexandra, thirty-nine, says:

It was so odd being so chaste. I grew up, sexually, in the late sixties. We were the sexual revolution generation. I love sex. I was supposed to be having lots of it, and my husband and I weren't.

ANGER IN THE HOUSE

Desperate to hang on to an ideal of goodness—and thereby to safety and connection—but longing to break out of it, all these women wind up wondering the same thing: Can I murder Donna Reed and live to tell the tale?

In 1942, Virginia Woolf wrote about her own decision to murder the earlier taunting image of the Perfect Woman, embodied at that time in a well-known figure created by the nineteenth-century poet, Coventry Patmore, who called her "The Angel in the House." You will recognize in this "angel" all the qualities of her successor, Donna Reed. And you will recognize Woolf's homicidal urge:

She was intensely sympathetic. She was immensely charming. She was utterly unselfish. She excelled in the difficult arts of family life. She sacrificed herself daily. If there was chicken, she took the leg; if there was a draught, she sat in it—in short she was so constituted that she never had a mind or a wish of her own, but preferred to sympathize always with the minds and wishes of others. . . . I turned upon her and caught her by the throat. I did my best to kill her. My excuse, if I were to be had up in a court of law, would be that I acted in self-defence. Had I not killed her she would have killed me.

Woolf killed the angel with no societal support. Paula, on the other hand, will find her role of assassin a bit easier. Coming to Paula's rescue is a new icon, another, more contemporary image of a wife, an ideal quite different from Donna Reed, whose story Paula feels quite drawn to. Born of feminism and the human potential movement of the 1960s, this woman is focused on neither men nor marriage, but aspires to her own personal development. Her goal is self-discovery, self-realization, and self-fulfillment. Not yet as tenaciously embedded in women's unconscious as Donna Reed, she is a model of womanhood neither defined by men nor assessed solely through the patriarchal gaze. She is not a woman confined to the conventional romantic tale, but out on her own, following a path of creativity and self-expression, a path requiring that "each person risk the loss of secure and known positions for the danger of new and exciting challenges," writes Annette Lawson in *Adultery*, in order "to achieve the peak of self-actualization—the height of maturity." It is a path of self-knowledge, stipulating that all who follow it "explore all facets of themselves, including their sexuality."

Theoretically, this new course of adventure and self-actualization coexists with the old; that is, the pursuit of one's own development should not conflict with the pursuit of a rewarding marriage—since these days marriage promises self-fulfillment to both partners. But while all these women entered their marriages fully intending to grow separately as well as together—to "have it all"—they found the two routes divergent, the moral imperatives of each jarringly incompatible, and the possibility of integrating the two daunting. Instead of feeling relief from the old selfless model in the promise of the new, more self-fulfilling one—they felt only conflict. Each model, forty-four-year-old Anna found to her horror, "carries its own bag of 'shoulds' to live up to—and boy, do they contradict each other!"

These women found that marital contentment required a stunting of themselves that they couldn't accept; yet personal growth required an insistence on a self-concern and pleasure-seeking on which they had difficulty insisting. Every woman of every age had trouble reconciling the two. Forty-nine-year-old Hope, married twenty-three years and with three teenage boys, said,

> My marriage works best when I genuinely care more for us as a family than for myself—which most of the time is how I really feel. I feel best then, sort of like most virtuous—you know, "Soup's on, everybody!"—and everyone else is of course happiest. But the truth? It leaves no room for me at all. It's full time. And the setup simply works best that way. Ask anyone.

Ruth, forty-seven, agrees:

> My marriage is really, I don't know, not about me at all. I now feel I've got to be the one to take care of myself because I've finally got it through my head that nobody else is going to. I don't even feel angry about it, just a little . . . surprised. It's just reality. I mean my husband just isn't running around worried about my growth as a human being, so if I *am*, I'd better do something about it myself or here I'll sit. And I'll become one of those women I hate, who go on and on about having poured the best years of their lives into husbands who long ago stopped caring, or who divorced them, and children who don't really appreciate all that they did.

Chris, twenty-eight, leans more toward the new model of womanhood—and with less ambivalence than the older women:

I find it odd that my family cares so little about my needs and finally I understand what the women's movement was trying to say to me. Men really aren't going to ask their wives, "Honey, are you getting your innermost desires attended to?" now, any more than they ever did. Anyway, at the risk of sounding like a boring hair-coloring ad—like *Hey, Appreciate Yourself, Honey!*—I feel I can't be much good to him or to the kids or to myself unless I feel good about myself. So I really try to go my own way.

This tug between marital and personal contentment—between what Lawson calls The Myth of Romantic Marriage and The Myth of Me—was ever-present in my talks and showed up in each interview I had, leading women right to the center of the selflessness-selfishness dilemma. As they come closer to making the decision to have an affair, the pressure to give in to their feelings is met by enormous reluctance to become "the kind of person" who does so. What had happened to their intentions, their goodness, their moral fiber? And yet, weren't they also supposed to have their own lives apart from their family, to be independent and self-sufficient, "to achieve the peak of self-actualization—the height of maturity"?

Terror of both options, of selflessness and selfishness—of being the new model but, as twenty-eight-year-old Chris says, "being crucified for it"—are threaded through their stories in equal doses. Says Chris,

Oh, that word! I'd heard it from day one. *"Chris, don't be so selfish."* Good girls aren't selfish. What bullshit! Little girls are called "selfish" if they're not concerned totally with the well-being of anyone but themselves. Every child is selfish—why are girls supposed to give it up, while boys aren't?

Adds Angela, thirty-four:

The most selfish thing I ever did in my marriage was to
decide to go to a spa. "How could you leave your child
alone?" some of my friends asked. "How could you
spend so much money for just one week?" my mother
wondered. I did get away, but the resolve to do so, to do
something for me that might be inconvenient to the family, was enormous. It was an interesting lesson: You
have to fight to get what you need, even R and R. You're
not supposed to. In any case, the two times I've been
most selfish were when I went to the spa and when I
went to bed with Charlie. And those are the two times
in my adult life that I felt the best the longest.

And forty-year-old Carla, married fourteen years,
says,

If I do what I really want, I'm not sure I can have my
marriage. I just wonder if a woman can really do what
she wants and be married.

They feel that even though the goodness role is "dishonest" and "destructive to women" and had led to the
stagnation, not the contentment, of their mothers—it is
also still very much "part of the marriage contract."
They would have to fight hard against its hold on them.
Angry about the collusion of women in the perpetuation
of the Donna Reed model, yet feeling simultaneously
very much in its thrall, all the women find themselves
walking a tightrope. If they succumb to total selflessness, they see themselves manipulated by a society that
still requires them to be good girls. They are furious
when they sense themselves giving in to this model and
this demand, when they hear their own voices becoming
muted, and feel their own desires giving way to the de-

sires of others, as if the process were somehow uncontrollable and ineluctable.

Says Chris,

I hate to sound like a self-help book, but I make it a big point to speak up and be myself, because if I don't, no one will. No one can, I suppose, or should have to. But it's so hard to always be weighing the pros and cons of my own needs for both dependency and independence.

And Carla,

I've begun this new thing. Every day I do something for myself. Something that pleases me. Anything; anything. It can be small, like buying a lipstick or something, but it's symbolic. If I don't do this, I feel in danger of doing nothing at all for myself ever again.

"I Don't Want to Be a Victim"

Suddenly the word "victim" is in the air; it comes into every interview at just about the same time, highlighting both the disdain these women have for the women who never fought against becoming Donna Reed, and their anger at their own vulnerability to her. Those women who saw their mothers struggle to reenter the job market, or who saw them treated badly by their fathers, or who watched them find new husbands when their marriages ended, use the word often throughout the interview. Says sixty-five-year-old Marcia,

Look, it's not my husband's fault. He never asked me to abdicate my needs. I was the one who said, I'll be your support system, your nurse, your housekeeper—wouldn't *you* say yes to such an offer if you were a young man? It was my job to not make such an offer, to not volunteer to be a victim. I can't be mad at him—I mean I could in a minute, but then I'd really be up a creek.

Vickie, thirty-two, says,

Sometimes I hear myself sounding like my mother, quietly desperate, acting like my family is everything and I have no separate needs, talking in that good-woman way about my kids and my recipes . . . and I can feel the anger almost choke me. Where does this *come* from? Why do I *do* that? For whose benefit? What am I trying to *prove*? Get *over* that victim crap!

And forty-six-year-old Renee says,

Nobody even questioned why my mother didn't have a life outside of us, except I remember thinking that she wasn't happy, and that she might get very sick some day, and that if she did, no matter what anyone said, I would know why. It would be *Victim's Disease*. Something deep that eats the innards; something weird that only victims get. I truly worried about that.

Needing to inject self-care into a model of caretaking; to write a new story about a new kind of woman in a new kind of love relationship—yet doing so with enormous anxiety and trepidation, all these women felt themselves falling short of both ideals, the old and the new. Julie, thirty, says,

You know, I feel screwed. I've failed to sacrifice myself and failed to be true to myself. I don't fit anyone's model of anything. I'm just out in the cold. Still, I wouldn't want the old way.

A twenty-four-year-old newlywed, Janie, says,

I've learned that "good" means "good for men." Or "good for the children." I've rejected that as *necessarily* good for me. But I still don't have the strength to do what's good for me when it conflicts with everybody else. It's not easy. It's not clear.

And so Paula, like all these women, comes up against the final questions she poses to herself before her change of heart, questions that challenge her image of her idealized self. Harry reminds her, as Jonathan reminded June, that pleasure is hers for the asking—but at a terrible price. To have it she will have to renounce her claim to a feminine goodness she has valued and maintained without question all her life. After about two months of deliberation, she can no longer weigh the questions with any equanimity; she cannot see how to remain this good woman, nor can she imagine leaving her behind. She knows there is no longer a right answer, and that the price of either choice is exorbitant. She is too filled with desire and resolve to go back, though, and suddenly and inexplicably decisive about her next move. Paula is about to attempt an outrageous life-saving maneuver, but one with terrifying consequences: Adultery, the single most stunning violation of "iron framework" wives have forever lived within, is the most powerful tool she can use for shattering it.

None of the women "drifted" into extramarital sex; nobody said to me, "It just happened." They all had made the decision after many thoughts and daydreams similar to June's, had asked themselves, "Do I really want to do this?" and had said yes. And once the decision was made to do the unthinkable, to take the chance, there was a sense of urgency, a replacement of "I mustn't" with "I must, and *now*."

Paula says yes. She leaps.

Chapter Eight

"WHICH IS THE REAL PROBLEM: MONOGAMY OR MARRIAGE?"

The following interview took place in Connie's New Jersey home, six months after our previous talk. Connie's marriage to Martin is still intact; and so is her extramarital relationship with Stephen.

DH: Tell me about Stephen.

CC: Stephen is a friend. An old friend. We began seeing each other, sleeping together, with so little fanfare it seems hardly even to be an affair. It's more like a terrific friendship. He was hugging me one night because I had been upset about my job, and he was just holding me. And I realized how long it had been since a man had held me, stroked me, been there. It felt like I almost couldn't remember the last time I had been held without any tension. And that seemed so odd to me—that I had done without it, not only good sex, but affection. Me! The outlaw! The Love Goddess! I suddenly felt like I'd been given an incomplete in high school; that I had had this incredible education and then just dropped out. Where had sex gone? Where had my talent gone?

DH: You decided to go back and get your degree—did you feel guilty?

CC: No. We made love, right there on my couch at home. Martin was visiting his sons. I didn't care about anything. Well, I did too care, I wouldn't have made love on our bed. But I just wanted more of his sweetness, his holding me like that. And we haven't stopped.

DH: Does Martin know?

CC: No. Martin had always made a point about this. He said when we first got married that it was all right if I had an affair; that we were both grown-ups and that it just wouldn't bother him that much. I never believed him. I really thought he was just being incredibly cool. It infuriated me at the time because I thought he was protecting himself by saying that, announcing what a cool and unpossessive guy he was when I knew he was wildly possessive. But it had the effect he probably wanted it to have: I didn't want to test it, because it would have been horrible if he really had not cared.

DH: You wanted him to insist on sexual fidelity?

CC: Yes. Sure. In retrospect, I think he was issuing a warning. "I am not necessarily going to fill your needs." Sort of, "Good luck." But what I didn't see was that I had put myself in a box: I had a husband with a lower sex drive than my own, and less of a desire for contact. I had traded in my own feelings and my own needs for this mythical state of being that I thought would provide for me. My assumption was that this was the price for being loved and cared for. I was angry at myself because I put everything in his hands, my whole well-being, my sexual life as well as the rest of my life, and what he was telling me was, in effect: Be available to me emotionally and sexually when I want you. But don't ask that of me.

He felt sex was due him. But due me? No—I was on my own—he even *said* I was on my own. What I didn't understand at the time was how much the word "sex" was limited to what he wanted and precluded what I wanted.

DH: And your own pleasure got lost in the face of his implicit demand that you please him?

CC: Yes. I was supposed to display an inherent, always-there pleasure for him, as if I had a reservoir of it, could dip into it and come up with some for him whenever he needed a glass of it. It was supposed to *be* there, be *in* me, in this smiling, contented wife of his.

DH: And so you lost the sense that you could ask for, or get, the same thing from him—you felt that the pleasure-getting process was one way?

CC: Yes. And so with Stephen, I suddenly felt, it's back. My life is back. I feel alive and free and wonderful. My body felt good again, and—oh, lord, this is like some woman's magazine—my *skin* looked good again. I felt suddenly that I was living in color and not in black and white. And those zombie dreams went away. And I almost wanted to share that with Martin, the whole thing.

DH: But you're not going to risk it.

CC: No. I've this feeling in my bones that it would be a disaster. And also that it isn't Martin's business what I do sexually. It was his business when it was confined to him, but he wasn't all that responsive, so, you know, he's lost the right. But now I feel I'm living in two worlds—my home world and my sex world. And if I tell him what I'm doing, it would be only to *get* him interested, in some perverse way, or to punish him, or to punish myself. I don't need to blend the two worlds in one. I already know I can't. Not with Martin. So again there's the choice: I'm happier getting what I need from

Stephen than forcing Martin to give me something he can't.

DH: Do you have trouble pulling that part of you, the sexual part, away from the marriage?

CC: Yes. Because of the myth, which tells me that I should get it all from Martin. And because I really do love Martin. I feel protective of him. Like he's too crazy, too traditionally male, to set straight. But you see, when you say that I pulled my sexual self away from the marriage, I didn't: It was pushed away. It wasn't required. What was required was a pretend kind of sexuality. A willingness to give, that's all. But still, I understand him. And I know he loves me.

But the *reality* is that it's no trouble at all. It's easy being with Stephen. It was hard being so sexually . . . fake . . . with Martin. That's what's hard; it's easy to adjust to getting what you need!

DH: Are you in love with Stephen?

CC: I don't know. I know I love him. And love what he's giving me.

DH: So you're not thinking that your marriage might end now that your sexual needs are being met outside it.

CC: No, just the opposite. My marriage feels better to me now than it has in ten years. My marriage might *stay* because I'm getting good sex!

DH: Many psychologists would say that you're stabilizing your marriage through the affair—adding trainer wheels onto a bike, as it were—and that without the triangle, you'd be back to the same old unsatisfying marriage. And also that this stabilization is only temporary.

CC: That's probably so. But what I've come to is that what's most important is not just to make the *marriage* work, but to make my life—which includes my marriage—work *for me*. It's a flip-flop in priorities. My marriage can't be my priority; *I* have to be. And now I am. And it works for me.

See, the thing is, I can have sex that doesn't mean my marriage is over. I can. You know how men who have an affair often say "It has nothing to do with my wife"? Well, not that sex with Stephen has nothing to do with my husband, but it doesn't have everything to do with him. It's a separate thing. I didn't plan to have an affair, but now that I'm having one it isn't bursting open the seams of my marriage, and I have no desire to run off with Stephen or anything. That's soap opera stuff. It's just that I'm not following the rules anymore—the rules that say, "You are a woman, and this is how it is for you. And you be good, and give your husband what he needs, and don't ask anything for yourself." And you know what? It seems to me that *not* going by the rules works as well as it always did for me. It reminds me that where I always get into real trouble is when I go by the rules!

DH: But when you got married, you thought the rules were for your benefit?

CC: Yeah. I did. But the rules are not created for women who want anything for themselves; the rules are created for women who want approval! Then they have to stay good to keep that approval. I'm a perfect example: Whenever in my life I've gone for what I want, I've had to break rules, and then I've been called *bad*. And nobody has liked me for it. And whenever I've been good, people have said, "Oh, Connie is a great gal. Let's invite her over"—and I've been miserable. Because "good" means "good for everyone else" and "bad" for a woman means "getting what you need"—specifically, getting *sex*.

DH: I want to ask you whether it's possible that you, as well as Martin, have trouble integrating sex with intimacy. Your sexual history was similar to a man's: You followed a male model, at least for a while. Lots of variety, but with little emphasis on the relationship. In that light, your affair with Stephen is a manifestation of that same pattern of separating sex from a close relationship.

CC: Well, I've thought of that. That I'm splitting off sex and love here for more than practical reasons. But remember it wasn't my intention. I mean I have had both together, I just haven't had it in marriage. I *think* I could have had sex and intimacy with Martin; I don't feel like I'm pretending it's him when it's me. You could say maybe I chose a man who wouldn't give me intimacy so it wouldn't be my fault we didn't have it . . . but I can't really believe my subconscious was up to that.

My sense is more that something happened to me in marriage—I both expected something that was far too great, and gave up everything else to have it. And Martin's expectations were more realistic, in that he didn't have to give up anything. But everything I knew about myself, well, I threw it all to the wind. I started doing the Wife thing, thinking that any minute, if I was good enough at it, it would all be mine, the whole bit, it would all be worth my while. Whatever genuine problems with intimacy I might really have, they can't show up when all I'm doing is trying to be wonderful—and not even pointing out that my own husband is not doing the same thing.

With Stephen I'm very close—we have amazing closeness and understanding, I think. It's mostly sexual, that's its reason for being, but the sex is intimate sex, fun and close and warm, not cool sex. Not just *sex*. And it's enough for me. I don't have to own him, marry him, as the next step. I got back to myself. That's what I really wanted. And I'm happy with it as it is. I don't believe in happily ever after anymore, not with one person. . . .

DH: Do you mean you don't believe in happiness anymore? Or happily ever after? You don't believe in the myth of perfect happiness or you don't believe you can be happy with one man?

CC: I believe in happiness, and I believe in the possibility of happiness within a monogamous relationship. But I don't believe it's given to women just because they're good. They have to fight for the relationship they want, the circumstances they want. NO one says, "Here it is." What they say is "Here's what we want you to have."

I went to a friend's house on Friday night and she said, "Sorry, I'm not serving the shrimp I told you about. It smelled a little funny, at least I thought so, although nobody else did. I couldn't get the idea that it was contaminated out of my head." And I think that the nineties approach to eating is going to be oriented around this terror of contamination. You know, the Russians didn't get us, but the seafood will. And I think that's operating with affairs. "Don't think your husband is going to give it all to you, because he's not going to, and you'd better as hell go out and get it while you can because you're going to be dead."

DH: So you do think, "There's not much time."

CC: Well, no, I don't think I'm going to die, not consciously. But I think every woman may have to erase all the tapes that play in her head that say altruism, altruism, altruism, and marriage, marriage, marriage, and men, men, men, and learn to think me, me, me. It sounds appalling. But the truth is, a man won't provide for you, and that doesn't jibe with what we were taught about love, does it? That sounds bitter. But it isn't. It's just not *romantic*.

DH: And you still feel the pressure to be romantic?

CC: Yup. I think nobody wants to hear that women are actually going out and getting what they need. That they are actually actively seeking, finding some way to provide for themselves, emotionally, sexually. Only if the guy was so abusive that she had to go out in order to save her own life does it seem acceptable for her to be that brazen. Nobody questions men's treatment of women; but if women respond to that treatment, respond in a diffuse way and they're not sure why, but they want to protect themselves somehow, get some pleasure somehow, they're shocking.

DH: Are you saying you think women who have affairs are reacting to bad treatment?

CC: I'm saying it's only acceptable to society *if* they're reacting to bad treatment, if they're driven to it. Nobody can accept the idea of a woman taking on a man for pleasure and for fun, the way a man takes on another woman.

DH: Were you driven to your own affair?

CC: No, not in the traditional sense. Not like I have such a terrible husband that I have to find someone else, or such a terrible marriage that I'm trying to find a new husband to replace the old one. I was driven to it by something within me; a sense that I would die without contact.

I can have that sex I need, and the contact too. Do you know what I mean by contact? Conversation. Play. Isn't sex just adult play? Interaction. Only not in my marriage. So the choice is, do I end the marriage and keep trying for that perfect marriage-with-monogamous-sex situation? Can I get rid of that frozen, married feeling simply by having sex elsewhere? Or do I only get rid of it by divorce, and then try to superimpose the same old losing myth on the next relationship? That's what most people do, but they fail, because second marriages are worse, statistically. My other choice was to keep my marriage and get sex, too. So yes, I was driven to that choice, but by life. By my life.

DH: And how do you feel, now?

CC: I've never felt so good, so that must say something, either about the arrangement or the sex or my rethinking how to get what I need. I'm less dependent on Martin and I feel happy in the mornings when I wake up. I feel sexy again. I think I look good. I feel like I finally took control of my situation as it really was and have made it work for me. If it isn't ideal—and it certainly isn't ideal according to the myth—well, so what? It's okay. I feel better. It's really okay.

Chapter Nine

THE AFFAIR

". . . If I cannot act without my own appro-
bation—and I must act, I have changed, I am
no longer capable of inaction—then I will
invent a morality that condones me."

—Margaret Drabble, *The Waterfall*

*B*ecoming an adulteress is not easy. Just to negotiate
successfully the lunacy of the logistics—When will she
see him and where? How will he contact her, or she
him? What will she say to her husband? Her children?
Where will she claim to *be*?—each woman has to become a master planner. When she realizes she can be just
that, and handle the even more complex, dangerous
emotions as well, she begins to feel competent and sure-
footed, at once frighteningly out of control and,
strangely, very much in command.

And then this forbidden experiment begins to become
surprisingly rewarding. There are no social rules gov-
erning it, no pattern for its development, no precedent
for how to behave, no defined *goals* for an affair. Because it is temporary and has no predictable outcome, a
woman is free to create an unusual entity—a sexual relationship in which she has no prescribed role. She can-

not slip into the idealized role of wife; this other man cannot slip into the idealized role of husband. With no sexual script guiding her actions, she begins to create something new, something she could not have experienced even before marriage, no matter how many relationships she had.

It will be she who decides if this relationship will take place, where, when, how often, and just what her part in it will be. She does not have to win a man, because she already has one; she does not have to plan the future, which is already planned with someone else; she does not have to worry about whether the relationship will end, nor if all her needs will be filled. She does not have to worry about whether she will have a date for Saturday night. She has one. She has a life. It will be day by day, this friendship; its only goal is mutual pleasure, without which it has no reason for being.

The women spoke about how revolutionary this arrangement felt. Laura, thirty-eight, says,

> This will sound crazy, but I didn't even know how to *do* a relationship that wasn't in some basic way about pleasing the man. I don't mean pleasing him in a geishalike way, but having it be essentially on his terms. Because I was always worried about the next date, about where the relationship was going, about whether we *would get married*. My enjoyment of relationships before I was married was determined totally by whether they had a future.

Joy, twenty-eight, says,

> He desired me strictly for who I was. For my existence, not my instrumentality. Seeing me was a lot of trouble for him, so I didn't doubt his feelings. I felt very important.

Commenting on the feeling of power and self-confidence she felt when she saw this relationship being formed around her and their mutual needs, Iris, a forty-five-year-old woman, told me,

> I called the shots. We met when I could get away. The places we went to were convenient for me. Sexually, it was as much about me as it was about him. I hadn't had this before. Where the deal was that I already had my life, so he'd have to, you know, please me sexually or it might end; where the relationship was all about me in some way.

And Ethel, forty-seven, said,

> I can't tell you how bizarre it was. I had never had this . . . just existing, doing nothing but being, and having the relationship proceed without my orchestration. There had been men who had chased me before, but what was different about this was that I wanted it too and *still* I didn't do a lot of work.

These same two women couldn't think of any previous relationship focused so entirely on them. If she were single and in an affair with a married man, or even single and in an affair with a single man, she would be entering a classic and classically unrewarding role. The single woman, still socially and personally less powerful than the married woman, is perceived to want more out of an extramarital relationship, whether she does or not.

The very structure of such a secret and forbidden relationship, according to sociologist Laurel Richardson of Ohio State University, supports only the married man. Because of the greater status that marriage, money, and maleness all confer on him, she observes in her paper, "Secrecy and Status: The Social Construction of Forbidden Relationships," and also because the single woman agrees to protect his marital status by keeping their relationship a secret, that relationship becomes readily idealized, her lover's power and status are reinforced, and she is further disempowered. If the status of one person in a secret, sexual liaison is given priority, "the relationship will be constructed to protect that person," Richardson writes. "Subsequently, that person will have greater power in the relationship." As always, the lethal combination of idealization and disempowerment add up to only one thing for the woman: loss.

The structure of the affair with a married woman reverses this power imbalance. Since, as Richardson concludes, "secret, forbidden sexual relationships . . . reinforce and perpetuate the interests of the powerful," the married woman will have no less than equal power if her lover is married; more if he is not.

And while both these women remembered courtship as a time during which they felt some of the same feelings, they also recalled the goal—marriage—always looming.

Ethel said,

> There is a brief period in courtship when a man sort of rushes you; but very quickly after that, about as soon as he knows you're interested, the whole thing shifts and boom, you start thinking about where it's going, whether you're going to get married, when and where and how he's going to ask you and what everyone will think. You begin to shape your sex life accordingly— should I give him more or less to get him to marry me? Meanwhile, he starts backing away. Here, though, there's no marriage at the end, so sex is not used, or use*ful*. It is beyond courtship; it's not restrained and there's no goal.

And Iris,

I couldn't have had this without already being married.
I would have been so different; so much . . . needier.

Suddenly, she experiences something else that is new:
an absence of the emotional neediness that often characterizes women's relationships.
Dora, forty-nine, tells me,

Always when I met a man I liked I moved immediately
into "When will I see him again?" mode, and then into
"Did I say the right thing, do the right thing, *be the
right thing?*" mode. Never before have I said, that was a
nice evening, or that was great sex, without immediately
obsessing about whether there would be another
evening; more great sex. Never have I been able to enjoy
the relationship as it was at that moment rather than how
it was developing, you know, how it would, could,
should be.

Sandy, twenty-six, says,

I don't have to choose between being myself or being
desired. I choose the former and get the latter—it's a
miracle! Before I was married, when I chose being myself, no one would look at me! So of course, I didn't. I
was too hungry for love, to put it bluntly. It's as if you
have to marry to fulfill the societal thing before you can
be free to have this honest thing.

Anne, forty-eight, says,

What he got was me. There was no other way I could be.
Me with all my fears and problems. I didn't pretend to
be otherwise, the way I would have if I had been out to

win him. We didn't have time for any of that. And he didn't shy away.

THE POWER OF "UNDAZZLING" MEN

In a dramatic departure from the way they had previously chosen men, the women selected extramarital partners without their usual careful consideration to age, employment position, social, financial, and marital status—for while these were important criteria for choosing a husband, they felt, they were irrelevant when picking a man for pleasure. Rather, what they became interested in were a man's personal, not his "checklist," qualities: what his body was like, his smile, credentials as a friend and lover and nurturer; whether he treated her respectfully and kindly, and as an equal.

The men tended to be the same age as the women, or, when different, as often younger as older. Research shows that since marriage confers upon a woman a higher social status than being single does, she starts out in these relationships more nearly equal to her partner. By choosing a younger man, or one who makes less money, or one who is single—as many women do—she finds herself in a relationship in which she has even more power than her lover.

I heard about "undazzling" men, "really lovely" men, from women who weren't able to find the words for precisely what it was they had fallen for; "gentle," "sweet" and "special" and "nice" men, whose touch was "accepting" and "reassuring" and whose concerns— always, always—were with, as Paula said of Harry, "giving me what I need, as if that was what he was living for and—more to the point—as if it should be what *I* was living for." They felt as freed from the usual male stereotype as they did from a need to fit the female stereotype.

Laura says that when she "hit fifty" she began to think she was being perceived by her husband as having matured beyond her sexuality, somehow, and knew she would ultimately become inadequate to the task of simulating the girlish sexuality that more closely fit his taste. But with her extramarital partner she felt less pressured to be girlish, more appreciated for being womanly:

I was so glad my friend wasn't into that Calvin Klein ad stuff. I realized that what I most loved about him for the whole first year was his deep appreciation of my stretch marks.

Margo, fifty-one, said something similar:

Now I'm not saying men shouldn't like eighteen-year-olds with taut bodies, but I found one who likes fifty-one-year-olds, thank you Holy Jesus, and that alone has broadened my appreciation of men. Not to mention of myself.

Victoria, forty-six, liked the emotional equality she felt in her new friendship:

The greatest thing is that I am judged on precisely equal terms as him. He doesn't feel that because he's forty-six he should look one way and I—at forty-six—should look two decades younger. His criteria are the same for both of us. We're both middle-aged and we both look it and we both like it fine. I think I saw most men as so vulnerable to this double standard that when this guy wasn't I felt freed.

He thinks I'm beautiful, you know. Really.

The model of maleness these women were subscribing to differed dramatically from that of the unmarried women I interview for my monthly column in *Mademoiselle*—a magazine whose readership is predominantly single. For those women, the familiar socioeconomic superlatives (tall, brilliant, handsome, rich, powerful) comprise the list of characteristics they desire in the men they hoped to meet and to marry. Conventional qualities of this sort were rarely used to characterize these unconventional relationships, however; another kind of checklist was being devised. But I had the sense that the words in this new inventory were so removed from those offered up in the language of romantic idealization that once spoken, they just landed flat.

Janet's sentences are clipped and self-conscious:

> I like him. He makes me feel good. We talk. And we tease each other. He's really . . . fun. Oh, I just can't explain it. It sounds so dumb.

Paula was just as embarrassed when she first described Harry:

> It sounds too revoltingly simpleminded to say what I love about Harry. Like, "Oh my God he's so wonderful, he looks me straight in the eye when he talks and he lets me finish my *sentences*, isn't he just wonderful?"

June, too, was self-conscious coming up with an adequate description of Jonathan:

> Here I am talking about this overwhelming feeling I have about this man, and all I can say about the guy is that he's short and dark and cute.

One by one, they found themselves unable to find the right words for this new man in their lives, and became flustered, like Nadine, twenty-seven, who said:

You must think I'm really a nut case telling you about this crazy time where I'm lying and running around and all for . . . *a nice, friendly guy* I can't think how to describe. But I know that I feel incredibly good. And that whatever I do to describe him won't really convey how terrific he is with me.

"Well, maybe that is why there is a song, 'He's just my Bill . . . an ordinary guy.' "

Except that he isn't ordinary. It's just that the words I can think of don't seem to suffice. Like they would convey something special to you, wouldn't they, if I said, "He's CEO of AT&T and he plays polo with the Prince of Wales. Now there, you'd think, is a guy to have an affair with. Right?

No Words for this Love

It was when we talked about their sexual feelings within their affairs—after the women had already described their partners and also their feelings for them—that I came up against a sudden and inexplicable wall of silence. It always happened at the same time, well after I was a trusted interviewer, and long after we were comfortable with each other. It was not that they were hesitant to speak, it turns out, but that suddenly, they felt what they had to say was ineffable. "I feel as if the language available to me cannot convey my meaning," said Tina, a thirty-two-year-old woman who had up till this point been open and almost garrulous. "I suddenly feel dumb."

Kate, an extremely self-aware and articulate woman of forty-eight—also relaxed and talkative—supported Tina's feeling:

I don't think I've ever talked about my sexual experience or feeling with anyone. I don't have a vocabulary. In my psychoanalysis, where I'm supposed to go on and on about my fantasies and feelings, it's like . . . a void. Even to myself, I don't have words. Somehow I've not integrated the experience of sex itself as a subject I can objectify. I don't have a concept for it. My feelings are *nonverbal.*

What I felt was at stake was the women's sense that their words might be misinterpreted. They feared that nobody would understand precisely what their relationship was like, or how much it meant to them. Any listener, they felt, would rebuke their stance, encourage them to reevaluate their relationship in a more negative light, hold up traditional mores. Most terrifying of all, the listener might take something away from their experience, some crucial essence of it they needed to have and to have understood. They questioned their ability to be persuasive enough to convey their pleasure.

It was as if the question, "*Why* do you appreciate this other man so?" was the most dangerous one. And so I began, as I did here, with Edie, a thirty-five-year-old professor of English, to pinpoint what exactly, at this predictable moment, was so dangerous.

"Do you love this man?"

"Well, yes, in a way. But I'm not in love with him."

"What is it that you like about him?"

"He is . . . I don't know . . . really, special. But I guess he won't sound so special to you."

"You needn't tell me his name, or even tell me anything about him at all. I just want to know how you *feel* about him."

"I'm afraid he won't sound worth it. Worth all this trouble."

"You mean, worthy enough for me to feel you are justified in seeing him?"

"Well, or that my feelings aren't big enough to be called love."

"And you feel *I* feel you should love him?"

"It would sort of give a reason for this thing I'm doing."

"Like I'm going to say, 'You left your perfect life for *that*? For a skinny, tall man with brown eyes who doesn't read *Shakespeare*? And you're keeping it a secret from your husband, a handsome, blue-eyed man who *does*? You must be crazy! You're calling that ridiculous arrangement *love*?' "

"Yeah, exactly. That he isn't good enough to make me feel this good."

"Yes—and that it shouldn't make you feel that good; particularly if it isn't love. Then it's really unconscionable."

"Yes. Right."

"But even if I said that—that your feelings were wrong or bad or peculiar or whatever—what would happen? What if I even said, 'That's not worth anything! You *have* what is worth something, right in your own kitchen. Now *march*, young lady! You go back home at once!'—what would that make you feel?"

"That you didn't understand anything."

"Which would make you feel hopeless, stupid, misunderstood?"

"Yes."

"But then you could explain it to me, no? 'Here's the feeling that is so important to me, or here's why *you* may think I'm crazy, but here's why I do not.' "

"I don't know. I don't know if I could convince you. I don't quite know myself."

"But you *do* know! You've come all this way to tell

me! Is it that if your love isn't endorsed somehow, it isn't real?"

"No. More like it will be taken away. The whole experience will be taken away from me."

"So that in some way without my understanding it, or my approval of it, or of you, you will be left with nothing at all?"

"Nothing but a stupid choice and feelings that don't make sense and a huge mistake."

"Yes. And here you have been trying to tell me how wise the choice was, how much sense your feelings have made to you. And I'm just going to wipe them out."

"Yes."

The women's sensitivity to having their feelings undermined, their experience devalued, and their relationships appraised, was inextricably connected to our discussion just then of their *sexual* feelings—feelings, you remember, they long ago learned were prohibited, unspeakable. They were entering that almost-forgotten, almost-familiar sexual territory again—where passion and punishment are intertwined, and where, in order not to be discredited entirely, women understand they must revise their real feelings, observations, knowledge, experience, and behavior and present more palatable, "better," and more acceptable ones. These women were silenced in the face of this obstacle as surely as they would have been if, at the age of sixteen, they had carefully explained to their father the total joy of having just had sex in the back of a convertible.

What seemed at first a verbal problem—a reluctance to speak about erotic feelings—soon turned out to be a more complicated one. They were thrown, right here with me, into the same central dilemma of relationship they had encountered both at adolescence and in marriage: how to speak honestly about their deepest feelings but not be called "bad"; how to say what they desired without sounding "wrong" to desire it; how to speak about sex without displeasing me and being punished somehow. Would I believe them? Would I ridicule them? Would I invalidate the pleasure of the experience they were trying to communicate?

Of course the women faltered when trying to describe the men they were sleeping with and the pleasure they felt! These relationships, these men, these feelings were explicitly, emphatically taboo. And so it became clear once again that adultery is *unmentionable*—a word itself defined as "immodest," "indecent," "obscene," and "shameful." To mention the unmentionable was very dangerous indeed.

It was only when I was able to mock my position as omnipotent arbiter—to joke about having the power to validate or repudiate their feelings—that, together, we began to understand whose role we were really mocking, whose booming voice carried sufficient moral authority to silence their own. They had to know that that role, that voice, do exist—one is the impersonation of society, the other, the voice of the patriarchy—and both have rendered all women both mute and dumb at some point or other. But it was not my role or voice. They had to know too that other women felt the same way they did at just this moment. Only then could we continue to talk about love, because only then could the words "pleasure" and "sex" be uttered without inhibition.

Then they spoke about something so radical, something that men have always had, the right not to exclude themselves from the sexual equation—even more radically, the right to put themselves first in that equation.

They spoke about constructing an emotional and sexual dynamic they had never experienced before and inventing their role in it. "Undazzling" and "gentle" men, "not-so-perfect," "playful," and "confident" sex, and "egalitarian" friendship in which they felt freed from the requirement to be "good enough" to be loved were the hallmarks of this forbidden, unconventional attachment. "It is hard to suppose a woman can mean or want what we have always been assured she could not possibly mean or want," observes Carolyn Heilbrun in *Writing a Woman's Life*, and nowhere is it harder to suppose than when a woman means and wants pleasure, and when she articulates who, and what, are giving it to her.

In one of three essays comprising *Contributions to the Psychology of Love*, which he wrote between 1910 and 1917, Freud observes that the tendency of men is to divide women into madonnas and whores—ideals of goodness on the one hand and objects to be taken to bed on the other. Women had no such inclination to "degrade the sexual object," he said, but he points to what he considers its corollary: "the necessary condition of forbiddenness in the erotic life of women." He notices in the third essay, that "[g]irls openly declare that love loses its value to them if others know about it," and that some women can love "only in an illicit relationship which must be kept secret, and in which she feels certain of being actuated by her own will alone."

It is possible that what so appeals to women in these forbidden, secret relations are the extraordinarily different terms of relationship they seek and find in them. What my women found is that within these gentle relationships they felt powerful and equal and freed from having to be pleasing—three aspects of relationship historically missing for women in conventional marriage. These feelings are what comprise and define their pleasure; these are what restore their authenticity and free their will and their sexuality. No wonder they do not want to risk exposing these relationships. For among other reasons, their own pleasure and power are not what they have been told to value or to seek, and equality is not offered in relationships endorsed by the patriarchy.

THE CHILDREN

I had noticed early on that women rarely cited their children as deterrents to their affairs. Only occasionally did they bring up the children at all, and when I questioned them what I heard was, first, how complicated the logistics were in making sure young children were cared for while the affair was going on. Mothers of very young children worried far more about how their absence for a few hours would affect them than about whether the fact of the affair, or their affection for the extramarital partner, might somehow hurt them. None of the women brought her affair partners home; and none had any impulse to introduce them to her children.

I heard again and again that the affair was a private issue, one the women intended to keep private, and the children were not a part of it.

All the women I asked said their major concern was not whether the affair itself might hurt their children—they did not think it would—but whether the consequences of the affair would somehow jeopardize their connection to them; they were fearful, in other words, about punishment for the affair; about the possibility of losing the children in a custody battle.

Several studies support my experience of women's reluctance to bring up the issue of the children. Annette

Lawson, for instance, while in the middle of her interviews, noticed,

> People in interview rarely mentioned their children as playing any part in their deliberations or in their feelings about having or not having affairs. . . . When I [raised the topic] then I would hear about the distress of a possible separation. . . .
> Perhaps, as increasing numbers of married women work . . . it seems more feasible to conduct such liaisons (just as it has always been for men) with less impact on the children.

Other studies suggest that some sociologists and therapists are concerned at the increase in extramarital sex, particularly among women, and are finding that children suffer when a parent has an affair. Andrée Brooks reports in *The New York Times* (March 9, 1989) that some specialists believe, "While an affair is taking place children sense that the parent is expending emotional energy outside the family," and as a result of the "subtle changes in an adulterous parent's behavior" they "may become anxious or frightened, or they may sense rejection and feel they must have done something wrong." And "When the mother is having an affair . . . a child who learns of [it] is in danger of losing confidence in the viability of marriage and the family."

On the other hand, sociologist Lynn Atwater's extramarital sex study suggests that, in the long term, a change in women's sexual behavior might conceivably have a positive impact on childrearing practices:

> For among the myriad ways in which women are changing, we cannot afford to overlook the consequences of sexual change that may well filter down to affect the lives of their children. . . . The stereotype is that parents are

supposed to be non-sexual beings, "uptight" in speaking about sex. As parents, particularly women, alter their own sexual expression and their ability to be open, their influences on their children's sexual development may well increase rather than decrease when children mature into adults. Changes in the development and expression of women's sexuality, then, may also influence their role as the principal socializers of children and, therefore, produce changes in the sexual socialization of succeeding generations.

My concern here is with the women, and if my findings of the women are surprising, perhaps subsequent findings about children will be surprising too. Certainly it seems necessary to keep open the question of whether women's affairs affect their children, and how. But where we suspect the effects are negative, we might rethink precisely *why*. Because the Perfect Mother is as tenacious an icon as the Perfect Wife, and we must examine our assumptions about a mother who rejects the role, and whether doing so hurts her child. The power of goodness to silence pleasure in relationships may be as detrimental to children as it is to their mothers. Children may pick up their mother's anxiety about the consequences of losing this goodness, including her fear that she may lose the capacity to be a good mother—or they might pick up their mother's excitement about finding pleasure.

ORDINARY RELATIONSHIPS

Even after the women began to speak openly about their extramarital relationships, they were tripped up by the language of "good" and "bad." Women who described their marriages as "more perfect" than their affairs, their lives as "great," and their homes as "wonderful" found themselves nevertheless not feeling as wonderful as the words suggested they should. They sensed that they weren't responding the way they were supposed to. And they described their affairs, for which they used words like "nice" and "warm" and "fun" and "egalitarian," as just . . . ordinary. It confused them. For while their lovers might be all these nice things—playful and experimental and involved and expressive—and be bringing them extraordinary pleasure, these qualities were not considered *"wonderful"* in the language of relationships they had learned.

I discussed these "ordinary relationships" I was hearing about with New York marriage therapist Dr. Laura Singer. She was hearing a similar story from her women patients who were having extramarital sex. "It's not about having a Prince Charming who is going to come and sweep her off her feet," Dr. Singer says. Instead, "the kind of man they seek is very real."

The women only attempt to reinstate the idealized "Prince Charming model" of men when they are leaving their marriages and looking for a new mate. Such a fantasy "is more likely to occur after a divorce," Singer has found, "when a woman is clearly looking for a new husband and she has a fantasy of remarriage to someone better than the former husband. It is then that a lot of comparison of the two men goes on." Choosing a new husband thus propels the woman back inside the framework, where certain criteria must be met to make a "good" marriage, and where these criteria are not, historically, those that necessarily best meet her emotional or sexual needs.

But choosing an extramarital partner hurls her outside this structure, where a different fantasy takes hold, notes Dr. Singer, one of "being treated like a grown-up."

Laura is thirty-five, married happily for ten years to a city worker named Vince. For five years, she has been having an affair with a colleague at the suburban New Jersey photography store where she works. The major difference she sees in her two relationships is that Cliff, her lover, "treats her like a grown-up" and by this she means that he sees her as a woman of many moods and conflicting desires, a complex and, as she puts it, "difficult" woman. Her husband, from whom she hides her moods "in order to please him and make everything go more smoothly" does not, she feels, see her in this light.

With Cliff, she is, she says, "moodier" than she is with her husband, by which she means she is far more open: more likely to tell him when she doesn't feel like making love or when she is feeling sad or angry or upset—and at the same time less likely than she is with her husband to anticipate punishment for doing so; less afraid that her moods will be interpreted as hostile, or that they will somehow be held against her. She feels less "rejecting," "demanding," and "withholding" with Cliff; "freer to do and be whatever I really feel at that moment." Laura senses a connection between her expressiveness with Cliff and her treasured sense of being "treated like a grown-up."

She feels she is in an odd predicament. In some ways, she believes, her husband gets a "better" part of her than Cliff does, because she's so much "less moody" at home, and makes herself so much "easier" to deal with, which then "puts so much less pressure on the marriage" than if she were to reveal herself more fully. And yet she also ascribes her closeness to Cliff to the very moodiness she has so carefully kept from Vince; finds, too, that Cliff "likes her more than Vince does."

Laura is struggling to understand why the unmoody and selfless wife she carefully presents to her husband makes her feel "infantilized," while the more complicated, authentic, and moody self she opens to Cliff allows her to feel grown-up and cared for. She understands the crucial role of her "moodiness" in all this—that it is somehow a major factor in both relationships—and is grappling with the idea that perhaps it is unwise and unnecessary to present her edited self to Vince—or to anybody. Certainly the astonishing freedom she feels with Cliff must have something to do with her authenticity and openness—her moodiness—with him. But she is not sure.

"It wouldn't work with my husband," she says to me quickly, anticipating my question.

"Why not?" I ask.

"He's moody, too."

"Yeah, so?" I say.

"Two moody people make for a difficult marriage."

"But not a difficult affair?"

"Difficult but not unworkable."

"Why the difference—why wouldn't it make the marriage, too, like the affair, difficult but not unworkable?"

"You can be a difficult lover, but not a difficult wife."

"But that's what I'm asking you. Who says?"

"You know why. We all know why. It just sounds so stupid to say it."

"Because when it's part-time there aren't so many consequences?"

"Yes, that, but I was thinking more that unpredictability in a wife may be attractive at first, early in a marriage, but soon that very inconsistency becomes unacceptable to a husband; one way or another, he finds he can't tolerate it—her lateness or her bad moods or her difficultness, it's too disturbing, too threatening. I mean like he doesn't *beat* her into shape, or anything, but *together* they find some way to make her a better wife, to change her, tame her."

"The wife, you think, is in collusion with him to be tamed?"

"Yes. I felt my husband's confusion and rushed in to relieve him by altering my personality. It's very subtle, of course, this complicity. I never felt I was 'being changed'; I just felt how unacceptable my personality was, how it wasn't quite sweet enough. I kept throwing him off. I just . . . softened myself. . . . It was all in the name of being . . . a better person or a better wife or—more to the point, a better *mother* to him than the one he had. But instead of becoming any of these, I just failed both of us. I hid. I became someone I'm not—a half-person, sort of."

"But you don't feel this need to modify yourself with Cliff?"

"Not at all. No. He hates it when I do. He calls me on it. 'You're not here to please me!' You already please me!' "

"Do you think, in time, you'd feel the same pressure?"

"No. I don't."

"How come?"

"Because it isn't my niceness he's here for, and time isn't going to change that. He really wants the opposite of that tamed part in me. Now if in time we got *married*, well, I might feel the pressure then. I don't know."

"Ah. Because if you got married, he might want to tame you too?"

"He might."

"Or *you* might. You might do just what you have done with Vince, don't you think? I mean, you may have responded to cues, but you made the decision to short-circuit your moods, no?"

"Yes, it's a deal."

"So you don't blame your husband."

"Hell, no. I blame *marriage*."

WIVES' "HAPPY DUTY"

Laura's "moodiness" is her touchstone to her real and "selfish" self—but she only allows it to show outside marriage. There, it is the rubric under which she can safely collect and display her authentic feelings. In the name of "moodiness" she could feel passion—"which," she says, "is neither nice nor controlled," and she could argue. Because she is "moody" she could be close to someone or distant, as she wished. Her moodiness, most of all, guaranteed that she would not be frozen in "niceness," which in turn guaranteed that she would be treated—by Cliff, anyway, "like a grown-up."

Other women felt the same way Laura did, and found that once they began an affair, they had no choice but to reveal their real feelings. Says twenty-nine-year-old Alix:

> It was a mood that pushed me into the affair in the first place, after all, and I've stayed close to my moods as a way to guide my actions. I think on a minute-to-minute basis now: Will I see him tomorrow? When? Do I feel like seeing him? I'm obviously relying not on protocol but on my real feelings to prompt me. I've become more aware of what I really want through this process, and of what I need, both of which are at the very heart of my new relationship.

For Alix, too, "moodiness" felt like the one thing that most upset her marital relationship—just as it is what established the basis for her extramarital one.

With my husband, there is always this feeling that I have to be in the right mood to make love. We seem to go into this sort of automatic "nice" mode when we come together, as if that's what's required—you know, like you take a shower and try to get into a nice mood—if it's going to work at all. It's very, very subtle. Like something out of *Ozzie and Harriet*. It's like if we're in that particular state—I don't know how else to describe it except as "nice," you know, like sort of without any effort; as if we were entertaining guests, he smiles, I smile; then all goes well. Otherwise, any other approach, any other mood—if I'm distracted or edgy or annoyed or in any way in the moment rather than in the reverie of niceness, it throws sex off totally, as if I've betrayed our bargain: You be nice and I'll be nice and then we can fuck.

I ask Alix, "What happens if you can't get into this nice mood?"

I don't know quite what happens. We've just never come together with our anger or our sadness or our ambivalence, even, right out there. What happens is that we must both in some way already *be there*, as if on cue. Ready, hon'? Sure, dear! My husband is simply not willing to seduce me—you know, like if I'm preoccupied he won't try to get me interested. If I'm not in the mood, he doesn't try to put me there. And that's so sad, because I love it when a man goes to that trouble, you know. I don't think I seduce him much either, because I feel like it's not part of our established repertoire; like it would only bomb, somehow. So I *always* feel like the heavy, because it's set up so that I'm the one who will determine WHETHER WE'LL MAKE LOVE TONIGHT because I'm the one least likely to segue into nice mode. I'm the bad one, the one with the headache.

"But how can you get in the mood in the abstract, for God's sake? Look at pictures of nude men? Masturbate before going to bed?"

I always feel this terror, before we start making love, that I won't be able to get into that weird "nice" mood that seems to be the only signal to him that I am ready, and that we can proceed.

"What do you think this is all about?"

Oh, being scared, being ambivalent, being unsure of our sexual power over each other. On a strictly sexual level it's simple: If I'm already ready, he doesn't have to do any work—there's no chance he'll fail. The fantasy of the woman just lying there, ready to make it at any time.

"Yes. Psychoanalyst Ethel Person calls this male fantasy image the 'omni-available woman.'"

Right! Anytime, any place, anyhow. But more seriously, it's about pretense. Sex is, for us, cut off from the world of real feeling; it's a duty. A happy duty. That's what all that niceness is. Are you ready to perform your happy duty, honey? It's not real. It's something you learn from TV or your parents. Some idealized thing a couple does that has nothing to do with real people, that doesn't come from the heart. And I deeply believe that we can't get out of it—not unless we can get into bed and express the rage and terror that we really feel.

"Have you tried that?"

I start out thinking I will. But by the time we actually come together, I just don't. I get nice. It's horrible, just horrible.

All the women understood this odd compunction to limit their range of expression in their marriages and to alter their moods to fit an ideal of goodness, of niceness—even if they were not successful at doing either. They considered this their role—what Alix calls her "happy duty." One woman said that the only difference between this and the "grin-and-bear-it" sex she used to hear her grandmother talk about was that her own generation admittedly loved sex, so nobody pretended it was an *unhappy* duty. But it was duty nonetheless, even if one that promised pleasure. And the need to live up to the ideal still made them feel infantilized, not treated like a "grown-up," and worst of all, that they were expected to be someone they were not.

It was not a question of whether their husbands were or were not overdemanding; did or did not rage against women for their own psychological reasons; hated or worshiped their mothers; needed or did not need to control their wives. The men may or may not have conspired to make their marriages repetitions of their original families—assigning their wives the role of being better mothers to them than their own were. The point is that the women bought into this self-transformation irrespective of whether they were pressured to by their husbands. They were their own enforcers of a system established ages before, and no longer in need of prompting by anyone.

Their adeptness at hiding their moods and their sexuality felt old and tired to them, both inevitable and inexplicable: they traced the origins of the mechanism to an early point in their marriages. Some said that they once had more expressive sex with their husbands, but long ago. There was a clear link between their determination to be better wives and their sense of not acting like or being treated like adults.

Laura, who continues to see the man she was having an affair with two years before, says that she had to let go of her idealized self in order to grow up, the first step in having the egalitarian relationship she feels she has with Cliff.

Maybe what I mean by "adult" is that the choices are so often my own, for me, and that *feels* adult, you know, not basing everything on what's best for someone else. Not capitulating or second-guessing or protecting some mythical fragile ego, where my pleasure is deflected, somehow, and supposed to come from giving him pleasure.

We don't manipulate each other, either, like pretending we're doing something for the good of the other to justify doing what we want. We don't act like father and mother or son and daughter; we act like equals who have complicated lives and who must negotiate and compromise and argue to love each other. It feels fair. Hard won, fair, and important.

By contrast, Laura talks about feeling "infantilized" in her eight-year marriage, more so now at thirty-five than when she was in her late twenties; and I am struck by her words, because again and again I have listened to this odd correlation between getting chronologically older while simultaneously losing a feeling of being a "grown-up"—a sexual anomaly that seems to happen when, after many years of marriage, women feel "old" but not "adult"—while in their affairs, they felt "adult" but not "old." I ascribe this again to the departure, in their extramarital relationships, from idealized models of femininity and masculinity, and to the return of easy, comfortable, unidealized relationships.

"I'm better at this than I am at marriage," Connie tells me ruefully.

"At what?" I ask. "What's 'this'?"

"At being in a relationship."

We both laugh. I press on with the obvious.

"Isn't marriage a relationship?"

"Well, yes, it is, of course."

"Why does this feel like a relationship, then; why did you put it that way?"

"Because marriage feels sort of one-way to me. Probably for both partners it feels one-way. There's this sense of a lot of work, and not a lot coming back—the way there is in a relationship."

THE RETURN TO RELATIONSHIP

In this new "two-way" relationship, old feelings began to flood back in; feelings the women traced to a time before getting married. Stepping out of the role of wife, with its implications of selflessness and obligations to fill others' needs, into the role of a sexually joyous and self-interested person—risking societal pressure and the possibility of hurting a beloved husband—infused these women immediately with a sense of competence and satisfaction, as though they had emerged from a trance to find that their personalities had been returned to them.

What if we call the "grown-up" selves these women recovered in their extramarital relationships "good" for a moment, and the "frozen" and "infantilized" selves they lost "bad," rather than the reverse? What if we call the "ordinary" and "egalitarian" extramarital relationships they formed "good" and the "perfect" marriages they had created "bad." What if we acknowledge that their own husbands may not be necessarily responsible for these frozen relationships, but the fact that marriage is in itself a kind of paradigm, one in which idealization cools relationships and, subsequently, the women and men in those marriages? Then we have to reevaluate the whole chilled climate into which the Perfect Wife is hurled; question the various images we call "wonderful" and "ideal" and "perfect" that are, in fact, freezing women to death. If we do this, we might just be closer to discovering what is truly pleasurable in a relationship, at least for women, and I believe for men as well.

Certainly it is clear that whereas before their affairs these women experienced their bodies as fragmented, their voices muted, some vital organ or aspect of their personality missing, during the affair and after it they became changed. They let go of those muffled feelings and entered a clearer reality, one filled with color and vibrancy in which they felt "alive" and "awake" and "strong" and "focused." They came out of the silence to find they had new opinions and loud voices with which to express them.

Two women—a thirty-year-old creative writing teacher and a thirty-five-year-old real estate broker— talk about the different picture they awaken to each day, both of them now many years into their affairs. Says Gloria,

> There's an energy in me that feels different from whatever it is that used to drive me every day. It was arousal at first, but now, five years later and he and I are still going strong, it's not that. But I don't know what it is. I'm suffused with it. It's like I can finally see the forest for the trees, quite literally.

And Margie,

> I got out of bed one day and realized that I was really happy to be alive. It was as if I had been living in a

perfectly pleasant dream, but it was in black and white and now I was awake and everything was in color. I felt sad for myself, in a way, because I'd never felt so good before and here I was, thirty-seven years of age, and here was this thing I was doing that I couldn't share with anyone because it was so out of the question and was making me feel better than anything else ever had, and it all seemed so ass-backward.

LIVES CHANGED FOR THE BETTER

Most striking were the women who were in pain—overwhelmed by the craziness of their lives since the onset of their affairs—but who still felt their affairs had changed them, if not their lives, for the better. "You just told me your life was a mess," I said to June, probing for regret, approaching her in the middle of her turmoil, before she knew what she was going to do about Jonathan, what she was going to do about her marriage. "My *life* is a mess," she corrected me calmly, "but inside, for the first time in my life, I'm a rock."

The clarification arrived with unannounced suddenness. These women spoke of feeling that something had "clicked" or "snapped" inside them at a certain point during their affairs, after which they never felt quite the same. They had now come closer to reaching a deeply comfortable internal persona, had finally recognized the woman each of them knew existed within herself but which, until now, she had not permitted to emerge.

For Alison, who you remember had been chilled all the time, who had described herself before her affair as having been "on ice" for many years, it wasn't a lost body part or vital organ that was found, but a more total physical integration, and a sense that her surroundings had "thawed" and were thus less hostile. Alison's perfect life became imperfect—leading her to wonder in horror, "Where have I been all my adult life?"

What had transformed them, apparently, was not having found something ideal in their extramarital relationship, but something imperfect and ordinary and comfortably familiar. Looking outside of what was supposed to make them happy, they looked inside and found that what really made them happy was something quite different. Rather than talking about how "wonderful" the new relationship was, they spoke about how wonderful they felt in it. Rather than describing idealized selves, they spoke of seeing and being seen, flaws and all; rather than describing relationships in which they never felt sad or angry or miserable, they described "ordinary" relationships in which the expression of anger was welcomed and conflict was as present as the playfulness and sex and conversation that had brought them and their lovers together. In this ordinary and flawed and unidealized relationship, their deepest, most authentic selves were welcomed; they felt not only relieved, but that they had unearthed the only thing that truly mattered in their lives.

What we have here is women saying again and again that their sexuality, which had been so disempowering inside the confines of conventional goodness, had, outside it, become empowering. They are saying that their love, inside marriage, had made them feel disconnected and devitalized, while outside it, in relationships they created for pleasure alone, they felt neither idealized nor debased. Their sexuality had "come alive" as surely and inexorably as they themselves had.

What had been lost was a simple, unidealized, warm relationship in which they felt completely at home, one in which their plain, true "unwifely" selves could thrive. And when they found these selves again inside such "ordinary" relationships—after wondering whether they had lost them forever—they also uncovered a long-buried voice. However fleeting the mechanism by which it was recovered, these women never wanted to let it go again.

Chapter Ten

"You Just Don't Get Divorced
after Twenty-Three Years of Marriage"

*P*aula thought about sleeping with Harry for about two months. She told him about all her concerns— whether they were seeing each other too much; what would happen to her if they kept it up—an affair was something so removed from her life and experience, something she wasn't sure she could deal with. She was not sure she was willing to jeopardize it by bringing sex into it. She told him how "out of practice" she was, sexually; that she was not sure he would even like her once they got into bed; it might be better if they just kept it the way it was, lunches and talks. Harry kept reassuring her: Whatever happened, it was all right. They could just keep having lunch. But he thought that they would be able to have sex, if she wanted to, without harming their relationship. He didn't expect to "not like her" sexually. And if it turned out to be uncomfortable for her at any time, they could resume their chaste lunches, he wouldn't be mad, and that would be that. They would have lost nothing.

"The truth is I got sick of thinking about it," Paula tells me. "I met him one afternoon and said, 'Today's the day. Where shall we go?'

"We went to the Lombardy. Didn't even have lunch. I said it was too expensive, both lunch *and* a place for sex. He said we'd have lunch afterward at the Laurent.

"He was altogether just . . . nice. Very much like, this is going to be fun, we're going to have fun. Like our lunches together. He seemed eager, but cared more about what I was feeling, whether I was changing my mind, or clamming up. He stayed with me, talking, joking, making fun of me. He's very wry, very low-key, and he knew I felt like a teenager. 'Would you feel more comfortable in the back seat of a car?' he asked as he took off my bra. God, that *was* the last time I'd done anything like this. He offered to take me to a drive-in and buy me a hamburger if I 'put out.'

"What it did was keep me close to him emotionally. He didn't want me to be out there in terror without him. And that's who he is: That's what I love about him. He does all this emotional work, worrying about what will make me comfortable, how to do that without letting me know that that's what he's doing. Very subtle things that I'm grateful for, precisely because he doesn't extract gratitude from me. He relaxes me.

"This relationship, in other words, is about *me*. Can you imagine that?

"Once we got through the preliminaries, it was amazing. I felt this was what I was destined to do—make love to Harry. Wherever it came from in me, I don't know. But everything just felt right. It's not as if any one thing pleased me, particularly—I mean Harry is lovely, but he's not a hunk—but everything from his skin texture to his scent, from his interest in me to his ease, made being with him feel as right as any decision I've ever made. It still feels right. And, no matter what happens, I have found something that is so good I can't quite believe it.

"I felt like a teenager for about ten minutes—the petting part, the undressing part—but after that I felt I came into myself, into my own in a way I never have before. I knew how to do this. I felt very free, very much me. I knew, immediately, I had gained something. And it couldn't be taken away from me, no matter what.

"It doesn't feel like an affair, or however I imagined an affair to feel. Am I in love? No. I am in *sex*. Did he seduce me? Kind of, but in some subtle way, I was the aggressor. Do I feel guilty? No. Am I planning to leave George? Was I out of control and just letting any old man have his way with me? Is juggling marriage and affair tearing me apart? No, not at all. Was I driven to it? No. Although I'm not dumb enough to discount that entirely, since my relationship with George isn't exactly close, although I wouldn't call it unhappy."

One day, Harry told Paula he'd left his wife, moved out, rented a place on Thirty-fifth Street. Paula didn't know he was doing it for her—that he had moved out specifically to wait for her to do the same. She realized later she should have known, that it was obvious; she remembers, in fact, a conversation in which Harry had said he'd be a lot happier if what they were doing wasn't sneaky.

"So move out, then you don't have to sneak around," she had said.

"If I do, will you?" he asked.

It was the last thing on her mind, and she remembers saying something like "Not till you do" or some such thing, something distracted, since it had never occurred to her. But Harry did move out. And made a point of telling her he was doing what *he* had to do, and that it definitely was not meant as pressure. They never even talked about divorce, except theoretically: "We'd talk about vacations we'd love to take together but knew we never would—Ecuador was high on the list," Paula says. "Or we'd decide what we'd do when we got old. I believed he was really so unhappy at home that he would have moved out no matter what. I decided to believe him when he said that it was what he had planned to do even before he met me."

But once he moved, she had the sense that he was waiting for her. Harry was too much of a gentleman to put more than subtle pressure on her, she says, and for a long time he didn't blink when she went home after their meetings. "And then one day he just pulled me over to him and said, 'Enough. You're a good Jewish girl, you need to be married, you *are* married, so then go *be* married.' And just as I was actually getting comfortable with these two relationships going on simultaneously—it's not that hard, you know, you just work it into your life—he decides he's had enough. The day he made that decision, I threw up and continued throwing up every day for two weeks."

"He didn't even come out with it and ask you what your plans were?"

"Yes, he did. I said, 'What is it you want me to *do*?' and he said, 'I want you to leave George and move in with me.'

" 'Leave George?' I said it just like that. 'Become president? Shoot my child?' What could be more outrageous than the thought of leaving George? Do you know, until he said that, such a thing had not even passed through my conscious mind? Do you know what George would do? He would end my life on earth. He would kill Flora, or kidnap Melissa or declare me crazy in court. In fact he actually said that once. 'If you ever left me, I would have no trouble declaring you crazy. Your shopping bills alone prove you're *an unfit mother*.'

"And anyway, you don't get divorced after twenty-three years of marriage; you just don't. Not in my family. Not in George's family. It's a family tradition to stay married." In her own Russian-Jewish family, as in George's Anglo-Saxon one, there was not a single member who had been divorced, not a single one they knew of who had had an affair. "No uncle, no great-grandmother, no wacky black-sheep cousin. Straight as arrows and all family, family, family," she says.

"To say that my priority was without question my marriage, well, it was an understatement. My mother used to say to us, no matter what went wrong, who got hurt, who died, who went into surgery—'Are you *married*? Then *Thank God*.'

"Harry was horrified when I told him it hadn't occurred to me to leave. 'What have we been doing for this whole year?' he asked. 'What do you think this is, a fling? A game?' I tried to say something, but I realized that he didn't understand. I loved him, I really loved him, but I never thought of leaving George for him. I think he was terribly insulted, and thought I was hiding an immense love for George that I just couldn't tell him about. But it wasn't as much love as commitment, and it seemed nonnegotiable. I had nothing to say. And so I left."

It was impossible, after that, for Harry and Paula to get together again. They were used to meeting every week at the same time at their Chinese restaurant, with no calls in between. Although Paula appeared at their table the next Tuesday at 12:30, on the slightest of chances that he would be there, she knew he would not be, and he wasn't. It was clear now. "I wanted to explain why I wanted to stay in my marriage," says Paula, "well, 'wanted' is a peculiar word here. Let's say 'chose to stay' in my marriage."

She felt stunned by Harry's decision not to see her anymore, and the nausea didn't go away. During the next two or three months she read everything in the library about affairs, poring over each book, each magazine, in search of the answer. She began eliminating, one by one, the "kind" of affairs hers might be, to see what the normal outcome was, whether one solution was better than another. "I wanted to find out what would happen to me. What happened to people whose hearts were broken? What happened to their marriages? Did everything work out all right? Was I going to be okay?"

She had no one to talk to, and her nausea only got worse.

"Let me tell you what I learned, during the second month without Harry, when I was still throwing up each morning like I had morning sickness. *You need someone who knows what you're going through.* You do. Anyone; your mother, a friend. God, I was tempted to tell Melissa. Somebody's got to know about the affair, so they can know about the loss you feel. Nobody knew about Harry! It was amazing to me. There was nobody I could talk to. It was like mourning the death of a man who never lived; of an imaginary friend. I was being forced to deny my feelings about someone I felt so deeply for. I wasn't even allowed to grieve—he was illegal. And so I didn't even feel I had the right to my own misery, believing, good girl that I was, that I wasn't supposed to love this man! I went mad.

"I had such a heartache, literally, a *heart* ache, that I

became convinced I had heart trouble. My heart felt as if there were a foreign body in it, a terrible little cramp that hurt more when I moved my neck.

"I went to the best coronary man in the city. He said there was nothing wrong with my heart. I laughed. The best heart man in the city couldn't diagnose a broken heart! It struck me as hilariously ironic. I asked him if maybe sadness could cause heart disease; whether there was a connection, at least—still laughing, just waiting for his horrible answer, for him to say, '*What you need is a hysterectomy!*'

"And he said, mildly, intelligently: 'Of course there's a connection. It just isn't visible. We probably couldn't pick up anything that sensitive with these machines.' I laughed even more, at my underestimation of him and at my feeble attempt to entrap him. I was still waiting for some medicalese—you know 'an incipient' something or other, or a pathology report.

"When I left the doctor's office, I desperately needed to call Harry. Just call him! Do it! Get this awful heart pain away. Call him. There was this song running around in my head, just rotating there, relentlessly. "Get back!" it said.

Her friend Carol saw her leaving the hospital. Carol, who used to call her about twice a month to find out where the sample sales were. She was a woman who, like Paula, shopped, and she consulted her regularly about what to buy. When they saw each other, Paula stopped short: "I was wearing the following, from my daughter's wardrobe: faded black capri tights, a huge old sweater that Lady Di had made popular years ago on some trip to Australia that had a big koala bear on it. Work boots. I tried to tell her I had just run out of the house that morning . . . but the way I looked, words were super-fluous. I stared down at the toe of my boots. I said something pathetic. 'Going to the country this after-noon!' She looked into my eyes and started to say something, but I ran."

Later, Carol called Paula. She was very crisp on the phone. She said she didn't know what was the matter, and that she was sorry she hadn't helped, or couldn't help, but that she had been depressed before and she knew the signs—maybe Paula was a little depressed?—and that she knew Paula was in trouble. Paula might be a genius about designers, but it was she—Carol—who was savvy about getting help. "She knew almost every shrink in the city," Paula says, "and boy, did she have a shrink for me, she said. Something like that. Nice. Reaching out in the nicest way."

Carol said, "Whatever you're going through, go through it with someone." It struck a nerve in Paula, since she was obsessed with the privacy of her grief. Paula said, "Yeah. Maybe someone smart can help." She needed to tell someone about Harry. About what she was going through.

Paula called this woman Carol said was as warm and kindly as chicken soup. Paula started crying the moment she got there: Where was the Kleenex? Weren't psychiatrists supposed to have Kleenex? Paula cried and cried. The doctor brought her Kleenex. "I am having an affair," Paula shouted.

"Oh," the doctor said.

"In that whole first session we never even got to George. She must have known I was married, since otherwise why would I be going through all her Kleenex? But we just talked about Harry."

Four months later, Paula began to examine her feelings about Harry—feelings she had never had before.

But she had trouble examining her feelings about George. In her family, and in George's family, she says, "*the marriage*—whatever the entity was and in whatever stage of degeneration it might be, was *it*. Nothing else mattered, not how healthy the relationship was, not how you felt about it. What mattered was that it remain intact."

While her mother would never question her choice, her psychiatrist did. "She kept saying I was vomiting because of the unacceptable material I was making my mind swallow." And what was unacceptable, apparently, was the possibility that her relationship with George might be in terrible trouble. To look at it, examine it, maybe even find it beyond repair, was intolerable.

One day, her psychologist shocked Paula. "I don't know whether we can keep on acting as if what you really want is to go back to this marriage wholeheartedly," she said, "when what is clear is that it is a deeply unsatisfactory, estranged relationship that you will not consider altering. So if you won't consider leaving George, or talking to him about your affair, or opening any dialogue whatsoever with him, would you consider seeing Harry again?"

Paula was stunned. "You're suggesting I resume my affair?"

"I am suggesting," she said, "that we are at an impasse. And yes, I think you should call Harry."

Paula started crying, choking uncontrollably. She cried without thinking of stopping, as if the crying would never stop. "My lungs were in some kind of coughing spasm that made me make these awful sobs that sounded like death rattles. I threw up all over the dear shrink's leather chair and started dabbing at the vomit with the damp yellow tissues I had shredded into my lap during the hour. She kept saying it was all right, that I would be all right, that this was good and that I needed to do it, and I continued dabbing the whole time. She left the room and came back with sturdier cleaning tools, and we cleaned up.

"She told me to go home and have a drink—or at least some hot tea. It was eleven in the morning. She said she would call me in a few hours. I had straight gin. Me, a nondrinker. My mother used to give me straight gin when I had my period. Something about the juniper berry and the ovaries. The shrink did call. I told her I had had one gin and was getting drunk. We made an appointment for the next day."

And then Paula called Harry. Relief flooded her, energy poured into her heart, and light seemed to fill the place where her pain was, the second she heard his voice.

They agreed to meet the next day. That was three months ago. Harry reluctantly agreed to see Paula—at least that once—without pressuring her to leave George, and found that although he was furious at her, he missed her so much he was willing to take her back; Paula continues to be in therapy—"We are talking about George now, finally."

"Do I want to run off with Harry forever and marry him and leave George behind? No. I don't."

"Any yesses?"

"Yes. I've found a someone I need desperately, who is loving, giving, funny, and I love being with him. I've found aspects of myself through being with him that I really don't think were there before—although I guess I thought I had a wild, extravagant, wonderful self just waiting to be resurrected from the dead. I'm really sexy with him, you know? And funny. Not idiotic funny, but, well, witty. My mind feels turned on, too. I feel smart. I feel he gets the very best of me. And that he loves it, loves me.

"And yes, I still shop. The old suppressed-libido theory may be all wrong, although I must admit I'm not racking up the same number of bills anymore. And I am getting a lot more work done—in fact I'm considering editing full time somewhere and stopping this hopeless freelance bit.

"You know, I have never, ever, had sex like this, conversations like this—even arguments like this—where I didn't feel like I was going through paces, acting some part. I'm not consenting to this relationship, I'm in it. And I'd forgotten what that felt like, that sense of being in my own life, feeling alive in it, not playing it but being it. I'm no longer feeling like I'm in a tower. I had forgotten . . . what my real nature was, how to act, not just react. I'm normal and open like I once was. You may question my use of 'normal.' "

"Nope. I question the *term* 'normal.' "

"Yeah. Well, I just feel, just sort of like . . . me."

"Are you going to stay in this relationship with Harry?"

"Yes."

"Is he really willing to see you now on this basis?" I ask.

"Yes."

"What if he can't stand it, and insists you leave George?"

"He's promised he won't. Not for now. Meanwhile, I'm looking at that possibility. At everything. I really am."

Hester Prynne doesn't get killed at the end of The Scarlet Letter, *she lives to die a natural death. Yet her fate is more depressing, to my mind, anyway, than Anna's train tracks or Tess's hanging or Emma's arsenic. Although clearly "some attribute had departed from her, the permanence of which had been essential to keep her a woman," there was renewed hope for her recovery of that attribute. Hester was free now to take from her breast the searing symbol of her shame and never wear it again.*

Alone with Dimmesdale, Hester rips off the letter and throws it into the forest, watches it lie at the edge of the stream "glittering like a lost jewel." Astonished by an indescribable relief and sense of weightlessness, she pulls off the formal Puritan cap that had hidden her glossy dark hair for seven years, letting it spill out as it had in the early pages of the book. And what a scheme she has for the two of them—to move away from Boston together! To love again! Hawthorne, unabashed, describes his once-silent Hester as her own passionate sermon renders the Reverend Dimmesdale speechless: "There played around her mouth, and beamed out of her eyes, a radiant and tender smile, that seemed gushing from the very heart of womanhood. A crimson flush was glowing on her cheek, that had been long so pale. Her sex, her youth, and the whole richness of her beauty, came back from what men call the irrevocable past." The attribute so long missing had returned.

As she basks in the promise of her brilliant plan, we witness for that instant the womanly Hester described earlier, as she breathes in with her lover "the wild, free atmosphere of an unredeemed, unchristianized, lawless region." We feel the impact of Hester's abundant sexuality once again, and of her happiness.

But she and Dimmesdale don't go anywhere. Hester

204

retrieves the letter from the side of the stream, puts it on, and never takes it off again. By resuming the scarlet letter voluntarily, Hester resumes as well the cell within the iron Puritan framework she had once eluded, reclaiming the deathly goodness she long ago renounced. She no longer needed those "iron men" and their heartless "goodwives" to enforce her punishment for adultery; she was her own enforcer. Finally, Hawthorne assures us, "the scarlet letter had done its office," and had crushed her.

Hester without hope and passion, without her voice and her plan and her sexuality, was now fit to join the other Puritan matrons—was eligible to become, in fact, the very, very best of the "goodwives"—for everyone knew that she alone "had no selfish ends, nor lived in any measure for her own profit and enjoyment." Sensing hers a selflessness and sorrow that exceeded even their own, the townspeople visited her daily, consulting her about their sadness and sins. Hester became the community counselor. Unhappy people—particularly "wounded, wasted, wronged, misplaced" wives, guilty of "sinful passion"—flocked to her cottage, "demanding why they were so wretched, what the remedy!"

Remembering that because of her unique knowledge and passion Hester was the one woman who possessed the remedy to cure what ailed them; that she had been slated to reveal "the new truth" that could "establish the whole relation between man and woman on a surer ground of mutual happiness," we can only share Hawthorne's gloom as we watch the outcome of the "lawless passion" that once made Hester a woman—the woman in his tale—now maim her, and the scarlet A that had once made her "Able" now disable her.

Part

THREE

Chapter Eleven

"I Don't Believe in
Happily Ever After Anymore"

*I*t always took Amanda at least a week to adjust to being home after being on the road. This time, the process of getting close to her husband again seemed particularly laborious, and she'd already been home ten days. Even her cats ignored her: "Oh, it's you, the brilliant actress," they seemed to say, while she tried to interest them in the can-opening ritual of their favorite kitty vittles. "How kind of you to come home." One, still a kitten, stared coolly at her past his tuna and refused to eat. "*Et tu*, Brambleberry?" she said, and he yawned.

Daniel was more overtly pleased about her return than the cats were but expressed it in his usual underwhelming way. Daniel was quiet. He was a careful and particular man, and decent, qualities she liked as much as his gentlemanliness—she thought when she met him at nineteen, ten years before, that he was reminiscent of Gary Cooper. That he had trouble expressing his feelings seemed to her inevitably and not distressingly male—

God knows Gary Cooper had that trouble—and she energetically extracted them from that reluctant soul of his, insistent that they communicate intimately. "Just say it!" she'd yell when she saw his jaw tighten and his gaze move away. "Daniel, you can't keep everything in. I won't live like that. Say it! You must, Daniel—it's for you as much as for me!"

And he would try. He would say it, whatever it was, and they would talk about it, and his jaw would unclench and his gaze return to her eyes, and she knew that this was their fate: While she expressed sufficient feelings for three people and more truth than anyone wanted to hear, he would listen and watch and learn from her how to be in touch, how to bare his heart. In exchange for her intensity and honesty, she would be the beneficiary of his solidity and strength and enormous patience.

So she didn't know, really, what the hell kind of response she expected this time. Something, though. She'd been away a month. It was such a stark change, going from the excitement of the theater, the familiar moodiness of the actors, and the constant free-flowing expression of feelings she had come to thrive on—to this, to home, where Daniel and the cats hid their moods and deftly obscured their feelings in an effort, it seemed to her, to prove to her yet again that they could keep their distance.

But it wasn't just the intensity of the theater and the relationships she had there that set her up for this letdown; it was the intensity of the affair she had had for two weeks while she was there.

A businessman who had seen her opening-night performance of the fourteen-year-old Hedwig in *The Wild Duck* had pursued Amanda—going backstage each night after the performance—until she had finally agreed to let him take her to dinner. He continued coming backstage every night, armed with champagne and flowers and a new place to go for a late-night dinner, and within two weeks she was going home with him rather than to the actors' residence.

Amanda is the friend of a close friend of mine, which is how I met her, and which, I think, allowed us to speak intimately quite quickly. When she came to my apartment on that bleak morning in December 1988, I saw immediately why a woman her age—she was then twenty-nine—could be cast as the fourteen-year-old in Ibsen's play. She had the clear, open face of a young girl, with pale blue eyes under lids that seem to be the rage all of a sudden—eyes like Charlotte Rampling's and Ava Gardner's and the model Tatiana's. She was, with those eyes and long, straight wheat-colored hair, a sultry but innocent-looking knockout.

She had, she told me, just told Daniel about her affair with Charles. I asked her how she happened to confess, what she had said.

She told Daniel exactly what happened, the events as well as her state of mind. "Charles had seen my performance the first night and had really bought it—bought my character," she said. "Hedwig is the only innocent character in the play, and Charles approached me as if I were she, this innocent and good child. He was entranced by me, because of who I was in the play. I was in his eyes a lovely, sweet, good person. And it was because of what happened on that stage. You can't imagine what that meant to me as an actor. I had woven a tale of illusion that had seemed real to him. It meant that I had succeeded."

"What about your feelings for him?"

"I had grown more and more lonely on this trip, be-

cause the communication between Daniel and me hadn't
been very good when I left. Daniel had been struggling—
he's an architect, but he didn't know whether he wanted
to teach or build. He wasn't sure what he wanted to do
with his life, and he was sort of hemming and hawing
about where to go—I mean, whoever knows what to do
with their life?—but he was in a bad spot, being really,
really unfocused. I, on the other hand, was very focused
in my profession, so I may have been impatient. And
also, Daniel and I were under a lot of stress last year. We
moved twice—did I tell you that?

"And I had had an abortion. I had gotten pregnant at
the worst time for us, but particularly for Daniel, who
just didn't know what he was doing. He really didn't
want the baby, and I was ambivalent, and yet we
mourned that decision terribly. And we became . . .
well, we were uncomfortable with each other, and I had
talked and talked about it but he hadn't, and then we
moved, and I was in rehearsals, and I don't know, we
just were not really tight at that time.

"All along, with Charles, I knew we were not meant
to stick together—I certainly wasn't looking for a permanent relationship!—but there were things I loved
about him. He is an ambitious, up person. Very positive, very smily—his upbeat personality really sort of
astounded me, it was so different from Daniel's—and
my own."

"How much of this did you tell Daniel?" I asked.

"I told him everything. All of it. All the background
and all about Charles. That he had come backstage again
the next night, and the next. That he took me to dinner
and to coffee and finally, after two weeks of this, to bed.
That I got sex from a person who made me feel good
about myself at a time when I was really lower than I
thought, someone who thought I was lovely and who

seemed safe, in the sense that I wanted companionship but not love. Even that I was glad that I had it for those couple of weeks—and I didn't need it to be more than that. It was over."

"And what was Daniel's response?"

"My initial reaction, when I told him the first time, was to push him to respond. 'You can hit me, you can do whatever you want to me!' I had said then. It was silly in a way, but it was my reaction. He didn't, of course. He withdrew.

"After about a week or so of not speaking to me, he said, 'This isn't fair, my being like this. This is exactly what you don't like about me. I'm as much to blame for what happened as you are.' And for a long time, we really communicated with each other. He tried to be more open. I had a lot of hope, then."

Why, I asked her, was it so important to tell her husband about this affair that had ended? Was it because she felt guilty? Or angry?

"No. I don't think so," she said. "There is just no other way for me. I have always been very honest. That is me. That's who Daniel married, and he knows it. A lot of people told me never to say anything to him— most people still say that, that I made a mistake. But I really never lived that way. I've never done that. Sometimes I think it would be easier on him if he didn't know, and harder on me—although I think that people have feelers, and they either choose to look at what they feel or they don't. That's what I always hated most about my parents' relationship—the denial. I don't like denial about anything. So I don't really provide the opportunity for it to happen.

"If I sense that Daniel's feeling something, I don't pretend it doesn't exist. Ever. He does that less—he can let things go more. I don't know how he'd be if I were more like him—he might be very happy!—I think he could live very nicely without facing some things. In fact, he does. But I can't. When something is very important to me, I never let the lie live. I mean, I go for the exposure. At least of *my* lies. I'm more tolerant of others' lies.

"I wanted him to see that there was a real problem here, or rather, problems. And that it was serious and *I wanted to work on it. We had to work on it.*

"It's very tricky. Because when I say that I wanted him to know that there was a problem, I am not placing *blame* on him for my affair. I'm not saying, 'I did *this* because you did or didn't do *that*.' I'm saying that all the things that went on last year, plus the distance between us, plus his lack of communication with me, plus my loneliness on the road, were parts of the problem, that they all need to be factored in, that they all needed attention. We needed to pay attention to all these things and we didn't—that was part of the problem. We should have talked about the moves as well as our separation as well as what I see as Daniel's overall lack of communication with me."

"Yes," I say, "yet he seems to have responded to the news with a reaction he later regretted, as if to suggest that you were entitled to your affair and he was not entitled to his bitterness about it."

"I don't think he felt I was entitled to the affair. Only that I was entitled to fairness in assessing why it happened. And entitled to credit for honoring my vow to him never to lie."

"Do you yourself feel that if you had had perfect communication with Daniel and if you hadn't been away for six weeks . . ."

"That I would *not* have had an affair? No. I can't say that. That's my point about not placing blame. That's

214

much too easy. Like 'I'm so uncomplicated and so good that unless I'm pushed to it by *you*, unless *you* do something to make me not good, I will always behave perfectly.' I hate that attitude. Who is really that good? Who behaves perfectly? 'She was pushed into the affair. She had no other choice!'

"I'm saying that this is what was going on with me, that these are the things we missed, and that together they must have contributed to the emotional state I was in, and that vulnerable state contributed to my behavior. That's all. My behavior might have been the same under optimum emotional conditions, maybe. I don't think so, but I can't know for sure because they weren't. What I do know is that we can work on the problems between us; that they may or may not be a part of my having an affair; and that I want to work on improving our marriage."

"Aren't you suggesting, though, that his recalcitrance, his uncommunicativeness, were issues that disturbed you enough to stray from the marriage? And doesn't that suggestion imply that a more communicative Daniel might have prevented the affair with Charles?"

"Yes. Our situation contributed to my willingness to seek sex elsewhere, that's for sure. But I wasn't *driven* to it. Daniel or the move or our problems didn't *cause* my affair. *I* caused it! Do you see? This isn't about my being forced. It's about who I am under various circumstances.

"I just don't want to suggest that I was pushed into something, or that I was lured into it. I mean, look: Charles chased me, but *I'm* the one who finally went after him, once the seduction at the theater shifted to bed. So I pushed it. Really pushed it. Daniel did not turn me into a person pushing another man to fuck me! That's what I mean—that was *me* there doing that. A part of me I never saw, granted, but me nevertheless. Should I blame that on *Daniel*? On my *marriage*? They're separate things!"

"I understand. But still, I think you're ambivalent about this issue, in spite of taking responsibility for your affair. I think we all get very confused about the extent to which marriage affects monogamy, because I think in our bones we believe that a good marriage is automatically a monogamous one, and therefore extramarital sex must mean that the marriage is, somehow, faulty. Even me—I'm probing around to see what might *really* be the reason for your affair."

"Yes, well, there are lots of those kinds of reasons. Daniel was angry, but very subtly angry, and he instilled in me a fear of things, all sorts of things, and I was very young. He'd take control in a very subtle way, and I began to feel inept. I could tell you a list of his faults, and a list of our problems—but I still don't believe that a 'better' marriage guarantees monogamy—isn't that backward thinking? There are good marriages in which both partners have affairs; terrible marriages where they stick together like glue. An imperfect marriage *justifies* infidelity emotionally, as if nobody would ever sleep with someone other than her spouse if marriages were perfect."

"I think that may have something to do with how you're defining 'perfect.' "

"Sometimes I think if Daniel had been less perfect— less Gary Cooperish and good and decent and all that, it would have been better for me, for us."

"Go on."

"I would be less like the woman who was trying to pry her man open, and he would be less like the man who was trying to keep his woman under control. It's such old stuff and we all, women and men, feel so righteous about those dull roles, like they're inevitable, or something. Like those roles are good roles. Yuck. You know what? The one thing I've learned in all this is that *I don't know for certain how I'll behave.* Good marriage or bad."

"Suppose you found out Daniel was having an affair."

"I would feel all kinds of things. But I wouldn't die. I'm not being philosophical here, Utopian. I mean this. I mean it. And *of course* I might be outraged if he did—I can be like a beast in a cage.

"What I'm trying to say is that if he *did*, it wouldn't be such a bad thing. I would feel all kinds of things, but they wouldn't kill me, those feelings. Is it better to stifle all your feelings so that you don't rock the boat for yourself or for another person? Is that love? Two people who agree to stay put emotionally, sexually, for their entire lives so neither of them ever has to have a negative, fearful feeling?

"When I was growing up, I thought an affair was absolutely the worst thing in the whole world that could happen. When I got married eight years ago, I didn't think twice about monogamy. I would be monogamous, that was all. That was just the way it was. So from that perspective, it would have been shattering.

"But because of my own experience I have a new perspective: I don't think monogamy is all that great. It's *okay*. But I've learned so much from these affairs and I've grown so much more tolerant of myself and of other people, both from my experience and from Daniel, that my attitude has changed. And if it had happened that Daniel had had an affair first, and I hadn't experienced it, if I hadn't understood firsthand what that really felt like, I don't know if I could have comprehended it. I don't know if I'd have been as tolerant as he has been. Daniel doesn't need firsthand experience to be tolerant; I think maybe I do. And I don't know if I'd have grown as much."

"Do you love Daniel more as a result of your affair?"

"Definitely."

"Because he did not punish you?"

"Because he understands me. And that for me to with-hold the truth about my behavior from him would be the real punishment for me, not only because it would be a lie but because it would *guarantee* my greatest fear in life—that I might not be understood. I'd much rather Daniel understand me than that he *approve* of me. I'm not interested in approval that comes from thinking the person you love is flawless."

"If I understand you correctly, you're saying that you have a problem not with marriage but with monogamy."

"It's true. Daniel does, too. The only thing we said to each other was, 'I will love you.' We didn't say we would be committed forever and we didn't . . . lie. We were both twenty-two years old and had very strong views and wanted to be married, but we left our marriage open for life's course."

"What about sex with Daniel now. Is it good?"

"It's better."

"Better than when?"

"Than it was last year. Daniel still isn't as expressive, sexually—well of course sexually as well as in other ways, as I've said—as I would like."

"Was it ever good enough in the way you need it to be?"

"It's not bad, even. I just want it to be . . . deeper. A deeper expression of our feelings for each other."

"Does he know that you might possibly have another affair?"

"He knows it's possible, yes."

"Could it be that he is too hurt to express his deepest feelings now?"

"I don't think so. If anything, he's more expressive

now than he ever was. I'm not asking for expression only of good feelings. I want him to reveal himself. Whatever it is. I'd go for angry sex, crying sex. But sex without expression, well, it's just a killer."

"If Daniel said you could not have another affair, said that it was sexual exclusivity or nothing for him, would you feel trapped?"

"It's possible; I'm not sure. I would probably put up with it for a while until something changed it. I would probably agree to it, but if something changed it, it would change. What I'm focusing on now is trying to be home. To be with him more. So I don't need to have an affair, maybe. If I have to have one, I will. And I don't figure on getting emotionally involved. What I prefer is to keep enriching our relationship. But we both have to want it. And we both have to be more open and more communicative about the problems."

Amanda and I stop to have something to eat. We turn off the recorder and make some toast and coffee. We start to talk of other things during our break, but we can't seem to leave the subject of sexual exclusivity. She says, "I have much more to say, and I have thought about this a great deal." So I grab some toast and coffee and turn on the machine again.

"You don't die or anything from affairs," she says. "You just grow. This Christian concept that we all have—whether it's Catholic, Christian, Baptist, or Jewish—that people keel over with these terrible feelings, that they die because of them or that God strikes you dead because of them—it's terrible. *We all have them.* Feelings don't injure other people irrevocably. It's life."

"Yes," I say. "But actions have impact, and nobody

has ever been able to explain the ferocity of the feelings elicited by sexual betrayal."

"Does that mean that all the people who have affairs should hide them? Maybe so. Not for me. I'd rather examine what the feelings really are that are so ferocious and primitive, where they come from, and how our attitudes about them are locked in this good-evil system. An affair is not evil. It's not a betrayal of Daniel, what I did; it's not a discounting of him in any way. This idea that if you do something that is *wrong*—like *commit adultery*—you *necessarily ruin your marriage or ruin your life or kill your spouse*—I can't stand it. It's a Sunday-school idea, and it doesn't fit my mold anymore. It's a lie, and it has very little to do with my life and my goals. Those rules don't work. And the repercussions of the rules aren't real for me, either. I'd rather grow than stay safe.

"And sometimes growth means doing something you don't understand. Years later, when your psyche is able to process it, you say, '*Now* I see what that was all about. Now I see why I did that.' "

"If you had to sum it up, could you?"

"Yes. I want connection. I need it. It's not a vague need, it's a pressing one."

"Then Daniel is likely to come up short again, no?"

"I don't know. There's so much about him that I like and need, too. He's so . . . kind. But yes, that's apples, and emotional closeness, sexual closeness, may be oranges."

"Does that scare you?"

"Not really. Love and marriage—I can no longer accept the hold on me that an old system has. I've grown past the myth of it all. I'm willing to stay married and to face what both of us have to face during our lifetimes. And I'm willing to not be married, if that is the case! I'm not willing to live with an outmoded belief system that is stultifying to both partners.

"We haven't been taught that a lifetime of sexual exclusivity is anything but totally natural. Does anybody get that we're now talking fifty, sixty years of marriage? Look, it *isn't* natural to have sex with one person for half a century—that's longer than the average person's life span two hundred years ago. And if it *were* natural, why are so many people not able to stay faithful for a lifetime? Or a decade? Why don't we face it? Why don't we at least examine other possibilities? Why am I so *bad* for noticing this?

"And why is our answer to affairs divorce? We say, 'Well, you weren't sexually faithful to me, so let's get a divorce.' Is divorce really the only outcome to an affair? Is marriage so rigid a relationship that it's lifetime fidelity—or bust?"

"Would you want to declare yours an 'open' marriage?" I ask.

"No."

"Aren't you saying you want an arrangement that allows for other sexual partners?"

"Allows for them, but doesn't stipulate you have to have them. And doesn't suggest that they're somehow without emotion—like *filling a need*. My sense is an open marriage denies the fact that an affair is a relationship; it turns it into a fucking experience and that's it.

"Maybe I'm just rationalizing, saying that I want the right but I don't want him to have it. But really, I'm not saying that. I think what bugs me about it is that it's a theory. It's dogma. I don't know. Like just another ideal system that isn't ideal for anybody.

"See, my marriage is unusual and doesn't fit a system and I like it that way, the way it is. It's not necessarily easy, but I mean it's good. What's great in the marriage—in the relationship, regardless of the marriage—is that we make each other grow. That sounds too forced, like we force each other. We don't. We grow from each other."

"One last question for now. Can you envision a better way? What you are struggling for, it seems to me, is freedom from old rules but within the structure of marriage. Would you wish to change the structure?"

"It's dependent on the individuals. I know that we were able to say we were not going to lie to each other when we got married, rather than take these vows that were basically, *fundamentally*, lies that then we would have to break."

Chapter Twelve

To Tell or Not to Tell?

We have no master-key that will fit all cases. . . . Moral judgments must remain false
and hollow unless they are checked and en-
lightened by a perpetual reference to the special circumstances that mark the individual
lot.

—George Eliot, *The Mill on the Floss*

If this book were a novel, I could have made Amanda
a more sympathetic character. I could not have created a
more revolutionary heroine: What she believes in is mutual pleasure and complete honesty in relationships, and
she is willing to live by what she believes. But my task in
making her sympathetic would be enormous: I would
have to bring you, the reader, to a place of recognition
and empathy; to make you care about her. Because the
way she cares about Daniel is not how we commonly
have defined a womanly care. If she *really* cared about
Daniel and his feelings, we figure, she would never have
had the affair.

If her honesty about her behavior had been accompa-
nied by remorse, say, or if she had gone back to Daniel
willing to change, asking for forgiveness—if she had

been *sorry*—it would be easier to sympathize with her. If she had been less sanctimonious or self-justifying, it would be easier to like her. Certainly if she were punished—if her face were scarred and she could no longer work as an actress, or if Daniel left her and no other man ever looked at her again—her story would resonate with other, more familiar ones.

But Amanda was neither punished, nor sorry, nor willing to change. And the audacity of such a position may be chilling to those who believe that a woman is entitled, perhaps, to her badness, her passion—even her extramarital passion—*once*, but who can forgive her for it only if she is repentant and, more important, willing to pay the price, and return to goodness.

Bound by the restrictions of her actuality, I cannot make her do that here. Amanda wanted Daniel to know the truth about her affair because "He had to know who I was," and whatever other motives are buried in that statement, she herself remains unambivalent about her choice. She did not tell him in order to be forgiven; and she did not promise it would never happen again. Amanda knew what she was risking. Perhaps deeper analysis of her behavior might reveal that she had been profoundly dissatisfied with Daniel before he became dissatisfied with her and that she was trying to end her marriage; or that she was discharging her guilt or anger onto Daniel in the hope that he would punish her. Or that her alleged desire to be understood by him was merely an excuse for telling him something hurtful, and a method for betraying him, and a scheme for leaving him.

In any case, the questions—was Amanda's behavior noble or vile?; was she really so "honest" or was she self-deluded?; was she attempting to forge a brave new relationship with her husband or trying to destroy him and perhaps herself?—are questions we could debate till we drop.

I suspect that ultimately what will emerge as most infuriating about Amanda in this debate is that what mattered to her most, if we believe her, is not what we are comfortable having matter most. In response to her insistence that she be in a relationship in which her needs as well as Daniel's are met, and in which neither must lie to the other, some of us would shout, "Utopian nonsense," while others would mutter, "She's a sactimonious, narcissistic, self-deluded slut."

Amanda cared less than the other women about sexual fidelity in general—her own or her husband's—and more about being deeply connected in a relationship that held no secrets. She was, if not subtle in her handling of her truth, extraordinarily consistent: She never agreed to promise sexual fidelity, even at the beginning of her marriage to Daniel, but always was committed to him. What she wanted all along was neither absolution nor idealization, but a genuine responsiveness and expressiveness—in return for which she offered Daniel the same. She liked being outside the bounds of goodness, needed that to be understood, too. She was saying to Daniel, I cannot promise that I will be a "good" woman, in terms by which wives are customarily judged, but I can promise you that I will tell you the truth about my feelings and my behavior. We can work it out and stay together if you can promise this as well; if you, too, bring yourself into the relationship with all your feelings and imperfections.

But nine years after they married, and two years after our earlier meeting, that hope—written into their marriage ceremony—fizzled. Amanda went away on location again, had another affair, and again came back and told Daniel about it. Finally, although there was no other man in the picture, Amanda and Daniel split up. Amanda, clearly defeated in her own aspirations for her marriage, left Daniel, whom she described as defeated as well. And so I want to go back to the question I asked at the beginning of the book, to ask you again whether you can tolerate such a story without condemning Amanda, without dismissing her as someone you don't want to know or don't believe. Can you experience Daniel's vulnerability without wanting to punish his wife for hurting him?—Can you stay with her if she does not regret pushing the relationship with Daniel to the breaking point by pursuing the relationship with him that she wanted? Do you think it would be better if she had not confessed?

If Amanda's honesty horrifies you, or if it exhilarates you, or if you find it cruel, or valiant, or hostile, or unrealistic, you nevertheless begin to get a sense of how visceral our responses are to the one question I discovered has eclipsed all others in this wild territory of women's adultery: *Should you confess an affair to your spouse?*

Whether to confess and when—and how, where, and why—is as hotly debated today as whether to engage in extramarital sex in the first place was debated in the past. Most therapists I talked with related an incident in which the telling—or not telling—led a woman either to redemption or ruination, which is to say, to a better marriage or to divorce.

Is it the *act* of extramarital sex that hurts the marriage or the *secrecy* about it? That is the question that catches our national obsession with marriage at a moment when women are reporting less happiness within it than ever, and when women initiate twice as many divorces as men. As Susan Faludi reports in *Backlash*:

A massive study of women's attitudes by Battelle Memorial Institute in 1986, which examined fifteen years of national surveys of ten thousand women, found that marriage was no longer the centerpiece of women's lives. . . . The 1990 Virginia Slims poll found that nearly 60 percent of single women believed they were a lot happier than their married friends and that their lives were "a lot easier." . . . A review of fourteen years of U.S. National Survey data charted an 11 percent jump in happiness among 1980s-era single women in their twenties and thirties—and a 6.3 percent *decline* in happiness among married women of the same age. [Emphasis hers.] If marriage had ever served to boost personal female happiness, the researchers concluded, then "those effects apparently have waned considerably in the last few years." A 1985 *Woman's Day* survey of sixty thousand women found that only half would marry their husbands again if they had it to do over.

Some say the act itself is not what is injurious to a marriage—that adultery can actually save it, or stabilize it, at least temporarily—but that the admission is what is destructive. Proponents of this theory say the confession catapults the "betrayed" partner into primal feelings of rivalry, exclusion, and abandonment. These people, theoretically, could have tolerated Amanda's affair but would be outraged at her confession.

Others believe the confession is necessary to reestablish contact after the affair, to renew intimacy and understanding—the only way to prevent future infidelities. For those who feel this way, the extramarital *secrecy* is seen to be what sabotages the marriage, not the illicit sexual act itself.

I attended a workshop for family therapists, called "Affairs: Getting the Message," and heard its founder, family therapist Emily Brown, the director of the Divorce and Marital Stress Clinic in Arlington, Virginia, present her views. When couples are in therapy and one spouse is having an affair, Brown believes, treatment must be structured around the revelation of the affair, and her message to fellow therapists and others who attended her workshop is emphatic:

> Always uncover the affair unless there is the potential for physical violence; or for legal violence—where a custody or alimony decision could be swayed by adultery; or when you haven't permission to explore marital issues— like if, for example, you are the kid's school counselor, or you treat one but not both members of the couple, or if the spouse to be told is incapacitated.

We practiced, in groups, playing different roles— some of us played marriage partners, others, therapist—in order to understand the complexity of the task of uncovering the affair. Brown reminded us of her view that if the couple's therapist knows about an affair, but the partner having it refuses to reveal it, the therapist should stop treatment of the couple, lest she be in collusion with the spouse in withholding crucial information from the partner—in perpetuating the secret. Moreover, she told us, if the secret comes out early in the couple's therapy, divorce is likely in only 40 percent of the cases; if it comes out late in treatment, there is an 80 percent chance of divorce—because with the discovery that the therapist was complicit in keeping the secret, "the spouse then feels doubly defrauded."

Peggy Vaughan, the author of *The Monogamy Myth* (1989), indeed felt herself doubly defrauded when she discovered her husband's numerous affairs—but says she has survived them through years of "talk, talk, talk." Vaughan was appalled at the "code of secrecy" surrounding her husband's affairs and, she maintains, everyone else's infidelities—a code she feels perpetuates the message: *"Never tell. If questioned, deny it. If caught, tell as little as possible."* Such a code thereby provides, she writes, "a buffer from the world that makes it easier for a person to engage in affairs and to avoid dealing with the consequences, or even to seriously contemplate the consequences." Vaughan's experience convinced her of the necessity for an honesty that she and her husband have now promised each other will be the foundation of their marriage from now on.

Many experts support such a pact. Frank Pittman, an Atlanta psychiatrist and family therapist and author of the book *Private Lies* (1989), is also a passionate proponent of confessing extramarital liaisons:

> The most-asked question from patients is this: "Surely you don't mean that I should tell my husband everything? That would upset him, he would never forgive me, the marriage would be over." Or, "I can't tell her this. She would (a) die, (b) kill me, (c) leave me. Disaster would befall us, etc." And I have to tell them that, yes, they should tell their marriage partner everything— even the big one, the secret of infidelity.

On the other hand, Fred Humphrey, a family therapist at the University of Connecticut who has researched the topic of affairs for over thirty years, insists:

> I don't agree with Pittman. I've worked with lots of couples where the affair was kept secret, who decided to end the affair and then put all their energies in the marriage. Whereas once the knowledge of the affair comes out, a barrier has been erected to the rest of their lives.
> Knowing about a partner's affair is different from other serious issues: Among those rare people who stay in therapy long after the actual affair has ended, I hear of

the affair being dragged out not once or twice later, but even years later, as explanation for retaliation. When old issues don't die, when they come up like this, they're not dead in the partner's emotions. The scab falls off; the scar stays forever.

And while Pittman feels the effects of the confession are essentially positive for the marriage . . .

It must be kept in mind that affairs thrive on secrecy. The conspiracy and adventure and tricks produce an alliance in the affair, while the lies and deceit increase the discomfort at home. All of us feel bound to those who share our secrets, and uncomfortable with those to whom we are lying. The power of an affair may be in its secrecy. The weakness of the marriage may be in the avoidance of issues.

To date, I have not had anyone die or kill anybody or even get a divorce over the revelation of a secret infidelity if the infidelity is now past.

. . . Humphrey feels the effects of a confession are salutory only in theory. In reality, he says,

We grow immune to the idea that an extramarital affair is devastating because movie stars have them and presidents have them and we don't see the really tragic fallout, the raw stuff that the therapist hears hour after hour.

You can't understand the impact until it hits you. Because extramarital sex creates so much shame—maybe even more than cancer or mental illness or mental retardation—many people don't talk about the pain it has caused them. Lots of the families of the people I see have no idea of what they are going through.

Humphrey also points out, in one of his clinical samples, that the commonest emotion a husband feels when he finds out his wife is having an affair is anger, followed by shock, while a wife's first response is shock—then anger. "Men are not socialized to think their wives will fool around," he says. "They are more shocked, and more angry." And studies indicate that the marriages of wives who confess their affairs to their husbands do not fare as well as husbands who confess theirs to their wives. Annette Lawson found that in her sample "as many as 40 percent of women, compared with only around 30 percent of the men, were clear that telling their spouses about their affairs had had *adverse* consequences for their marriages." Their marriages had "worsened or ended." Perhaps this differing response is key to the fact that a wife's confessed affair is more likely than a husband's to lead to divorce—further suggestion, he says, of the double standard that tolerates men's but not women's affairs. It suggests, too, that a therapist's advice to a wife who considers confessing might be different from advice given to a husband.

And so it goes, round and round: To tell or not to tell? It begins to sound like the question of a tree falling in a forest: If no one is there to hear the fall, did the tree make any sound as it fell? Is damage done to the marriage if the partner is never told of it—or is damage done irrespective of the telling? How damaging is an affair, anyway? In their response to a survey by Dr. K. Daniel O'Leary, professor of psychology and the director of the marital therapy clinic at the State University at Stony Brook, Long Island, 116 therapists ranked an affair ninth in terms of damage done to a relationship—with issues like power struggles and poor communication listed before it. Experts disagree over an affair's significance: Feminist psychologist Betty Carter told me an affair is "insignificant . . . just the tip of the iceberg . . ." while Fred Humphrey told me it is "one of the most deadly crises that could happen to a marriage." In one of his studies, he says, of all the 200 couples who came for marital therapy, at least one partner in all cases was having an affair. And half such couples separate or divorce at the time therapy ends.

Some therapists refuse to enter the tree-falling debate and, in essence, suggest that a woman may know more than the experts about the forest she lives in. Dr. Carol Nadelson, a Boston psychiatrist and past president of the American Psychiatric Association, told me:

> It really depends on the circumstances, and I have seen it go both ways. In some relationships the nontelling has been more hurtful because it's led to more nontelling. And sometimes the telling has been very destructive. I have to respect a woman's judgment about what makes sense to her. What I'd like to see her do is at least look at it and make a decision. I have seen women who have made a definitive decision that it would hurt more than it would help, and that has turned out to be right: They've never told, and their marriages are fine, and after a while the whole thing passes and they don't think about it much anymore.
>
> I think you can't call it categorically. And I think you have to stick with the individual and make sure that she is clear on what's best. It's the working out of how to call it that is what's important.

The common thread that runs through the furor over telling or not telling draws our the attention back to marriage—it is now therapists who are debating what a woman should do, asking the question, "How can you remedy the potential damage of the affair on the family?" and precluding the question, "What is the best way for *you* to proceed from here?" The deeper priority given marriage and husband is over and over again made clear—as is the assumption that what is good for wives is to find a way back to the marriage and the family, and to find it in a hurry.

THE NEW MORAL DILEMMA

My overwhelming feeling is that the subtle shift in the emphasis on extramarital sex from doing it to telling about it captures our attempt to come to terms with but not condone its increasing frequency. Moving away from the simple contention that *having* an affair is evil for women toward the murkier morality that attaches the evil to a wife's deceiving her husband and not taking care of the relationship, gives us a whole new, possibly endless, area for debate: How should women act in relationships, especially where husband and children are involved? "In analytic terms, our culture has lost its coherence," says New York psychoanalyst Martin Bergmann. "I'm not saying that coherence was good, but in a culture in which every woman caught in adultery was stoned, one would be somewhat hesitant." In such a coherent climate, then, what a woman did after her affair would be a moot point. She would not live to do anything.

The shifting of attention away from the act of adultery and onto the vagaries of the confession of it as the place where the potential relational violation lies has brought with it a new moral discourse. Of the two choices a woman has—to tell or not to tell—the former has become the moral choice. At this moment in our culture, we place unprecedented value on openness in relationships. We have redefined "intimacy" to mean a sharing with our partner of everything we do and feel, so that "telling" has been elevated to the status of "true"—while "discreet" has come to mean something vaguely tainted, something closer to "deceit." Annette Lawson calls this shift—which places the emphasis on the sharing of information as the primary gauge of intimacy between married couples, rather than on sex itself—a "displacement of honor by honesty" and points to the Pill as its source.

Once a man could no longer literally possess a woman's body, she writes, the sure knowledge of his lover's sexual history and current sexual activity became unavailable; he was therefore dependent on *what she told him* for assurance of her fidelity. After the Pill, monogamy, if it was to exist, could only be guaranteed by the giving of one's word. Knowledge and information literally replaced the woman herself as the commodity of exchange.

The rage that one man might feel at another's possession of his wife's body became, says Lawson, "a fury about a breach of contract—spoken words—the theft of information, of shared secrets, shared knowledge." Fidelity in the relationship "was to be counted on through a willingness to depend on the other, to be told about failures in the relationship, to achieve high levels of communication, to avoid secrets." While the ability to rely on one's partner has always been central to marriage, she concludes, "what is new is the greater *salience* of the idea of openness and honesty and the stress on the achievement of intimacy through talk, especially through self-disclosure and the confession of sexual secrets" (italics hers).

Honesty is the nineties form of exclusive possession; dishonesty is potentially lethal because of AIDS. Sharing one's sexual past has unprecedented relevance to one's future. Although the specter of AIDS was, as I said in the first chapter, very much in the background for these women, I mention it here because it so heightens the moral edge of confession. For while few of the women considered AIDS other than desultorily, they all considered the issue of sexual secrecy a crucial one.

I ask Amanda: "If you had had affairs and had *not* told your husband, would that have been dishonorable?"

"Yes."

"Because of the chance that you might be HIV positive?"

"No, I wasn't thinking of that. There is that, but my concern was I would have been adding to the misunderstanding we had about who I am, what I need, and what is going on between us. It would have been a symptom of something that neither of us was facing and so neither of us could deal with."

"When you say something neither of you was facing, do you mean the connection you missed so much?"

"Yes."

"You feel it would be living a lie?"

"Yes. Exactly. And a dangerous one at that."

THE SOUND OF SILENCE, AGAIN

Honesty's moral edge is questioned by some experts, who feel it is being touted as a cure rather than as one possible choice for solving immensely complicated marital problems related to extramarital sex. "Honesty gets so misused," says Carol Nadelson. "The concept of honesty becomes almost like *scrupulosity*: You have to tell *everything*. Does 'honest' really mean that? Or does it mean you tell when you're asked? Does it leave room to construct what you say? To weigh honesty versus cruelty?"

In our attempt to save marriage, we are ignoring the people—especially women—and adding to the idealization of it, which makes saving it, if anything, more difficult. Responsibility for marriage, if you look closely, remains the woman's, for the most part. It is her responsibility to take care of her husband's vulnerability and protect the relationship. Her vulnerability, never mind her pleasure, is often still not given a second thought. In the idealization of marriage women, as ever, have the most to lose.

As I listened to the experts counsel confessing or keeping the secret, I did not hear the statistics with which I had become so familiar: That divorce for women is associated with impoverishment and that marriage for women is associated with depression; that divorce for men is associated with an increase in income and that marriage for men is associated with longevity. Listening to experts, I lost the sound of women voicing their needs and their vulnerabilities. It was hard to stay with both the experts and the women, and in the end, as in the beginning, I have chosen to stay with the women.

The furor over telling or not telling, then, betrays more than just two strong points of view as to whether a woman should remain silent. Our culture is sending women a double message. A woman having an affair is presented with two opposing values simultaneously: the moral imperative to speak the truth to one's partner—"being honest in the relationship" and the moral imperative not to hurt others or—to "take responsibility" for it.

While these same opposing values are there for men who have extramarital sex, of course, women seem to be in a different position with regard to both—more readily undermined for being dishonest, secretive, manipulating, lying, and more promptly held responsible for causing hurt. Annette Lawson found the women in her study particularly sensitive to the effect their behavior might have on their marriages and their husbands—more aware than men of their power to wound, and more concerned about using that power as a weapon. The commonest reason wives gave for not telling their spouses was "to avoid hurting the spouse particularly . . . to save the husband's face." Men having affairs, Lawson reports, "never expressed any concern for a wife's reputation; they clearly did not see their extramarital affairs as reflecting on their wives in the same way. . . ."

So while women "seemed to feel a greater need to confess" because of the value they placed on openness and honesty as a measure of intimacy and moral decency—a measure, in effect, of their love—they were simultaneously "restrained in [their] desire to tell by the greater risks still inherent in her telling than in his." This included the risk of his loss of face, of his physical violence, of his walking out, of his ending the marriage—and therefore the added risks of financial insecurity and custody battles—risks that do not exist in the same way for the adulterous man who decides to confess to his wife.

The truth is, a woman who chooses to tell her husband for the sake of relationship often finds the relationship over. Telling, now the moral choice, is also the one statistically most devastating to women. For the wife who confesses, divorce rather than reconciliation is the more likely outcome: Pepper Schwartz and Philip Blumstein, coauthors of *American Couples*, found a "high correlation with breakup" when women told their husbands about their affairs. Fred Humphrey did too, and Annette Lawson. This holds true even for couples who enter therapy: And perhaps as a result, Humphrey found that by the end of their joint therapy sessions one in seven of the wives had not revealed their affair; while only one in sixteen of the husbands had not.

Of the hundreds of women I have talked with over the years, very few decided to confess—and then usually only when they wanted to end their marriages. Those who did tell report the kind of craziness we are by now familiar with: One husband chased his wife, at gunpoint, down the road, shouting at each neighbor within earshot, "My wife's a whore." One husband drove his car into his wife's, turning it into a "trash heap," she says, "right after emptying our bank account and canceling our insurance policies." Another threw his wife's clothes out the window of their tenth-floor Chicago apartment. Several husbands kidnapped the children. Other stories of husbands' physical and psychological abuse are wild and often bizarre and range from murder threats to suicide threats. The divorce—if it comes to divorce, and it often does—is uglier. The adulterous woman is tainted, and the divorce process tainted also. Margaret Atwood summed it up when she asked women what they most feared in the other sex and they answered: that a man would kill them. Men responding to the same question said: that a woman might laugh at them.

Back to the Iron Framework

The culture's double message—tell him if you want to be true; don't if you want to be kind (and if you want to stay married)—presents a woman with a dichotomy reminiscent of the one she faced in her marriage before her affair: Be yourself if you want to be true (and lose relationship), be selfless if you want to be good (and stay married). And just as she found it futile then to attempt to be herself and also to be virtuous in these terms, she now finds the old good-girl/bad-girl issue presented anew and in a newly complicated way: Would the telling be a noble attempt at renewed closeness, or a cruel unburdening of guilt and unnecessary punishment? Is it more selfless to tell him, or more selfish? More caring or more uncaring? Which is better for him, and for her marriage? And thus the earlier question—What does a good woman do?—is recast as the knottier What does a *bad* woman do to become *good* again?

Do you see where we are? We are right back inside the frame of reasoning where rights and wrongs and shoulds and shouldn'ts career about as wildly and blindly as bats inside that dim cave the woman fled when, sick of such no-win choices about giving and taking, she said, "I can't deal in these terms anymore." How odd, then, here in this new place—where by doing something "bad" she has begun to feel good, and where, freed from such bleak choices that pit caring for her loved ones at odds with caring for herself, she is able to clearly see the possibility of forming another code of ethics that include actively pursuing her own needs and her own pleasure—becoming herself—to find these old questions again: How will *you* make this illicit act good for your marriage? What will *you* do for your husband and family to make amends for doing something so pleasurable for yourself?

Urging her back inside the framework are those who perhaps unwittingly ask her once again to think only of what is best for her marriage and her husband, to return at once to the selflessness she so rudely abandoned. In what sounds eerily close to magazine-style advice given to an eager young newlywed, Dr. Malcolm Hill, a New

York psychiatrist, offers her these words, which I read in an article on women's extramarital sex in *Parade*:

> You should not, as a rule, tell your husband you've been untrue. Remember—it takes only minutes, seconds, to destroy a marriage. And that confession could do it.

If she is tempted out of overwhelming guilt to tell, he suggests she stand firm in her silence and instead

> . . . find ways to add to *his* comfort. . . . Give your husband a massage when he comes home from work, make sexual advances, respond enthusiastically to his sexual overtures, prepare his favorite meals. Go backpacking with him, if that's his hobby, or to the theater if he enjoys that. Try making him happy, to improve his life—and your lives together. This will ease your guilt and might so improve your marriage that neither of you will ever be tempted to stray again.

If she was unsuccessful at being Donna Reed *before* her affair, maybe now—presumably chastened and guilt-ridden and ready to reform forever—she can do a better job of it. Counseling silence, a return to the framework, and a renewed all-out effort to please her husband, the ethic being emphasized is one of care and nurturance *of him* in such a way as to restore the old setup, where "making him happy" and "trying to improve his life—and your lives together" will alleviate her guilt, absolve her, with the bonus that if she pulls it off well enough this time it will be sure-fire insurance of her own *and* her husband's sexual fidelity forever. She is given another shot at successful integration into the romance plot. She can reidealize her marriage, become responsible once again for everyone's well-being but her own, and have the happy ending at last. But it will be riddled with the same old terms she rejected: the return to what historian Tony Tanner calls "the past and its binding patterns," getting back, in other words, into her husband's good graces.

Wanting to be Open

I have seen women who have confessed their affairs to their husbands, and women who have not. Mostly, they have not. With few exceptions, though, they *wanted* to be able to tell—but not in order to be forgiven, or to be punished, or to return to an idealized marriage. When I asked, "Did you consider whether to tell your husband about your affair?" they were more likely to weigh the question this way, with concern for their own as well as their husbands' needs.

Karen, thirty-eight, said she waited until she knew what she wanted:

> I decided about whether to tell [my husband] when I decided how to incorporate my marriage into my life again. First I had the [extramarital] experience, and had to protect it, and telling was out of the question. But then I said, "Now what? What is the place of my marriage in my life? Where will my affair be in my life?" And once I decided what I would like, *then* I considered the issue of whether to tell him.

Caroline, forty-six, said,

> I decided not to tell him. Not out of consideration for him only, but for myself. I was, in fact, ready to give up the affair, but even so, that didn't seem a good enough reason to go tell my husband about it. If the secret ate

me up, as people kept telling me it would, that was my problem to work out, not my husband's. Because there was *no way* this secret was going to bring us closer. No way.

Elizabeth, twenty-seven, said,

I really felt I would do what was best for me. I was handling it [leaving the affair], and I would keep handling it. I think the temptation to tell may have something to do with needing some comfort—here you are giving up this incredible thing in order to save your marriage—but that's crazy. I still don't plan to tell him, and I doubt I'll change my mind.

Because of their respect for openness as the measure of a good relationship, and also because of the value they placed on closeness, they were all deeply concerned with the *issue* of telling—and consistently wanted to be "truthful" and "caring" and "open." Some said with irony how tempted they were to tell; what various justifications they found in their fantasies:

It sounds insane, but in many ways he would have been the first to congratulate me. That I did something for myself that no one else would approve of would have pleased Joe. In theory. He really would rather have liked that aspect of it, and I felt sad that he, who really was on my side in my overall push toward autonomy, couldn't be part of my, well, victory. I felt terrible that it might be at his expense.

Somebody should be proud of me for this, I thought. And I really, you know, thought that Joe would have been. But I just couldn't. I just couldn't.

It didn't seem like such a big deal, in the end. I had slept with Lou before I got married, and I slept with him again, and my husband didn't know about it. I think if my husband had been suspicious, had asked me outright, I wouldn't lie to him. That I wouldn't do, because it would be crazy-making for him. My fantasy is, though, that he would understand if I told him; just as my fantasy is that I would understand if he had an affair with an old girlfriend. That may be naive, of course. I see what I've done as crucial and essentially not disruptive—like a night at the opera with an old friend—I can't be absolutely sure he would agree.

Connie struggled for a year over her decision, feeling caught between several conflicting impulses. On the one hand, Martin had told her he "wouldn't care" if she had an affair and therefore "gave me permission" to do so. According to that logic, she figured, "What could he say? He wouldn't have had the right to be furious, since he had told me to go ahead." But she didn't really believe him. Pushing her to tell, even more than her husband's dubious permission, was her enormous impulse to release the secret, to be free of it, to stop having "to cover up everything concerning who I really am." At the core of her feelings was this sense of being sick of pretending, sick of being quiet; of wanting to

just come out with it, for God's sake. As long as I can remember, I've felt this pressure to keep quiet. About everything—my feelings, what I thought, what I believed—and of course to cover up everything having to do with my sexuality. When I was a teenager I just said the hell with it, and my friends and I shared everything. We weren't quiet about anything, sex, or our own desires and feelings or anything. As exhibitionistic as it may have seemed, it provided a way of talking about what we were really doing and feeling. I hate covering all that up again.

But she didn't tell Martin. "Reality won out over reason," she says. June concluded similarly, after long deliberation, saying she and her husband "are both only mortal" and mortals "can only take so much you don't really want to hear." It was one thing, she decided, to tell your husband if you plan to give up the affair, but

you don't go ahead and tell unless you're willing to be told you can't continue. I mean, how many women are going to say to their husbands, "I've found something that's making me very happy, and I'm not going to change that, even if you don't like it"? When telling comes up at all, it's because you feel something's got to give, some change in the status quo, and you really then have to be ready to end your affair—or end your marriage. You're not going to be given *permission* to keep both, that's for sure.

Jenny decided her affair, although it had lasted almost two years, was, finally, an aberration, a fling, a departure from sanity, something she linked with "turning thirty," an age she experienced as the beginning of the decade during which she would "really have to make something" of herself. She had had an affair with a man her own age who had already made something of himself, and in her own field—point-of-sales advertising—and whom she met through her work. She had lived, she felt, "a double life" for these years, and while she got great pleasure from her affair, she finally felt an overwhelming need to unify her life; to get "everything she needed" from one man rather than two, and told her husband

just everything. That I had done this thing and I knew it was wrong and not good for our marriage and that I didn't know what had gotten into me but that it had been something I really needed, but that it wasn't the way I wanted to live and that it had been incredibly selfish.

Her husband, hearing her outpour, questioned her at great length,

almost obsessively, it seemed to me. He wanted to know where I went, what we did, sexually, where—in bed? In the bathroom? and what . . . positions. He just couldn't stop with the questions. And I just told him everything he asked, like I was handing the experience over to him if he wanted it, or like he was entitled to it. The thing is, he just kept asking and asking and things between us were horrible.

The Price of Telling

At first, he just screamed and screamed. He would get up in the middle of the night, leave the house, and not come home for two days. In the middle of dinner, he would throw something, a lamp, a plate, a shoe. Or he wouldn't talk to her for weeks. When he approached her sexually, "very roughly," she felt "she couldn't turn him down." But she was unable to have an orgasm with him, and began to dread sex. "There was no love in this union, believe me; I felt like a captive, a prisoner of war—someone my husband hated but felt he had power over. I think he felt I should do anything to make it up to him, but that he was entitled to hate me and be abusive, no matter what I did to try to make things better. I thought it would go on forever."

Jenny's effort to reestablish emotional and sexual exclusivity with her husband through total honesty was, she felt, a renewed effort to make her marriage do what it apparently had not done before: Be everything to her. But what she discovered is that she was using honesty as a tool for reentering the myth, updating the "happily ever after" ideal, asking to be reconsidered as a candidate for the Perfect Wife. As Jenny put it,

> What I was saying was, "Here's how this marriage can be everything to me. Here's how it can be intimate and perfect and everything I ever dreamed it should be." By saying it that way, I could pretend there was something in that version of marriage that would really make me happy—something I already knew was bullshit.

One woman's story makes it clear that honesty about an affair can be used in an idealistic attempt to bring the "real" self, the "total" self back into the marriage— instead of bringing marriage, as a partial thing, into one's self.

Deborah was thirty-one at the time, feeling wonderful as a result of her year-long affair, and empowered by it. She eagerly told her husband the truth about it, and about how it was making her feel so good, with a kind of missionary zeal that she now admits ruefully did nothing more helpful than "rub his nose in it." In a burst of newfound confidence and strength, she attempted to share her "high" with her husband,

> as if he would be pleased. I felt I had come back to myself again in some way that was permanent and wonderful, and armed with this power and energy I just bulldozed him like someone just out of a weekend of est training. I asked him to welcome this new me as if he would be thrilled to, as if he should be thrilled for *me*. I didn't factor in how aggressive that request was, how naive and how . . . impossible. I forgot that while I had gained enormous power, I had broken something pre-

cious in the process in order to do so, and my husband had . . . well, *lost* power.

Not considering that—considering him sort of omnipotent and constant—was a terrible mistake. I wanted to be able to upset the balance of power—I *had* upset it—and have his love just the same as I always did. It was really . . . ignorant. As Rollo May puts it, you can't have your power and your innocence too.

Deborah said she felt insensitive to the change in the power balance of her relationship; that she had felt, from her own point of view, that it was in fact more balanced, but she neglected to see that her erotic voice would devastate her husband

who I think I saw as somehow invulnerable, as if he were constant and I were the variable. I saw myself as getting stronger and therefore thought the balance of our power would be better, more equal. I never thought he'd perceive the new dynamic as somehow less favorable to him.

But more devastating than her insensitivity, she felt, was her illusion that she could smash the framework with no consequences, either to her husband or to herself or to her marriage; and it is this that is the real danger inherent in the myth of truth-telling. Armed with renewed energy and power, and a societally supported sense of righteousness, Deborah forgot about men's vulnerabilities, and about her own.

Deborah had gone in feeling honorable, assuming honesty to be its own reward, with "honesty as well as energy fueling my decision to tell Joel, and a conviction that my marriage, if it were any good at all, would accommodate the new me." She suffered terribly once she realized what that assumption entailed.

Even the therapist, who urged me to talk, had this attitude that once I had told the truth I should be rewarded for it, like, *There. I said it.* That Joel should immediately be both grateful that I had told him and aware of his part in making me have an affair. It was cuckoo. I really hadn't ever blamed Joel and suddenly I was hearing the shrink say, "Let's discuss your role in this" to him almost without even letting Joel react to the news. In retrospect, I see that the therapist and I shared this nutty idea that Okay, I've told the truth, I've done *my* job: His job became to deal with it graciously.

Deborah hoped by confessing to make her marriage everything it could be for her all at once, everything that it wasn't before. She had in effect reidealized it. This time, she hoped, it would become what it never was before, and more. A relationship that is renegotiated—as any marriage after an affair must be—must indeed expand to contain both partners more fully. But it is one thing to shatter the old structure and then carefully rebuild it out of a more pliable material; it is another to try to rebuild it out of the same old stuff. It is not enough to say, in effect, "I have become myself again—yet I want you to accept me just the way you did when I tried to be your fantasy."

Whether attempting to slip back into marriage or to storm back into it, it is the intent to reidealize the marriage that is guaranteed to fail. With few exceptions, the women understood this. They had demolished something, and while it could be put back together again, it could never be *the way it was.* Those who did try to renegotiate the terms of their marriages struggled not to see themselves through the critical eyes that judged their goodness, but to keep their gaze fixed on a more complicated equation that included both their husband's needs and their own. Their decision regarding confessing was based on their evaluation of what their husband could take *and* what they themselves could take.

Their flight from goodness was revealed by their language, which encompassed his feelings *and* their own. They talked about "what would be best for us both." The complexity of fitting two people wholly into the equation meant resisting a simpler equation, whereby the wife recreates a dynamic in which she either suppresses her own feelings or ignores what she knows about how her affair will affect her husband.

LEAVING GOODNESS BEHIND

What was most significant about the decisions these women made, whether they decided to confess or not, was how much concern they gave to the reality of their situations and how greatly lessened their need had become to return to the old framework. They were not eager to put the experience of extramarital sex behind them; they did not feel torn apart by it, nor perceive themselves as either blameless or guilty. My sense was that their decision to confess was not for the purpose of eliciting forgiveness or approval, nor to "dump" their guilt or hostility on their husbands or punish themselves. I am not suggesting that these motives weren't present, but that there were other motives as well. Like Polly, the heroine of Laurie Colwin's *Family Happiness*, who says to her lover, Lincoln, "I love Henry and I love you. I know I'm supposed to think it's wrong, but instead I think it's *mine*. It's my destiny, and my complication."

It was this very destiny and complication that they had sought—a story, an adventure, with an ending not yet formulated—neither idealized nor self-punishing. "It may not be easy to deal with," June tells me, "but my life feels alive and . . . appropriate." And much to their surprise, the women were not inclined to try to simplify things, to end the adventure the old way, with a return to the marriage as it was, or to idealize the affair and turn it into the next "perfect" marriage. They were content to tolerate this emotional upheaval without needing to equalize it, to renounce it, to mend it, to end it.

I was not talking to wives with fractured souls or divided hearts; I was talking to women who were resolute: Whatever the cost, they would no longer lose connection with themselves for the sake of being in a marriage that forced disconnection on them. They would have to stay prominent and powerful in relationships with others. Remember that Amanda had said she was willing to do whatever was necessary *not* to become frozen again in her marriage, even if she had to cope with terrible fear and ambivalence, and even if she forced Daniel to do the same: "Is it better to stifle all your feelings so that you don't rock the boat for yourself or another person? Is that love? Two people who agree to stay put emotionally, sexually, for their entire lives so neither of them ever has to have a negative, fearful feeling?"

In the words of Ellie, a decade older than Amanda, "I will put my marriage in me, not me in it. From now on, I will not be subsumed by love—or rather, someone else's definition of love."

If this reentrance into marriage on this new basis meant they were in a mess, they would stay there. The certainty that their vitality depended on the egalitarian and passionate relationship they found by being authentic, left them unwilling to be in a relationship in which they renounced pleasure.

Chapter Thirteen

"MOST PEOPLE THINK
I SHOULD HAVE STAYED"

When I spoke to Amanda again, she and Daniel had separated. It was one year after our last conversation. We made an appointment to meet at my apartment a week later.

DH: The last time we talked, you were going to stay home for a while, and Daniel was working on being more communicative. What happened?

A: I stayed home for quite a long time. Eight months. I had very mixed feelings about it. On the one hand I felt warm and secure and stable and I had someone sleeping next to me; and on the other hand, I was just miserable. There was part of my soul that was not attended to. It's not Daniel's fault—it's nobody's fault. But I was very sad.

I'm a person who needs to work; I'm an actress; I'm an artist—no, I *will* be an artist; I'm an actress now. I became more and more depressed. And then I went away and I got this role—I was Nina in Chekov's *The Seagull*.

Now. Nina is a woman who leaves home—she's an actress. She leaves her family—who have all these leashes on her—in order to do what *she* wants to do. If you're the kind of actress I am, you can't get that role without having it deeply affect you—vampirize you, you could say. Here's a woman who decides that all those dreams she had about acting as a bright young woman—about the fame and glory—aren't what acting really is. What it's truly about is learning to endure.

DH: You mean "endure" in the sense of having the strength to follow one's dreams?

A: Yes. And this character, Nina, had that strength—and she gave it to me. I mean I know she was part of me, but she helped me to see it in myself.

DH: Had you made the choice, then, to leave Daniel?

A: Not yet I hadn't. I'd made the choice to be an actress, to not stay home, no matter what difficulties doing that presented to my marriage. And I was working with this director who knew what I was going through. Who understood me. And I got involved with him. And I'm very glad about it, even though I was really criticized by people because of it. And in the end, I think it's none of their business. It's my path. I held absolute private counsel with myself, and came to my own conclusion about it.

DH: Did you tell Daniel?

A: Yes. Of course. I would have been *out of the relationship* if I had lied. Not acting in good faith.

DH: What was Daniel's response when you told him?

AC: Well, all the other men I have ever heard about go nuts—try to kill their wives, or kill the other guy, or kill *someone*—but Daniel's anger went further inward. He wouldn't talk about it; wouldn't let me speak; wouldn't even get angry at me. He was always withholding, but now he was like a stone. He was defeated, I guess, and unreachable. Maybe he had always been unreachable, but now he certainly was. And that, finally, was my reason for leaving. I say "my" reason for leaving even though I think the truth is that Daniel was gone emotionally long before I left. But I did the unforgivable: I did the actual leaving and I take the blame. I knew then there was something in me, something I couldn't let go of, that was just going to keep torturing Daniel, and that his unavailability, his stoniness, was going to torture me. I don't know which came first, or who really left whom. And I thought, what was I *thinking* when I went ahead and was honest about all this? And I thought, I can't do this again. I'm thirty years old, and if I found something in me that means I'm going to be killing Daniel, then I have to leave him.

DH: What did you find in yourself?

A: I found the life in me that I had been missing.

DH: Are you saying you were sexually awakened?

A: No . . . but yes. I mean, I had been "awakened" before—I mean, I had had good sex. What this was was a thing that burst out of me, a clearsightedness, almost a reshaping of the world. It was no longer appropriate to say to Daniel that his and my relationship was what really mattered—because protecting this thing in me, this awakening, was what was important to me now. My priority was no longer what it had been before. And I decided that to look at him defeated time and time and time again was not how I wanted to live, and would be sadistic. Like reporting back to him about my sexual adventures. That was not what it was about before—then, it was about us. About what our relationship was and might be.

DH: This was more about you, alone.

A: This was about me. I might be wrong about all of this, I realize, but I still have chosen the path that I have chosen and I'll take the consequences. That's what I'm saying to myself. That if in ten years I look back and think I was wrong to leave, wrong to end this marriage, I'll say to myself, "I made a mistake," and I'll be able to take it.

DH: You're extremely sanguine about it.

A: Now I am. I wasn't last year at this time.

DH: What did Daniel say when you told him you couldn't see him defeated anymore and that you wanted to leave?

A: His response was to not deal with it. To not be able to talk about it. But that's his way of dealing with his pain—to withdraw. His response was sadness—he didn't cry, or scream or yell, he was just like, if you could feel a weight on another person's body, that's what you would feel.

I presented my affair, I saw his response, and I said I would leave. He didn't know how to react at first. I didn't either, even though I was the one making the decision. I came back home to Connecticut and I stayed in the house with him for two weeks. I lost a sense of myself during that time; more than I usually do. It was hard. We talked about separating, and talked through everything. We talked about what things belonged to whom. And this is where I didn't think clearly: I gave him everything. Everything. I gave him everything!

DH: Were you aware of feeling that amount of guilt?

AC: Sort of. I'll ask him for a couple of things. I did it subconsciously, blamed myself, because it's literally impossible not to. I was more successful at not blaming Daniel.

DH: Blame him for what? You're presenting him as blameless.

A: No, he's not, in the sense that he's so . . . passive. I couldn't handle the isolation, the sense of being the life in the relationship and of having to literally instill it in him. But it's hard to criticize him for being that way, because he was also so nice.

DH: Does he blame you, do you think?

AC: He says he doesn't. But how could he not? I left him. I had two affairs and told him. That doesn't sound so good, he couldn't have liked that. He has tremendous anger that comes out in all kinds of ways, but it's not a malicious anger—he's just not a malicious man. The worst thing he did was to kick out our cats, to say that he wouldn't give our cats a home. He said, "They're your cats, not my cats." And I didn't have a home. So I gave them to a friend.

DH: Does he feel you ought to feel guilty about the affairs?

AC: Yes and no. He and I tried something that we deeply believed in, and it was hard, and he was as willing as I was. We were going to try to be honest with each other. He, remember, would have stayed—because I had honored our own pact. But of course he was mad about it. And in the end, we both feel profound, deep sadness. In me and in him.

DH: This tremendous anger of his, it must have been there during your marriage, don't you think? Might it not have contributed to the lack of expression, emotionally and sexually, you found so difficult to deal with?

AC: You bet. Daniel has a lot of rage—and it's all internal. I think I felt a lot of his hostility *for* him. But I got to a point after nine years where I felt like "I'm *tired* of talking about this. I'm *tired* of explaining to him what's going on with him as well as with me. I'm *tired* of trying to make it work, sexually. I want to go to a man and *I want this man to know how to make me feel good*. And I want *that* to be the starting point of a relationship. And *then* let's see where we go."

So you can see already that that would show a whole different kind of potential. But I don't think that's very *nice* of me.

DH: Not nice because you feel you abandoned the marriage or because you feel you're asking for so much?

A: Well, both, but mostly because I left the marriage. Because part of the point of our relationship was always wanting to help the other person to grow, I mean, that's what I kept saying to Daniel—and then I gave up on it.

DH: Did he understand why you left?

A: Yes. I told him I was leaving for two reasons, and they are both the same, I see now. One, that we could never communicate on the deep level that I wanted to communicate on—our spirits never seemed to meet, sexually or any other way. And two, that once I had begun to feel that feeling elsewhere, and couldn't seem to bring it home, home became less important to me than it was. Now *that's* a hell of a lot to swallow.

DH: So you almost feel that you betrayed Daniel by finding out how good you could feel—not by finding another man, per se.

A: Yes. I don't feel I could have *not* told him: I wouldn't have had any relationship at all with Daniel if I had hidden that crucial a fact. And I don't feel bad about the affair, which is over. It's that I want sex to go deeper. I want to go deeper. Deeper than Daniel can go, at least with me. I had to keep trying to bring life into our relationship—good life, bad life, whatever, but energy and honesty—and then in the end I split. That's what makes me so sad. And him, I think.

DH: You say he was defeated when the second affair came out, but you were defeated, too, no?

A: Yes. And I keep getting the feeling that everyone, my friends and family, wish I had said, "Well, okay, clearly I can't get what I need from you, no matter how hard you try and I try, but for the sake of your desire for me to stay, *for the sake of the marriage,* I will dedicate the rest of my life to you." That's what makes me feel so awful, now. That I hurt Daniel by telling him the truth and then by acting on the truth. I know that lying would have been kinder. But so is staying in the marriage no matter what.

DH: Which you feel would have been more destructive than leaving.

A: Yes. I wasn't satisfied, and he wasn't going to be able to satisfy me and so I felt like a failure. I felt over and over that I was the one killing him. Because I *know* that he wanted to satisfy me. And he couldn't. And when I found someone who could . . . it was just a whole different thing.

DH: What happened once you felt what it could be like?

A: Oh, God. Well, I felt like I had been born. Like I was alive for the first time. That I *wasn't* a failure. That I *didn't* have something wrong with me. What your mind does to adapt to not experiencing pleasure is amazing—you feel like such a mess. And then suddenly everything was right. Like it was supposed to be. My body was alive, my mind was alive, I felt good and right and like a woman and like me. Only before, I never knew what was wrong.

I felt like doing things I had been afraid of doing.

DH: Like what?

A: Driving in the city! Daniel always drove. I'd become terrified of it. Like doing things alone! Going places, to the movies, exhibitions. When I was home, when I was with Daniel, I wasn't one to fly out and do things for myself that are fun. I've been busy doing things I've wanted to do for years and never did. I'm starting to conquer many of my own fears. Many. And

I feel that I have a lot of potential now. There's a lot that can happen to me now.

I have to spend some time loving myself—oh, I know how stupid and New Age that sounds. But it isn't easy to do. You know, this is another trap in a marriage: You can end up giving away everything. You give—to children, husband, but the thing that becomes hard to do and that marriage erases, somehow, is you giving to yourself. You forget how. Or you don't learn how. I think "selfish" is *good*. I like this word a lot.

I ask myself over and over, What is love? And I can't define it. But one thing I think it is is to give unconditionally. But it's not a nice thing to give with no expectations of getting anything in return *if* that erases you.

And I know we're talking about infantile, primitive emotions when we talk about affairs, and about confessing about them to your own partner, but I'm saying that I know I can grow beyond those emotions. I know I can. I know I can deal with the truth, if I'm in a relationship in which I'm deeply loved. People just can't always behave in a way that works for their partners. I know it hurts, but I think that you should be willing to hurt each other, because you are looking for some growth in the relationship and in each other, even though honesty can be really abused. But I was committed to Daniel, deeply and truly.

Chapter Fourteen

THE PRICE

Men tend to move on a fairly predictable path
to achievement. Women transform themselves only after an awakening. And that
awakening is identifiable only in hindsight.

—Carolyn Heilbrun, *Writing a Woman's
Life*

*I*t is impossible to tell you what will happen to these
women's relationships: I have seen and talked with
young, middle-aged, and older women who have had
one affair or several; whose extramarital relationships
lasted for two months or two decades.

A fifteen-year-affair might be over by the time you
read this book, and a monogamous marriage reinstated.
Some of the men who were single at the time I wrote this
will, by the time you read it, be married—either to their
affair partners (although statistically that is unlikely) or
to someone else—and this newly formed couple may or
may not opt for sexual exclusivity. A very few women
confessed to their husbands and wish they had not, fewer
still are glad they did. Some women found that their
husbands could never forgive them; some found that
they could, and did. Some wives loved their husbands all

along; some did not. Some women fell in love with their affair partners, some did not. For some, the marital relationship turned into a stronger love during the affair— for others, only after the affair ended; for still others, it turned into hate, regardless of the outcome of the affair. Some of the women's marriages were not ostensibly damaged by the affair, some were temporarily devastated, others, permanently destroyed; still others were strengthened immeasurably. Extramarital sex can ruin the best marriages—and it can improve the worst ones. And vice versa.

Some experts suggest that there are discernible patterns of extramarital sex, with predictable reasons and outcomes for each, and offer clearcut rules for handling the aftermath. Such rules introduce a new psychological framework of reasoning into what once was an institutional, legal, or theological one, and I wonder if these modern rules address any more than the old ones did the individual wife's wants and needs, or whether they still guide her toward what she "should" want, or to what others want her to want. The rules, new or old, still threaten to thwart a woman's authority of her own feelings and needs; they still tell her how to behave, how to get love, how to get "better." They still silence her. Psychological laws are still laws, and they still push the woman back in the direction of the conventional goodness she so emphatically renounced when she entered what Hawthorne called that "lawless region" outside the structure of marriage.

Getting her back to or out of her marriage was not my goal, and I would warn women away from those whose goal it is and urge them to be their own guide to the handling of an affair's aftermath. I believe the passionate woman who leaves the confines of goodness, however temporarily, is an outlaw today as much as she ever was—as much as Hester Prynne was in Puritan Boston over 150 years ago—and that she must never forget it. She is the expert on her own feelings and relationships, and if she gives away her authority now, after having once seized it, it will be small comfort to her that she has done the "right" thing. Think of poor Hester Prynne, who did the right thing, became the best goodwife in all of Boston, won the trust and love of the entire community—and gave up her sexuality altogether.

Some things for the outlaw to keep in mind, though, if you are considering the fate of your marriage: Statistics show that an affair is one of the commonest reasons couples go into therapy, and over half of those who do so either divorce or separate over its impact by the time therapy ends. The average income of women of all social classes who are divorced in this country decreases by roughly 30 percent. Do not forget about institutional power; about jealous men; about money. Do not forget that women will look at you with the same cold eye as men. Do not forget what it feels like to speak without being heard; to appear without being seen. Do not forget the society you live in—that it views an adulteress as *adulterated*; she is tainted, still. I cannot emphasize this enough: Women are seriously punished for having affairs, today as much as yesterday.

Do not forget that even your children may wound you when they find out about your affair; they are living in the same society you are, so their sympathies are very likely to be the same as the culture's. If you lose institutional power, they may align with it and not you—at least at first. Above all, do not idealize affairs. It was the idealization of relationships and marriage that started all this in the first place.

The one thing I can tell you about these women, however uncertain the fates of their relationships—however devastated by circumstance—is that they all felt they had been forever altered by the experience and were without regret for having it.

Each spoke of seeing things from a different perspective, looking out at the new view with the unaccustomed clarity and surprise of the nearsighted who are fitted with corrective lenses for the first time. There is, in fact, an optical instrument called a stereoscope, used to impart a three-dimensional effect to two photographs of the same scene taken at slightly different angles and viewed through two eyepieces. The women spoke of viewing their own lives from these two different angles, from both the vantage point of the married woman in her position of conventional goodness, and from that of the outlaw roaming some uncontained, unframed lawless region. They were now able—magically, they felt—to adjust their vision to encompass a larger scene, one that spotlighted both the picture of their married "good" selves and their adulterous "bad" selves—and the resulting image was clearer and more whole; it had more depth and dimension than either snapshot on its own.

Looking at themselves from both inside and outside the frame, they felt they could begin to reassess their lives and their relationships more honestly; with this new perspective, they could use different criteria for evaluating themselves and the world.

Their self-assessments, once minutely descriptive of what was wrong with them, changed. Their language changed, too. Freed from condemning self-judgments—either about being a "not-good-enough" wife, a "too-selfish" person; from having "too-fat" thighs, and "too loud" a voice—what they saw and talked about was no longer "too" or "not enough" anything. They stepped out of the silence and gained access to the "lost" vocabulary of their own real feelings again.

It was a vocabulary as devoid of the world of "shoulds" as it was filled with colorful words of pleasure. With Donna Reed no longer their model—for they had lost their claim to perfection by having the affair in the first place—they began to experience the undertow of their lives, no longer trying to swim in the deceptively still waters above it. Here, where there was motion and life and the sound of their own voices, their physical selves were restored: their body parts reappeared; laryngitis vanished; zombie dreams ended; wax dolls melted.

Returning to bodies that felt like their own and felt intact again, they began to track their own feelings as they experienced them, frankly, simply, clearly. They felt sad sometimes, but also happy; they had paid a stiff price but it had been worth it; they had lost an ideal to which to aspire, and felt remorse over their loss of innocence, but were elated about both, too. Things were not ideal in their lives, but they no longer used "perfect" as a gauge for anything. That feeling of confusion to which so many of the women had earlier confessed— that "marriage is supposed to make me happy and I'm sure I'm happy and therefore I'm happy, I guess, I mean, I am, yes"—dissolved, as did the sense they once had of feeling compelled to do more and more good in order to feel less and less bad, but always failing to accomplish either. Freed from the model of silence and goodness—an image that in no way enriched or enlarged them—through the consummate act of transgression they once would have labeled "selfish" and "bad," they now felt "released." They felt good. "I feel freed from this cumbersome purity," Paula said—and, like losing her virginity, there was no going back.

"I Got My Brain Back"

"I got my brain back," Clara, forty-two, told me.

"Your *brain* back," I repeated. "From a sexual experience, you got your brain back? Where had your brain gone?"

"I don't know," she said. "I lost it along the way, I guess. I just know I can think straight again."

"How so?"

"I mean that I feel, now, when I go through a day, that I'm using my faculties. Like I'm aware, that I've got real say in my actions and that I'm not on automatic pilot."

"How long had you felt on automatic pilot?"

"Years."

"Think back. Were you on automatic pilot in graduate school?"

"Yes."

"Were you married during graduate school?"

"Yes."

"Do you associate that state with being in graduate school or with being married?"

"Well, with both, in a way. Both were choices I made that were good choices but that were not really my own. I don't regret them—I'm happy about my marriage and my profession—but at that time I sort of stumbled into both of them. And while I'm glad I didn't make self-destructive choices, I don't know, really, what criteria I used to make them. As bizarre as that sounds, I feel like another person stepped in and said, 'Okay now, Clara, here's a good profession for you and there's a good man.' And I obeyed. And I'm damned lucky I didn't marry some ax murderer or decide to become a professional lambada dancer."

"Because you were not conscious, in some way, in the selection of your choices?"

"Yes, right. I know that sounds odd. I'm not an Ibsen creature, stuck in a doll's house. But no, that's not true; in a way, in some real way, I was. My friends and I would marvel at what had become of us. I have an awareness now. Some 'on' switch flipped in my brain. It sounds crazy. I was always wondering, 'Does he like me?' and never once asked myself, 'Do I like *him*?'

"I also began to feel, now that I had this operative brain, more grown-up. Like I am now one of the living, breathing, thinking, *fucking* people, finally; in an intense relationship I'm comfortable in. You can't imagine what that feels like, that change. At forty-two, I had begun to feel like a heroine in one of Anita Brookner's novels—a really good person, half-alive, with a rusting brain, becoming arch and eccentric from being smarter than a lot of women but at the same time stupid in the art of getting what she wants."

"And you feel like you're smarter, in that way, now?"

"I think I am more able to get what I want."

"Like what?"

"Like anything. Every decision I make now includes me in it. I don't exclude myself anymore the way I used to. I would organize family outings that were absolutely not what I wanted to do. I'm allergic to the sun, I can't stand beaches, and I get seasick. So I'd go along on my husband's fishing trips, and have to take drugs for seasickness just to get through them, not to mention massive amounts of sun-protection stuff. And no one in the family blinked an eye, except to be a little annoyed that I wasn't enjoying the trip."

"And you wouldn't take that kind of trip today."

"Not in a million years. Last year my husband and son wanted to go fishing, so they went, but I went to London. This year we're going to Germany."

"And all because of your affair?"

"It's all because of my affair that I made a choice that was for me only. Like that was unheard of. And it was so incredible, I mean, I got too much from it to go back; it would be literally impossible for me to make a choice that didn't have me in it. My brain is back. I'm my own person."

For Clara, it was her "lost" brain that was found. For other women, it was their hearts, their humor, their voices, or their memory—a recovery of some integral part of them crucial to their functioning—that led them to see they had "become whole" and "come alive" again.

A Return to Relationship

Alison, who had been chilled all the time, now challenged her own view of the perfection of her marriage; opened a dialogue with her husband that didn't require her to see him or their life as ideal, and in so doing, she says proudly, ended a twenty-year silence. "And so," she adds, "we began to fight."

"About what?" I ask.

"About *everything*, at the moment. I think I began picking fights. To see if this thing was real, this new thing we had where we didn't just shut up when we were annoyed. He was nervous about picking on me. But once I started to pick on *him*, the whole thing blew up. We're in a huge fight, now, but I feel a lot better, for some reason. And you know, I think he does. I really do."

Leslie, forty-seven and married twenty-two years, ended her four-year extramarital relationship with Paul two years ago, because she felt it had "emptied out" emotionally; that she "couldn't keep two relationships alive and well." She had hoped to keep both, but after her third year with Paul, could not manage it. She confessed her affair to her husband, Thomas, and says that, although it took these two years for him to forgive her, the relationship they are building now "is more like the marriage I always wanted to have" than it ever was before her affair. She too is fighting with Thomas "over almost everything," but the quality of the fights seems to have changed from "a kind of meaningless bickering over nothing" to "major fights about very meaningful things"—like who really controls their family and why; who does the work at home and why; what their views of each other are, sexually—and why.

Leslie and Thomas are renegotiating the terms of their marriage, something Leslie feels she could not have done, would not have even thought to do, prior to her affair with Paul. She is giving up some ideas about herself she had held dear and that she was not aware of previously.

I liked being the wife of his dreams. I really did. I wanted to be the woman of his fantasies, and for years I molded myself to what I thought his fantasies were. So it was weird to confront that after I had become the woman of his *nightmares*. I found myself at first trying to get back in good with him, shifting myself around as if I were some kind of moldable plasma, wanting so much to be accepted again. It made me defensive—"I *am* that woman you married, honest! It was just a glitch!"

And then I got it. I was not that woman anymore, if

I ever was, and what I couldn't seem to find my way to was who I really was now. It was a crisis for us. Who am I if not the good woman I'm used to being? Can I change the way I'm perceived? Can I accept being perceived that way? Can I be loved? It's very tricky.

Leslie was asking to be forgiven for breaking something precious, but something she frankly did not want to restore. She feels shaky about giving up the role of the innocent, of the harmless person who never did anything for herself that might interfere with her family's wishes and needs. And she is trying not to reinstate her old self—to do, she says, "what people who are powerless try to do—make the husband the forgiving parent" and ingratiating herself to him.

First I blundered around trying to make him less angry, promising him I really was the same person I used to be. But I wasn't. I broke something and I'm never going to be the person I was before I broke it, and I feel responsible for that, but I'm never going to ask my husband to conspire with me to somehow make me that person again, either. And that will be harder for me than for him. He might be able to love a bad wife. But I may be the one deeply invested in the good-wife routine, because it's so safe, and promises so many rewards.

Leslie says she thinks she likes the role of "bad" wife better than the old role, but only because it seems to have "brought out something wonderful" in Thomas. His attitude toward her has changed, and while sometimes all he does is "torment" her about her affair and remind her how she broke the trust between them, he also now seems to listen to her responses. He is trying to make sense of what she is saying. He has begun to

take me seriously in some way he did not before. We talk much more about things not related to the family's functioning; he listens to my thoughts about things, whereas before I really never felt he did. I can't tell if he is just more comfortable with me because we have talked ourselves to death, or whether we've broken through some wall between us that has always been there. Or maybe it's just that I think twice before I answer questions and don't come out with my predictable answers. Maybe that's just more interesting to him.

Amanda, living alone and talking about the "mess" she made of her life as a result of her affair, tries to figure out why she is not depressed about it:

I'm alone. I'm not seeing either man. I have no money. And what I feel—I feel *released*. I know I should feel regret, but what I really feel is reborn.

Paula says,

I did the worst thing in the world, the worst thing for a woman in this entire culture. And you know what? It was the best thing I ever did. It opened my eyes to so much . . . it opened my heart.

The women began seeing everything now "in color" and feeling more "alive." In all my interviews, the most remorseful words I heard were these, from two women, Lynne, thirty-six, and Loren, forty-nine. Their affairs had ended, both had stayed in their marriages, and neither was now involved with other men.
Lynne:

I have worked things out with my husband, and I honestly believe we have a relationship that is better than it used to be. But, Jesus Christ, what a route to it. I wish it had been simpler, less painful for both of us. We're still hammering it out—he's still furious, I'm still furious, and I honestly don't see an end. But I don't think we're going to split up. Maybe we're too mad to split up. Maybe we'll split up after we stop fighting. I really don't know. It's been very hard.

Loren:

I wish I'd chosen a man I cared about more. I would love to have been with someone who appreciated the changes in me that I experienced in myself—a man who loved me, and who I loved. I really liked myself in this affair; I thought I was funny. Very much myself. Even this body of mine, which I've tried to make thin—with clearly not much success—became something I rather liked. It's round and soft, I found myself saying, and what's the matter with that? I'd have loved the man I felt these new feelings with to be someone permanent, you know, someone I could turn to and say, "Wow! Do you believe it? How much I've changed?"

Sometimes the changes were scary. One twenty-nine-year-old woman, Phoebe, who has been in a tumultuous affair for five years with a man she continues to see, feels the fallout of her newfound assertiveness in all her relationships—"the new me," she calls it—and in every area of her life:

Oh, I kind of wish I could go back to the old me. It was . . . easier. I'm angrier. I'm not as gullible. I challenge everybody. I feel sort of insistent, like I exist, like I have a voice and must speak out. It's a little tedious for other people. I'm like a one-woman ad for filling the census form or something: "Ladies! Stand up and be counted!" I'm shouting all over the place and it's weird, because no one knows what to do with me. But I feel good. I go around feeling bossy, like I did when I was in eighth grade.

The particular change the women most wanted to protect was of this new sense of both seeing (and having access to) the scene inside the frame, but also seeing (and having experienced) the scenes outside it; of being in the picture ("I hate to say it," said Paula, "but I keep thinking of that image of 'seeing the forest for the trees.' "), but also being in their own skin, in their own lives. Some women expressed a fear of losing this new clearsighted, openhearted self. They weren't sure enough of their ability to hold on to it, and spoke about that jeopardy in the most physical terms, fearing that maybe they lacked some crucial protective mechanism to defend themselves against losing it again. Each of the following women talks about the need to "protect" something:

As Leslie says,

I feel really entitled to this happiness. I really feel the need to protect this good thing I got that's now in me. Somehow I'll keep it.

Dina, fifty-six, says:

I take more actions to protect what's important to me now; because I won't let what's important to me get submerged again. I know that I tend to get into this thing where I'll say, "I'm going to do something that's just for me this year. I'm going to go skiing, even if no one else wants to. I'll go alone." And if my family doesn't practically arrange it for me, I don't go. I'm waiting not only for approval of what I want to do, but for my plane ticket. Needless to say, I haven't been skiing in ten years. I can tell when I'm doing that kind of complicated sabotage now. So if I say, "I'm going skiing," now I also say, "I'd like to go the first week in January; anyone have any problems with that?" And I book it, fast, before the list of reasons why I shouldn't start pouring in.

Annette, forty-five, says:

Maintaining my psychic boundaries is like protecting my immune system. Really. I now get a herpes thing on my lip when I feel invaded; and that always means I'm getting very depressed. I have this sense of a psychic fence being knocked down, and my not having the energy to put it back up. So I really have to learn how to protect myself.

Some women no longer felt the need to protect themselves, sensing that the change in them was irrevocable. Paula says,

All those shoulds that used to fill my day—I should be home to cook, but I should stay at the office longer, but I should see my child more, and I haven't made any phone calls and I should . . . well, I don't feel them screaming at me anymore. They come up, but not often. And not so loud.

IMAGES OF SEX WITHOUT SILENCE

Sexual feeling no longer rendered the women mute. "I have come to love my sexuality," a sixty-five-year-old woman named Roberta tells me, "and not a moment too soon."

"I treasure the feelings I have now, how my body gets so filled with colors and feeling" when she is "at that edge" she falls over before orgasm, Belinda, fifty-four, says. "And then, as I go back and forth over the edge, just about to go over it, the color shifts. I know when I'm going to really go over that edge, to lose control completely, because it starts to shift from the orangy, fiery shades to green and blue, like the night sky in December.

"And then, moving into orgasm and letting everything go—moving beyond consciousness, beyond control, I move from color into sound. I feel as if I'm in a sound studio, where it's dark but you can hear every note. As I release into that out-of-conscious place, my body takes over and my *voice comes out*, and it's not controlled, it's like a flood" (italics mine).

"You can ride on that feeling if you know how," Belinda says, "that blue feeling, and you can catch the wave."

Colors paint sexual response for Ellie, forty-six, as well, who says that sometimes orgasm carries her "into a warm sea of blue oil, cozy, Caribbean-colored; and other times, I see rockets with orange and yellow flames. I feel like I'm soaring. There are red rockets in the sky, and it can stop and start like the grand finale of a fireworks display on the Fourth of July in Monaco, a wonderful and continuous spectacle. And I have learned—no, I was taught by my lover—how to keep soaring, what it takes to harness that feeling, to make it like a guided missile—I can now make myself ride that feeling."

"I orbit into this totally physical realm that is so deep," says Rina, thirty, "that I lose my mind there, let it go, and my whole body resounds with feeling. There's a desperate quality to it, a pulsating sensation, and I feel this deep lust, and I get flushed and the hair on the back of my neck feels like it's sticking up—well, it's like being intoxicated, it's so heady—and I just feel heat. . . ."

In a culture that declares a woman's sexuality over at menopause or even, some of the women felt, at forty, I was surprised at how many of the wives I interviewed were in their fifties, sixties, and seventies, and involved in long-term extramarital relationships. I had predicted that most of the women I would hear from would be in their twenties, and that their affairs would have begun soon after marrying: This was the "new" social phenomenon about which I had heard before I began this book.

But this prediction, like so many others I made about what I would find, was wrong. I ended up interviewing almost as many older as young women, and their reports confirmed that the story I was hearing from all of them was ageless: It was a *woman's* experience, not a *young woman's* one. Older women, perhaps, felt more pure joy because it was so unexpected—the extramarital experience and the joy—and so radical. Some, after all, had not had sex prior to or outside of marriage; the younger women all had had premarital sex. The older women had for so many years agreed to, if not accepted, the terms of being an American wife; the younger women were still hoping to negotiate new terms. The older women held out great hope for the ways by which women could defy the system, but were more convinced of and sanguine about the necessity for doing so secretly; younger women more often doubted the system's power to effect negative change in them or, when they believed it, had more hope of changing the system itself. Finally, older women's flight from conventional goodness was a more daring and unprecedented trip; younger women, less accustomed to life within the institution, and more comfortable with the role of sexual outlaw, were slightly less awed by its power. Older or younger, though, they all reported similar feelings about their flight—and recounted astonishingly similar changes in themselves.

"I'm No Longer Who I Was"

"How, exactly, have you changed?" I ask Eleanor, forty years old and with a thirteen-year-old son and a nine-year-old daughter. I'm sitting in her house in Staten Island, to which she has invited me after several earlier conversations. Today we've been talking for hours about her former husband, Bill, and about Joe, the thirty-three-year-old electrician she'd had an affair with for four years, whom she hasn't seen now for a year.

Eleanor answers my questions without hesitation, telling me about the course her life has taken since meeting Joe. Her marriage and her affair have both ended; she is living with her children in a small apartment near the water. Pictures of Bill and her children surround her on her couch in the den.

> I'm no longer who I was. That's really the only way I can put it. The way I think is different. I buy different food and watch different shows and buy different books. I talk to my mother differently. I won't let anyone talk to my children about being good or bad anymore—I fired a babysitter who kept telling my daughter she was being "bad," I'm no longer as interested in their teachers' assessments either of their work or their behavior. I ask them, my kids, for the information I need about how they're doing, not some authority who makes me second-guess them. I listen to their feelings more. I pay attention to my own more. I see the gray matter. I have less of a need to organize my opinions of things in advance, according to right and wrong. I guess you could

say I'm assessing right and wrong differently now; thinking for myself, and I feel more human, more myself.

"Can you think of anything specific that you do differently that you didn't do before?" I ask.

I can get my children's report cards and literally read them differently. I can get a note from a teacher saying—like this, about Jessica—"She is the brightest girl in the class—but she doesn't have the most drive to learn," and think, That's right. She doesn't. She wants to play. She's nine. She's very intense, but her intensity isn't focused on schoolwork yet. I can say that and mean it—like, who says a nine-year-old shouldn't still be playing? And, so what if she's going to take longer than other girls? And—and this is very different for me—so what if she *is* behind a bit? Do you see what I mean? I mean, this is a different way to live. My anxiety level has diminished. And my children trust me. I don't fall to pieces because my children don't fit some norm; they don't go crazy because they have to. It's a different ball game.

"Do you behave differently in the world as a result of this change?"

I called the teacher, thanked her for her observation, told her I've noticed how intensely Jessica plays with other kids, and that if in a year it seems to be a problem—not an incipient "problem" because of her failure to fit certain age-norm requirements—we'll discuss it further. I can do this without feeling defensive or hostile or righteous. Just like, really, I don't think it's a problem, but I'll be happy to discuss it if it persists and if I deem it a problem then.

"You would not have made this call before your affair?"

I wouldn't have made the call; I wouldn't have felt the need for such a call—the teacher was always right. If I had felt the need, I wouldn't have dared to challenge the teacher, or even thought to challenge her. See what I mean? It's like in layers. I would have thought I'd be killed, or my child thrown out, or the family attacked by the school board or something dreadful. Hell, I wouldn't have had the impulse to do it. I would have automatically, reflexively believed the teacher and believed my child was a failure, that she was in trouble, that her life would be a mess, that I was a mess. You know, the whole package. Being good was a big deal to me. All of that.

"A therapist might say that Jessica's distraction from her schoolwork is a result of her knowledge, if even unconscious, of your affair. Does this worry you? That she knows there is a secret and is upset by it?"

Of course. But that's the thinking I've moved away from; that blaming myself for whatever the hell I do, the idea that you can't *move* or your child will die. Jessica has changed very little—she was always called "not intense enough about her schoolwork," so it's hard for me to blame it on my affair. And I see her blossoming, not suffering. I see her speaking out in another way, both to me and to her friends. She's freed from this crap just as I am. Because I am. A psychiatrist might also say I was filled with denial, or that I was really, truly profoundly unhappy and *didn't know it*. But what I know is that a psychiatrist also declared me happy when I was borderline suicidal—simply because I had what should have *made* me happy—and that there was therefore something wrong with me that I couldn't feel happy. What I see is that I was once depressed but I'm not anymore. What I see is that far from hurting Jessie, and in spite of the real possibility that she sensed something, and that my splitting up with her father is obviously not the best thing for her or what she wants—I think in the long run I'm a much, much better mother. I don't see, in other words, that the change in Jessica's situation has had as much impact on her as the change in me has. The children are reaping benefits far greater than whatever harm the fallout of the affair might be having or might have had, because in a potentially bad deal they're getting a mother who is able to be with them and present.

"With them emotionally, you mean."

Yes. Because I get it now, get this whole thing about mothers and children I didn't get before. I mean, look: Before I had the affair, I used to detach from my children because of my own insecurity and depression, buying the teacher's verdict about people I knew better than she—siding, in effect, with the authorities. It's a small issue, maybe, but I now see that as such a gross injustice, such a betrayal of the people I care about, such a betrayal of my own real feelings. It's as if something snapped into place in me and I can see now, and feel my own real feelings. As if I had manufactured feelings before—This is what a mother feels; this is what a wife feels. The affair has made me feel the feelings of the outsider, while still giving me the authority and concern of the insider. Me. I feel like me.

A New Look at Right and Wrong

"Right" and "wrong" suddenly mattered less to the women as "pleasure" began to matter more. Two women, Jessie and Corrie, both in their twenties, both married three years and involved in affairs for one year, tell me:

It never used to occur to me to question what I got out of a relationship, as long as I *had* the relationship. Its existence was the point; I worked totally around that, whether it made me feel good or not, like you would please your father when you were a little girl.

No pleasure? Then why would I be in it? Do I need a man who gives me grief? I need a man who brings me pleasure.

They began to value their own responses, their own responsiveness. They wanted partners who, as Jessie put it, "want to please and want to play."

You know, I don't hear that little voice that says, "Get serious. Relationships are no joke. They're hard work. Get on with it." Not anymore.

THE CONVERSION

It is not a simple matter to calibrate change, to measure what it is that is different in a person once she says she feels different. I did not know most of these women before they said they had changed. I had to trust that conveying the profundity of their experience, the magnitude of their inner change was, in fact, the reason they were spending so many hours with me. "Conversion" is what William James calls the process of change in religious experience in *Varieties of Religious Experience*—an inner event that seems to be as elusive as it is unscientific:

Now if you ask of psychology just *how* the excitement shifts in a [wo]man's mental system, and why aims that were peripheral become at a certain moment central, psychology has to reply that although [s]he can give a general description of what happens, [s]he is unable in a given case to account accurately for all the single forces at work. Neither an outside observer nor the Subject who undergoes the process can explain fully how particular experiences are able to change one's centre of energy so decisively, or why they so often have to bide their hour to do so. We have a thought, or we perform an act, repeatedly, but on a certain day the real meaning of the thought peals through us for the first time, or the act has suddenly turned into a moral impossibility. All we know is that there are dead feelings, dead ideas, and cold beliefs, and there are hot and live ones; and when one grows hot and alive within us, everything has to re-crystallize about it.

I believe the women I talked to had come to me to tell me about their conversion, about a recrystallization of their thoughts and feelings and a refinding of some long-missing vitality, all of which facilitated a reintegration of their sexual selves. This recrystallization came about mysteriously, but always with an extramarital relationship acting as the catalyst. In this relationship they found—even if briefly, even if temporarily—something profoundly and, perhaps, irrevocably satisfying: an experience of a relationship that had no reason for being except to bring pleasure.

The words the women used to express the experience of such a relationship and the pleasure it brought—"reborn" and "released" and "recaptured" and "rescued"—suggests that what they found had existed before. What they had unveiled was prosaic and recognizable—resonating with love given and received before they felt obliged to turn boys into princes, before they themselves were turned into quiet sleeping beauties adrift in an erotic void. They simply experienced, I think, a reversal of the transformation they underwent when they covered up their real selves in an effort to become first, the Perfect Girl, and then, later, the Perfect Wife—and the self-repossession felt both familiar and good. For each of these women, *this* was the recovery: of a relationship before it was idealized, before sex was idealized, before *she* was idealized, and a time when relationships were as ordinary and comfortable and difficult, as sexual and playful and moody, as she herself was.

That sense that they should be happy within their marriages, but then *why weren't they?*; that they should be grateful that they had so much, but then *why were they feeling so deprived?*; that they loved their husbands and children, but then *why were they feeling so bad?* went away. The feeling, "I thought I married this alive person who was fun to be with" or "I thought my husband married an alive person who was fun to be with, *and then something happened*," vanished. And so, as James said, "aims that were peripheral become at that certain moment central." Pleasure becomes central, and it is such a powerfully resonant feeling because it is not new—they had felt it before, and here it is again. And all those "dead feelings, dead ideas, and cold beliefs," as James calls them, suddenly turn into "hot and live ones." There is then, almost magically, a healing; a rebirth of the woman.

The band of outlaws I interviewed, the intrepid women who left the safety of conventional goodness, did so because that very goodness deprived them of an essential connectedness they missed, and by leaving it they recovered not only their capacity for pleasure but an amazing vitality and clarity. And while I was struck by their resilience and resistance, I do not know whether either will last, or whether the women will sustain their vitality, or even whether their stories hold true for other women. But my questions about them spill over into other questions about women's sexuality: Is there another way to reclaim it? Experts suggest that economic independence, or even a good job, or therapy, or close family ties, or strong female friendships, are the answer to recovering diminishing selves and lost relationship. But these experts do not speak, for the most part, of sexuality.

Some additional questions come out of my work, I think, that need amplification: Must a wife's recovery of her sexuality necessarily take place in a relationship that is sexual? Must this relationship be illicit? And, once she has recovered her sexuality, can it be brought back into a licit and monogamous relationship? For all of these women, the answer to the first two questions was yes; and for some, the answer to the third question was also yes, at least the last time I saw or spoke with them.

And what about women who have affairs with other women? What about women of color? Women of different social classes? For all women, I suspect, the white, male framework is suffocating, but for some women, automatically excluded from it—and therefore from the whole petrifying idealization process—that framework may have extraordinarily different dimensions and an affair different consequences.

An Opening, Not an Ending

Rereading *The Scarlet Letter* was as wondrous a journey as my conversations with the "scarlet women" in this book—and equally as surprising. I had expected to be reading the old morality tale I read in high school, the comforting triumph of repentant goodness over sin, and what I found was another book in disguise, a stunning criticism of puritanical America, a passionate lament of the loss of one woman's sexuality and the implications of that loss for her and her daughter, and for the entire community. And I found there, too, in Dimmesdale, a model of the American psyche, the determination to keep up appearances of sexual innocence, of belief in the Spirit, in Purity, in Selfless Love, and in Pure Consciousness—while Hester, wearing her badness on her breast, pays for this hypocrisy.

I was twice surprised. Expecting to interview women deeply divided about their decision to have extramarital sex, devastated by it, I first called this book *Wandering Wives*, anticipating the many wives who would be sorry they had wandered—wives who, like Hester, had learned the bitter lesson of "lawless passion" too late, after they were branded, when they could not go back and could only yearn to return to the safety and the approval of goodness within the framework.

In a later version, finding this not to be so, I thought of calling the book *The Death of Forever*, as I began to think that perhaps I was not hearing any of these sad tales because monogamy was simply dead, and that, for whatever reasons, few of those who promised sexual exclusivity were capable of keeping their promise. I was struck by what Arizona State University sociologist Bernard Farber calls "permanent availability," by which he means that, increasingly, all married partners—men and women—are looking, always looking, for their *next* marital partners; throughout their lives, they are permanently available for another marriage. I noticed too that young women, coming from divorced families and often divorced themselves, used the word "forever" but brought to the word a different meaning from Webster's "of a limitless time; eternally." Never having witnessed a permanent relationship, never having known premarital abstinence or long-term sexual exclusivity, they might never comprehend the original definition of "forever." I planned to devote the book to examining just what their new meaning of forever might be.

It seemed to take *me* forever to take the intellectual step outside the framework myself; to notice that the reason these women came to talk was not to discuss divided hearts or new meanings of forever but the recovery of their sexuality, and the dramatic physical, psychological, and emotional ramifications of that recovery.

I will be asked whether I am advocating affairs, or whether I think wives should simply eschew sexually exclusive relationships. Certainly not, and neither would these women themselves, many of whom yearned for and preferred emotional and physical commitment to one man, and believed in sexual fidelity in marriage. Often, as I have said, a woman's affair can have overwhelmingly destructive ramifications for her, and a confessed affair can add devastating financial consequences from which she might never recover. Further, many women do not "lose" themselves in goodness in the first place, but find that, in their marriages, they can express themselves freely and completely, and share a relationship of honest connection, pleasure, and passion.

I want to make clear once again that it is not *marriage* per se that causes a woman to lose that compilation of attributes I am calling her sexuality; on the contrary, that relationship offers her enormous possibility for discovering and expressing it. It is at the occasion of marriage, though, that she is greeted with the potential thief: The Perfect Wife. It is *she*—not husbands, not men— who endangers the emotional, psychological, and sexual well-being of our bride; she who is the most insidious sex offender of them all. She, a product of that "iron framework of [men's] reasoning," as Hawthorne called it—is certainly a familiar remnant of the patriarchy. But she still exists, and it is no longer men who invoke her; they do not need to. Women themselves unwittingly, often unconsciously, opt to emulate her—even as they hate her—and the traditional marital arrangement still depends on their decision to do so.

I *am* saying that for all these women I interviewed, sexually exclusive marital relationships were made joyous only when they first killed off that Perfect Wife, and shattered this rigid institutional cage in which she flourished and which imprisoned their sexual selves. The conventional goodness the women entered when they married, and through which they found they still assumed status and approval, was precisely what was killing them—and their husbands, too—and they felt they must smash that framework in order to save them both. Then they found that, ironically, the tumultuous process of leaving goodness not only freed them but also their husbands and their marriages from what Connie called "that frozen, married feeling"—rescued them all from the "tower" inside which Paula says she had for so long felt exiled.

I will be asked, too, whether an affair can benefit a marriage—and again, I will say it depends on the marriage and on the couple. There are studies that suggest affairs need not break up marriages; indeed some research suggests that marriages have improved—or are even saved—by affairs.

Many of the women I talked with who ended their affairs and returned to their marriages report that their marriages are better now, and their husbands are happier, too. Paradoxically, the men sensed that the vital, warm, sexual women they married had over the years turned into someone else—and their own vitality had been sapped in the process. Having risked their marriages in order to find that vitality, these wives managed—against the odds—to bring that life back home. Transformed by pleasure themselves, they transformed their marriages, and brought more pleasure to their relationships. Many of the women who chose to return to their former sexually exclusive relationships are, like June and Clara and Dina and Annette and Leslie and many others, thriving in them. Other women, like Amanda and Paula, created a different arrangement for themselves.

Marriage—so much what these women wanted—had provided them with a relationship, but within a framework that was in many ways not at all what they wanted. Their distress came about, I suggest, not because their marriages were "bad" or fell short of the dream, but because they in fact met the dream. But the dream never really was *their* dream. The women never really were looking for that happily-ever-after story in which the door slams on the little cottage once the couple is ensconced inside. The story these women are telling does not have closure; the heroine is not locked in a place where she can have no more adventures. For them, in fact, an affair was the opening of the door; their stories are just beginning.

My sense is that all woman, even if they do not shatter the social structure so conclusively, must learn how to straddle it—to step outside it, if only to look at what's going on inside it—if they are to keep themselves—and by "selves" I mean their expressive, creative, sexual selves—from going underground. Some women accomplish this feat early, and do so in lively, nurturing marriages, often with their husbands' support. They never become erotically silenced. But one way or the other, the battle of American wives against stifling virtue, the hallmark of the iron framework, will be unending, at least for now. And the marriages they struggle to create and renegotiate, marriages that can assure them the mutual happiness between men and women that they seek, are anything but idealized. They are as filled with conflict as with harmony; they are complex, imperfect, difficult, ordinary relationships.

Chapter Fifteen

"WHERE HAVE I BEEN
ALL MY LIFE?"

*O*ne afternoon, a Thursday, one of the two days each week she met Jonathan, something happened that made it clear to June that there was a change in her extramarital relationship. She was at Jonathan's apartment, and they were in bed.

"The day had been particularly good," June told me. "I remember we had tried to have sex and I wasn't wet enough and so we just sort of forgot about it for a little while, and we were just fooling around and he was very aroused and suddenly just attacked me, with all the ferociousness that I associate with him, but expressed in a way I had never seen. He just went wild. He was usually so controlled—intense, but always alert to any changes in me, or any possible changes, even. I mean, God forbid I should have some sexual feeling anywhere in my body, some sensation even, he didn't witness!

"But this time he wasn't too interested in what I was feeling. It was a relief, really, not to be so carefully observed; in fact, I wasn't observed at all. I was like an acrobat's wire, or an athlete's ball, just kind of out there for his pleasure. The word—and I swear I've never even thought of this word before, let alone used it—is ravished.

"And I loved it, loved how he lost himself, how he came so hard and so violently. I loved the feeling, after all his careful nurturing, all his watching and waiting and wanting me to have the quintessential orgasm that would bind me to him forever, that I was being *used* this time; that I was a body for him to do what he pleased with; that he didn't even have to look at me, worry about me."

What June was feeling, really, she says now, was that it was not she who was being used, but Jonathan. She was using Jonathan. But she did not know that yet.

"It was the first time I felt he let it all go, trusted me enough to really go at it with me. I felt like that night he was out of his mind in love with me.

"But he was devastated. At first I thought it was because he was embarrassed that I might have felt used, that he had been insensitive. But it wasn't that. He knew what had happened and he knew I knew."

"Which was that you had reached a point of no return? He loved you too much, and that broke the deal?"

"Yes. We had both refused to discuss love, we were so intent on feeling that our relationship was equal and that one did not love or need the other person more, and were so intent on proving to each other that we could handle this affair. But Jonathan was odd all the rest of that evening. Shaken. I hoped it was a kind of wondrous quiet—he had just let go, sexually—and that he was happy. But then in the middle of dinner, which he made and brought to bed, he started crying. He didn't say anything.

"I had the sense that This was It; he was going to say

something I didn't want to hear. I panicked. And then I started crying, too. 'Well, we'll just continue,' I suddenly said lamely, as if he were about to say, 'What are we going to do?' and I would save the day. My words sounded so fake. So falsely brave."

"Because it was you who did not want to continue."

"Yes. It was. I couldn't anymore. But he was the one who said it. 'You know we can't continue,' he said, annoyed. 'I can't do this for the rest of my life, this every Thursday shit.'

"I knew that in fact this was exactly how this affair would end. That it wasn't going to just die. We weren't going to get sick of each other. It was going to blow up. It had to. And I knew it had just blown up.

"I kept thinking that I somehow had the advantage because I was married. I kept feeling that this was totally unfair to him and that I could afford this relationship because I could walk away and lose very little," June said. "But increasingly, the stakes were getting higher for Jonathan, and my power in this relationship only began to sicken me."

Jonathan knew all along that she wouldn't leave Russell, couldn't take Chloe away from her father, because she had told him that right from the start. "It was out of the question," June says now. "Even if I had hated Russell, Chloe loved him with all her heart. And frankly, I not only didn't hate him, I loved him. Even with Jonathan in the picture. Leaving was never a possibility."

She told Jonathan that she felt guilty now, guilty not only because of her feelings about him, but about Russell. "Jonathan always told me that the minute our relationship was over and I again needed Russell to be a companion and husband and lover as well as a father, I would remember that he was not perfect."

"Did you think Russell was perfect?" I ask.

"No, of course not, but Jonathan had a good point; he knew he was stabilizing my marriage, in that he kept me from being The Wife Who Needs Too Much and Russell from being The Withholding Husband. As long as Jonathan was there, he was saying, things went smoothly for me. But I don't agree with Jonathan that my love for Russell diminished and *then* I met Jonathan, you know, that my affair grew out of a burning need to have more love, or anything. I can't say what went on in my unconscious, but I know I wasn't thinking I needed another man. I mean, that's such a tricky argument, because who couldn't use a little more love? Who is so satisfied that the mere thought of a great orgasm is out of the question? You know? It's a chicken-and-egg thing—was it Jonathan who turned me on or was I ready for a turn-on and Jonathan appeared? I think it's the former; and I don't think my willingness to form a relationship with Jonathan had all that much to do with Russell."

But in time, it became about Russell. Suddenly, the balance shifted in both relationships, and each seemed to empty out, leaving June with an inordinate concern about hurting Jonathan's feelings. She didn't tell him, the way she once did, why she had to leave earlier than usual, if the reason had to do with Russell. He hated the reality of their situation—or at least she believed he did. And she in turn hated the thought of reminding him of it.

"The worst thing is when a relationship gets touchy," June said. "I kept thinking he'd turn to me in fury one day and say, 'Oh, why don't you just go home to your husband and child and forget this?'"

Not to mention the fact that she felt that was precisely what she should do. But she couldn't. And to keep him from pushing it, she began withholding the truth from him. She'd say she had to go to the library. She no longer spoke much of her little girl; rarely mentioned anything having to do with her home life at all. It began, she said, to feel odd. "He'd ask about Chloe, about my 'other' life, but I avoided the answers. It became my problem, not his: I was lying to both Russell and to Jonathan. I was weighing everything I said to everybody. I was keeping secrets from both men, not sure which man I was eager to see, pleasing no one. I just got very confused."

She says she went from having everything to having nothing. "I had half an intimate relationship going on with two men. It was like two bad marriages. There was zero pleasure in any of it—I just became a superwife, or rather a madwoman, racing around caring for two men, two homes. Which household had the toilet paper? Which one needed the Tide? I'd buy milk and jars of honey for home, then remember it was Jonathan who was out of both. I just was a wreck.

"I began to hate sex. Even with Jonathan. I felt as if I was married to two men, serving both of them, servicing both. 'Didn't I just *give* you head? Don't you realize now I have to go home and give it to *Russell*?' I became wild, resentful. I suddenly thought: Yes. This is my punishment. 'For having sex with two men, young lady, you are now doomed to have *two husbands* for *eternity*.' I felt like I was in hell. 'Okay, okay, I'll give head to everyone. Just get me out of this.' "

They stopped seeing each other a year ago, and June went into a decline for about six months, and her account of that time resonates with Paula's breakup with Harry. "I lost thirteen pounds. I couldn't wake up in the mornings. Russell, I guess, thought I was having a work crisis—and indeed among other things, I was. I couldn't write, I wasn't interested in my job at all. I certainly couldn't appear at psychological meetings—which had been, before Jonathan, my real beat. I couldn't talk to anyone about Jonathan—no one, not even my old therapist, who I decided not to tell because I was afraid she probably knew Jonathan. Not that she would do anything or tell anyone—but I just didn't want anything to be any messier than it already was. I never had told anyone, and even the idea of telling my best friend now was ridiculous. She'd just wonder why I hadn't told her earlier.

"I'm telling you, with all the self-help groups, why isn't there one for broken-hearted lovers?"

"Affairs Anonymous? 'Hi, I'm June. I'm having an affair.' What a good idea for a singles' group!"

"Yes, right. Lament the loss of a love and find a *new* love."

Just as Jonathan had prophesied, June began to put all her energy back into her marriage. She was determined to try to get the pleasure she had found in her relationship with Jonathan, emotionally and sexually, in Russell. Now that she had begun to understand what she wanted and needed—how to even define what was pleasurable to her—she began to express herself more openly than before. In turn, she figured, so would Russell.

But it didn't work out that way. "Russell seemed to be waiting me out; kind of like, 'Well, this woman has lost her mind and become all sexed up, and it will all go away soon when she gets her mind back, which should be any day now.' I really tried. It's not like I suddenly deluged him with demands, I just tried to get closer. I told him more about myself. I'd set aside a real, organized cocktail hour for us each evening—really, with martinis, or Rob Roys—and ask him about what was going on with him and tell him about myself.

"I didn't tell him about Jonathan. I agonized over that decision because in some perverse way I knew that was the way to *really* get his attention. But in the back of my mind I kept thinking of Jonathan's words: 'Don't tell. Whatever pain it brings Russell, it will bring you more.' I kept thinking of that and the old Lenny Bruce line: Even if he finds you making out on the couch, *say it's your hairdresser*. I had such a sense of its being too destructive—to me—that I overcame the impulse to tell him. It was a strong impulse, too: You figure, well now I won't be alone with this thing. Now someone else will have to deal with it with me. Now I'll be understood. Now I will be honest."

"Now it will all work out?"

"Yeah. And now I can load my guilt on him and say, 'See what you made me do?' "

"But do you think Russell knew, or knew something?"

"He had to know something had gotten to me, that I was trying to deepen our friendship for some reason, that I was wanting—actively—a more involved relationship with him. I mean, you don't have to be a genius to notice that your partner in life is trying to get your attention, and that it's important that you give it."

"He must have noticed that much."

"Yes, he did. I could tell. And it's not that he did anything wrong, I mean he didn't overtly *not* notice—he said several times, 'I like this cocktail hour, don't you?' But he didn't get it, get the purpose of it. Or else he did get it, and knew perfectly well I was trying to get closer, establish more contact."

"Or maybe he knew, but didn't know, yet, quite how to respond."

"I wanted him—the man I live with and sleep with and talk with—to go to the trouble of making a few gestures that say, 'What a good choice you made; look, here we are together, isn't that nice? Isn't this fun,' or 'Let's have some fun together, you and I!' "

"But, June, he didn't know about your choice. It sounds like you wanted him to guess how close you came to leaving him and to make you see how right you were not to."

"Yes. I did want that. But I did not want to say, 'Y'know, I had something really terrific and I let it go and . . .' I didn't want to do that."

"Yeah, I understand why you didn't want to tell him. I'm just saying that what you hoped for was an epiphany on his part, but without all the facts."

"I guess that's right. What happened, though, is that Jonathan was right. Once I had to put all my eggs in one basket, back in my marriage, I realized how futile it was to extract from Russell something I had never even articulated I wanted. I felt wonderful, in an odd way, even as I felt disgusting about losing Jonathan. I felt alive, clear, on target. Like yes, yes, this is it! This is wonderful! Where have I been all my life? I had this feeling that I could instill it in Russell if he'd only let me—that he would wake up like I'd awakened, that he'd say, Oh, yes! So that's what we should do to make our sex better! Now I get it! Come on, let's go!

"But I realized soon enough that if I wanted to have what I needed, what we both needed, we were going to have to change something fundamental in our marriage, both really come together in a way we never had, make some crucial turn. I had ended the old marriage, and if we were to have a new one, *if*, we'd have to take it out of the *marriage* ball game altogether, somehow, and into some other more satisfying one. I think that's what my urge to tell him about my affair was *really* about. That I could then say, 'Now that there's no way we can have an exemplary marriage, we'll have to start with another idea in mind.' "

"What other idea did you have in mind?"

"Oh, look, I felt this was *it*, our chance to see if we could connect deeply enough to have a real . . . relationship. My idea focuses on us rather than on the partnership or on Chloe, alone. On our life, our pleasure—I have been trying to say this to Russell. To rethink why we were together in the first place. Did we want to be? Was there anything really happening between us? And what scared me most was that Russell was going to say, 'What is it that you want here? For me to change my whole personality? Well, I *can't*.' "

"And you'd find out there was nothing going on, and that maybe you didn't really even want to be together."

"Yes, and I wanted to talk about that. Should we do this some more? Is it the way you want to live? Shall we go for another decade together? That's where I was. Out of the affair, out of the old marriage; waiting to see whether there could be a new arrangement."

"So what did you do? How did you tell him all this?"

"I just poured it out—all my feelings, although nothing, ever, about Jonathan—like I'm telling it to you. Just got hysterical and said it. I started by being mad, about his passivity at my cocktail hours that got no response. And then that anger grew into more anger, and I don't know, I guess I just blew up—at him, at the world, at the gods. I wanted . . . to keep this feeling of being alive. I had let Jonathan go, but I still had this. I had this need to have this very alive thing going with Russell, to have this feeling of expressing it all. And whatever I said, something worked."

"Why?"

"Russell fought back. Said he thought I had been the one who was so contented with my life, and that I had what I had told him I wanted. And he was mad because he thought he had to guess what I wanted all the time, and that I never told him, and how the hell was he supposed to know? He said I never told him what I needed sexually or, really, in any other way; that I just seemed so . . . fine. So now he felt like a jerk because all along I was expecting him to guess how to please me, and he had assumed he *was* pleasing me—that my life was pleasing me—and here I was accusing him of not giving me what I needed."

"He seems to have a point, there."

"Oh, absolutely. And he said he thought he was seen as the 'incommunicative' one, but that he was taking his cue from me. And it's true: This was a deal we made. I knew that. I knew it wasn't, you know, *his fault*. I didn't even know what 'it' was that might *be* his fault. He was being a husband for all those years, I was being a wife, and my message to him was 'I'm being quiet and sweet and this is how it's supposed to be' and he took my word for it."

"Only you were dying inside."

"Only I was dying inside. And . . . Him, too. How could he not have been? We were keeping this ridiculous deal going. I mean, not ridiculous in the sense that it was bad, or anything, but . . . not real. Not me and not him and an 'us' that was only a tiny little part of each of us. And that 'us' was what we were living off of, emotionally."

"Do you ever wish you had never met Jonathan?"

"Never. Jonathan was the best thing in my life. I was closer to that man than I've ever been to anyone. My life changed because of him. All my ideas changed, about me, particularly; and all that understanding about the 'us' that could be created if you really did it from the heart. I have a completely different sense of myself now—nothing I thought about myself before is true. Nothing at all. For instance, I'm trying to make my marriage work for me, for this new person, and I will give everything to it. I wouldn't see Jonathan now, or anyone. I'm *in* this marriage now."

"Is it better?"

"Hmmm. Well, better is an odd word, since all Russell and I do is fight and storm around and let out old, stupid grievances, at the moment. We talk and scream and get exhausted and start all over again. 'But I thought *you* thought,' and 'Well, sure, but I thought *you* wanted . . .' And I'm mad at him and he's mad at me. He's saying, I didn't *know* you were this kind of person, and I'm saying, I didn't *know* you were that kind of person. So is it better? Well, yes, actually, it is. Because we both have this sense we're fighting for our lives. To have this really alive thing between us, which is not necessarily 'pleasure' in the sense of the word that anyone else might think, but oh, yes, it's better."

"And sex?"

"Well, it's sometimes terrible and it's sometimes good, you know, the way sex always is."

"But I'm really back with Russell; I mean, he *feels* like my real partner, my real alive mate. My marriage means more to me now that I sort of left it. More and less. I'm bigger than my marriage now, too. I mean, this isn't the old June who couldn't ever imagine leaving her marriage. I can imagine it. I'm no longer afraid he'll say, 'What do you want?' He'd now more likely say, 'Here's what *I* want,' and that isn't so scary. I can handle all of that. But if I had to leave, I would. And it *still* wouldn't be because of a man. It would be if I started to feel that rote feeling again, that death-in-life feeling. Now I feel like I'm alive and sexual and true, and that's how I am. If I had to go back to being the old way, I'd leave, I think. I'd have to. But in some crazy way, now, I feel good. Fierce. Fighting for this makes sense. To both of us."

Epilogue

$\mathcal{T}$o go back to my first story, the one about Anne and Kurt: I have decided to alter the old narrative throughout: I will keep the heroine, adjust the inevitability of her demise, eliminate her poignance as a victim, and not elicit pity for her. I will definitely not kill her off at the end, nor sentence her to some marginal half-life on the fringes of society. I am sick of the romance plot, which lures our lady into love only to promptly erase her (or give her the alternate ending, death), thereby endlessly repeating the old story until we do not even question its validity or examine its bizarre implications.

After listening to these women, I have made a space for another plot about women's lives, one that is ongoing and has no finish, not even the seductive happily-ever-after ending. Once we conceive it, this tale that some women are actually living, the more power it will have to generate new lives. Once her voice is heard—my Anne's, say, who is after all based on all the women you read about in this book—then the voices of other women speaking out about pleasure will become less jarring, easier to listen to and really hear, and Anne's story will become a possibility for other women.

Like the grooves that transform a piece of plastic into a CD, these voices ensure that Anne's story can be heard again and again. The more we strengthen Anne, the more she strengthens us, for she is a sexual woman—a woman women know themselves to be and love being, a woman men love. Anne can become the new Anna—or Tess, or Hester—a woman neither unable nor disabled. "A" will stand simply for Able; Anne is Able. I will not adulterate her.

Anne's story might go anywhere: She could continue her relationship with Kurt or she could end it; she could start another affair or she could return to a monogamous, joyous, complex relationship with Alex. She could have more children, or not. I can assure you Anne's fate will be one of lifelong vitality. She will be able to stay in relationship while staying true to herself, without being called selfish, thereby providing a model for marriage in which both partners thrive. The one thing Anne has sacrificed in my story is her claim to goodness. She is permanently out of the running for the title of Perfect Wife. But what a trade: In exchange for the title, she has gained—or regained—the voice to speak about her pleasure. That will not guarantee her happiness or a perfect life, or promise forever. But as long as she holds on to her sexuality and does not try to reclaim goodness—and as long as she does not forget where she is living—my Anne will live.

Acknowledgments

I am grateful to the psychiatrists, psychoanalysts, psychologists, researchers, sociologists, therapists, and other experts who so generously shared their time, knowledge and opinions with me: Dr. Nancy Arndt; Lynn Atwater, Ph.D.; Dr. Martin Bergmann; Jessie Bernard, Ph.D.; Betty Carter; Dr. Dorothy Dinnerstein; Dr. Marion Dunn; Bernard Farber, Ph.D.; Norval Glenn, Ph.D.; Virginia Goldner, Ph.D., Frederick G. Humphrey, Ed.D.; Dr. Otto Kernberg; Annette Lawson, Ph.D.; Dr. Harold Lief; Dr. Carol Nadelson; Dr. Maj-Britt Rosenbaum; Maggie Scarf; Pepper Schwartz, Ph.D.; Dr. Judith Sills; Dr. Laura Singer; and Dr. Alexandra Symonds.

For hours of discussion, valued comments on all or parts of this work, and the best possible counsel and care, I am indebted to Ginger Barber, Lesley Dormen, Mary Evans, Pat Goldbitz, Jean-Isabel McNutt, Lori

Oliwenstein, Kathy Rich, Carol Rinzler, Jacques Sandulescu, Judith Stone, Jennifer Rudolph Walsh, and Eileen Winnick.

Special thanks to Joni Evans, Carol Gilligan, and Kitty Ross.

My deep gratitude to Annie Gottlieb, whose inexhaustible intellect and support sustained me.

And my greatest debt is to the women whose voices fill this book and whose feelings and lives are at the heart of it.

ABOUT THE AUTHOR

DALMA HEYN has written extensively for most major magazines. She was formerly editor in chief of *Family Health Magazine* and executive editor of *McCall's*. Her column, "The Intelligent Woman's Guide to Sex," appears monthly in *Mademoiselle*. She and her husband, Richard Marek, live in New York City.